ERRATUM

Page 106, line 35, should read:

English women are at last beginning to realize that they

Radical records

Radical records
Thirty years of lesbian and gay history, 1957–1987

Edited by
Bob Cant and Susan Hemmings

Routledge
London & New York

First published in 1988 by
Routledge
11 New Fetter Lane, London EC4P 4EE

Published in the USA by
Routledge, in association with Chapman & Hall Inc.
29 West 35th Street, New York, NY 10001

Set in Baskerville
by Witwell Ltd, Southport
and printed in Great Britain
by Richard Clay Ltd, Bungay, Suffolk

Library of Congress Cataloging in Publication Data
Radical records: Thirty years of lesbian and gay history,
    1957–1987/edited by Bob Cant and Susan Hemmings.
    p. cm.
    1. Gay liberation movement—Great Britain—History—20th century.
    2. Gays—Great Britain—Political activity. 3. Lesbians—Great
    Britain—Political activity. I. Cant, Bob. II. Hemmings, Susan.
    HQ76.8.G7R33 1988
    306.7'66'0941—dc 19   87-27004 CIP

British Library CIP Data also available
ISBN 0–415–00200–1
     0–415–00201–X

Dedication

The editors jointly dedicate the work of putting this
collection together to Sue Cartledge, lesbian feminist sister,
who died aged 34 in February 1983 after many years of
spirited writing, working and campaigning for women's
and for lesbians' rights; and also to Mark Ashton, gay
brother and comrade, who died in February 1987 aged 25,
after many years of keeping gay issues alive on the left and
in the unions, campaigning alongside lesbians and gay
men in supporting the Miners' Strike of 1984–5.

Contents

Ways to organize – looking back at past efforts in
CHE, GLF, GLC; failures and successes; party
political postures on our issues; new waves of
energy and a focus on social policy/legislation
issues; why coalitions and alliances could now be
crucial.

Acknowledgments

The editors acknowledge all the help and support they have received with this book, both on personal and practical levels (typing, photocopying, dogwalking, hot meals, pep talks and generosity over phone bills), and also thank the contributors for putting up with pressure and bullying at a time when so many demands were being made on so many of them for political solidarity and action. We hope you will feel that it has all been worth the effort.

1 Introduction

Bob Cant and Susan Hemmings

I

Susan Hemmings: This book is a history book. The lives and struggle of lesbians and gay men are at last being recorded, not just as 'coming out' stories, but in terms of full, politically active struggle. During the past few years we have seen a steady movement to archive the experiences of older lesbians and gay men, with writings, audio-tapes, videos and films. This book is part of that desire to record, before it is too late, our recent efforts to change our lives and the wider context in which we live them, before a pall of silence falls on the important events of the post-Wolfenden era.

The history of a movement (or, as it is in our case more accurately, a complexity of movements) is more than the sum of the personal histories of its individual participants. But, until those stories are told, we cannot make sense of it all. Nor is any history book particularly gripping or inspiring that leaves out the heart of the matter: changing, growing people, in relationship to each other and under the conditions of the time. A book like this can give us the opportunity to *make* history: to describe our lives and to reflect simultaneously upon ourselves as social and political beings.

When we embarked on this project in early 1985 there was still a climate of considerable optimism among lesbians and gay men. Although the Metropolitan Authorities and the

Greater London Council had just been abolished, the support engendered within them for aspects of lesbian and gay concerns had placed some of our politics on the public agenda in a way that was quite new in British history. Meanwhile new alliances within the trade union movement (such as the mutual political benefits experienced in the Lesbians and Gays Support the Miners Campaign), as well as the growing number of lesbians and gay men working on issues of oppression in both local government and voluntary organizations, gave many more of us a chance to learn about, and to be influential within, sites of public policy-making from which our ideas had previously been entirely excluded.

Many lesbian feminists, mostly those from the radical feminist tradition which has always remained sceptical of working in mainstream, male-dominated sectors, did not feel particularly optimistic about any of these opportunities. They interpreted them rather as co-options and coercions. In fact, most of us who *were* optimistic also retained a healthy scepticism, while at the same time gaining experience – and sometimes, for us, extraordinarily regular and respectable paycheques for doing what we had for years been doing for free. While both the optimists and the cynics worried about the corrupting power of the paycheque and of funding, because of its ability to undermine the power of voluntary commitment to the movements in which we had all been so involved, this period brought about a new generation of lesbians and gays with experience in public administration – its possibilities and its limitations.

Bob Cant and Susan Hemmings: This was also a time when a public concert of homophobia returned in a strength that perhaps young lesbians and gays had not previously experienced. Day after day the media attacked us, through exploiting fears about AIDS, as British deaths rose. The media again fanned the flames with constant stories of money spent on lesbian and gay projects, especially when it was, as it rarely was, anything to do specifically with Black lesbians, and especially when it had anything to do with giving information, fair and square, to school students.

Because our existence is now so much a matter of public 'concern', even if our issues are completely distorted, it is

more important than ever for our history to be documented
– and to be available. There are those of us who have been
working for many years for lesbian and gay rights, working
as well to explore the relationships between our oppression
under heterosexism and the other oppressions which affect
both ourselves and other people in society. *We* need to take
stock, to look back, and to assess what we have learnt and
how we can exploit it for further progress. Those who have
more recently become lesbian or gay – whether young gay
men or lesbians, or older people who have changed their
sexuality – also need to know what has gone before, and
because our history is suppressed, it is up to us to tell them.
This book is also for heterosexuals, particularly those on the
left, who have much to learn. For too long sympathetic
heterosexuals have (when not actively opposing our work)
hidden behind façades of tolerance, never questioning the
roots of their sexuality or the patterns of their own
relationships, never supporting our campaigns, and –
giving nothing – learning nothing from the radicalism
which has been part and parcel of our advance and, indeed,
our survival.

All these issues, and many more, are explored by the
contributors to this book. Clearly, as editors, we are on the
left, and define ourselves as socialists, although Susan has
never been aligned to any party. So we wanted the book to
contain themes relevant to socialism. Not all our
contributors define themselves as socialists. Some may
prioritize certain issues over others, and almost certainly
some would strongly disagree with some of the paths of
progress proposed by others in the book. There are also
contrasting – and sometimes irreconcilable – analyses of
what it is that fundamentally causes society to be so split and
to give privileges to so few.

Susan: However, we have not aimed to make the book from
one perspective. It is meant to reflect the reality of the
political enterprises in which we have been engaged, and to
bring out the splits, the stops and starts, the uncertainties, as
well as our planned and lasting projects and our
spectacular, euphoric moments of success. We know, too,
that the book has gaps: it can't be comprehensive. And it's
quite untidy, like real history is: however you read it – right

the way through in order, or picking out the bits which appeal to you, you'll come across the same issues, the same events, even the same venues, but each time as part of someone else's perception, someone else's political growth.

You will read a nostalgic report of Gay Liberation in one place – followed by a cutting critique elsewhere. And there's a geographical spread. Then the contributors themselves: spanning a wide age-range, with the older contributors able to give us much important documentation fast vanishing from our collective memory, and the younger ones able to remember vividly the short-lived revival of seventies' student politics, everyone pinpointing what it was – in the political climate of the moment – that confirmed within them their lesbian or gay pride and strength.

Many of the contributors haven't written before (a few are seasoned writers): again, we wanted to have new voices, and we also wanted to ensure an authenticity that comes from a fresh approach to the subject, and that doesn't try to neaten up what should be left ragged and suggestive, nor to marshal everything into a convenient polemic.

So while we hope this is a highly *readable* history book, it may well be one in which you, as the reader, have to do some of the work, as you trace the themes, recognize the repetitions, piecing together – perhaps from your own memory of the events mentioned, and the feelings identified – your very own interpretation of the events of the past thirty years which have been so influential on our lives as lesbians and gay men.

II

Bob: There were, during the seventies' a number of celebrated cases of lesbians and gay men being dismissed when they refused to continue concealing their sexuality. Employees who saw themselves as progressive were often just as homophobic in practice as those from whom one would have expected reactionary behaviour. One such case, which symbolized many of the issues at stake, was that of John Warburton, the teacher sacked in 1974 by the Labour-controlled Inner London Education Authority (ILEA) for refusing to lie when his pupils – teenage girls – asked him questions about his sexual identity. A report in *Gay News* had led him to believe that ILEA, which defined itself as the most progressive education authority in the country, would not discriminate against gay teachers. His dismissal made it clear, that while they might not dismiss teachers whom they knew to be closeted, they would not tolerate teachers who challenged the homophobic climate in schools.

John Warburton was not reinstated. This defeat, however, rather than marking the end of the struggle for lesbian and gay rights in the Labour movement, represented the beginning of a new period of self-organization. Groups which had been set up, particularly in public sector unions, began to mobilize support around some general principles of civil rights for lesbian and gay workers. Conference resolutions often became a focus of such activity and in the late seventies a number of unions, starting with the National Union of Journalists (NUJ), debated and passed resolutions of support for their lesbian and gay members. This succeeded in generating a public consensus among trade union activists that we should not be victimized on account of our sexuality.

A number of workers – in teaching, in social work, in local government – have begun to look at the way their profession endorses society's view that heterosexuality is not only the superior, but even perhaps the only natural form of sexuality. Even to make such a critique meets with enormous resistance from people who may, in a liberal way, have formerly been allies but now feel obliged to defend patterns of institutionalized heterosexism. Liberal and reactionary alike, they often share the view that the lesbians or gay men who criticise the heterosexism operating within their own profession or their own workplace are endangering whatever else has been won in terms of equal rights. When we challenge heterosexism, it is easier for others to labels us as 'extremists'.

The collectivism of the Labour movement is, however, unique in British society. It represents a whole history of working people coming together to resist their exploitation, to improve their standard of living, to make their working conditions safe, to enrich the quality of life of their communities and to defend their weaker members. It is that living tradition of collectivism that makes lesbians and gay men continue to struggle within that context. Sometimes there are major victories. The achievements of the GLC and the formal support of lesbian and gay rights by the Trades Union Congress and the Labour Party Conference in 1985 were not simply fortuitous. They reflect the drawing together of a number of collectivist traditions.

It would be foolish to suggest that many in the Labour movement are not uneasy about these developments. The fact that the economistic traditions of Labour are being challenged not only for their heterosexism but also their racism, their sexism and their ableism makes this sense of unease profound. The common ground that exists between the politics of the Labour movement and the politics of oppression ensures that these attempts to create a new collectivist politics will continue.

III

Bob: The major focus of gay male politics has for many years been coming out. For a man to admit that he desired other men was to endanger himself. He became a laughing-stock, a hate figure, an outcast, a legitimate target for violence. The bravery of the first men to come out and thus reject some of their male privilege is unquestionable. Their declaration made it clear that their homosexuality was not just an occasional activity but an identity. For much of this century gay men have perceived their homosexuality as a condition into which they were born. It served as a useful defence against the claim that homosexual activity was a wilful, and therefore curable, perversion. With the development of a movement, and of greater confidence, more gay men began to see their homosexuality as a social identity. Much of the politics of the early seventies was about the construction of communities within which this identity could be sustained. In the city centres and the campuses, this role was taken on by GLF; in the suburbs and the smaller cities and towns it was taken on by CHE; in Scotland by SMG. All of these organizations were open to women as well as to men but right from the start most were, with some remarkable, short-lived exceptions such as Lancaster GLF in 1972–3, male dominated.

The process of community construction began simply by bringing people together into groups. Group meetings helped people to develop the confidence to organize more public events such as socials and dances. The pages of *Gay News* in the early and mid-seventies chronicle the growth of an increasingly open social self-organization. 'Out of the Closets' became more than just a slogan as these social events ceased to be isolated phenomena and ceased to be confined to cellars and private clubs. Originally very much part of the movement, they became less so as gay entrepreneurs opened up discos in the upstairs rooms of pubs around the country. The cheap and friendly Tricky Dicky discos in north-east London and Essex have been among the most durable and most successful of this trend. By the mid-seventies the focus of the burgeoning gay male community was moving away from the political meeting towards publicly acknowledged pubs and discos.

The process of apparent de-politicization developed further with the emergence of the mega-disco. Ron Peck's 1978 film, *Nighthawks,* ended with the central character entering such a club whose all-encompassing atmosphere of controlled light and sound seemed to offer the potential of fulfilling every fantasy, of enlivening every dream. Gay men had become not just a political force or a community but also a market. Although the Pink Economy in Britain has never achieved the scale of its US counterpart, it has tapped the spending power of gay men successfully and generated a new service industry. The quest for the realization of gay male fantasies would not have been possible without the de criminalization of some homosexual acts and, even more, without the growth of gay politics, but those who now controlled the form of the quest were light years away, in terms of political consciousness, from the earlier campaigners. No-one who is in any way dependent on an environment which is the object of constant police interest can be totally apolitical, but as the gay male scene grew in prosperity so organized politics in the community appeared to dwindle.

The image of affluent hedonism was, however, far from being the reality of most gay men's lives. Most were unable to belong to the world of the Pink Economy – although many of us made use of it. Many more continued to be closeted and the number of men arrested on criminal charges for which there is no heterosexual equivalent continued unabated. The 'permissive' society may have permitted more tolerance for parts of the gay male ghetto but even that was fragile – and normally conditional on 'good behaviour'.

The advent of AIDS seemed likely to endanger the fragile tolerance. The premature deaths of gay men in the industrialized world led to a revival of prejudice and homophobia, as well as enormous fear among gay men themselves. Commentators predicted (some gleefully) the end of gay male lifestyles, but they proved to be wrong. AIDS, on the contrary, stimulated a new sense of resistance among gay men. The development of a Safer Sex culture, the growth of support networks, the lobbying of governments, the links formed with other AIDS–affected groups all revealed a political energy in the gay male community that had seemed possibly absent and certainly on the wane.

All of this was only possible because of a dimension of the gay male experience that had been hidden from the outside world – the development since the gay movement, of friendship patterns and social networks that embraced both the 'political' and 'non-political' alike. Nameless and undefined, these networks acquired a new purpose and took on more public forms in the struggle against AIDS. What the AIDS crisis has revealed is that gay men have learned to care for one another not just on an individual level, but also as members of a community. Everyone knew that sex had come out of the closet since the early seventies, but it was the AIDS crisis that helped everyone realize that affection and public values among gay men had come out as well.

IV

Susan: Coming out – and dealing with the ramifications on both personal and political levels – has been a key theme in most books dealing with gay and lesbian issues, and most of the contributors here will give their own accounts of this radicalizing act and its effect on their lives. What is perhaps clearer in many of the women's pieces, more than the men's, is that coming out is a continuous act, with clusters of meanings and implications, depending on the oppressions affecting us and the current attitude of the state towards sexuality, the family and 'morality' – as well as pressures of unemployment, housing and general social policy.

The exhilarating release of coming out with the Gay Liberation waves of the early seventies, or within the Women's Liberation Movement of the mid-seventies is documented here – but so is the painful realization that if you are other than white, middle class and male there may well be serious consequences. Valued support from family sources which you may well have depended upon before to survive racism, for example, might be thrown away as you move, in a state of optimism, into a gay or lesbian community, only to experience racist acts and attitudes, including having your difference denied and ignored. Several pieces document this process: it is significant that it is mainly lesbians, rather than gay men, who are open to describing it carefully and forcefully. This is because it has been in the lesbian feminist communities that issues of multi-oppression have been most vigorously debated, to the extent that they have become, in the mid-eighties, central to most of the discussions about what it is to be a lesbian.

Furthermore, coming out has had profound effects on employment rights. 'Equal opportunities' became a major issue as locally-based Labour groups confidently surged into power to practise their manifesto commitments: manifestoes which, for the first time ever, had been open to influence from lesbian feminists and gay men working long-term in the community and, sometimes, in the party itself. Lesbian and gay rights came into focus because of the experience of feminists in demanding women's rights, and alongside Black activists' insistence on anti-racist policies for local authorities. As local councils set up women's committees and race relations committees, activists continued to demand that policies – and funding – took into account the needs of lesbians, and of Black lesbians and gays. Lesbian and gay sub-committees gradually began to emerge on a few councils – all this with constant media harassment – and personnel departments all over the country, but particularly in metropolitan areas, began to find themselves obliged to consider the oppression of lesbians and gay men alongside gender and race oppressions. This in turn reopened, on a more public level, the discussion about coming out: if departments were to monitor their employment practices to ensure equal and non-discriminatory selection procedures ... how would they know if they had the 'correct' percentage of lesbians and gays? Absurd, of course, firstly because there cannot be any sense to many lesbians and gays in coming out in a situation where your sexuality is or should be irrelevant; secondly because in this climate you might choose to come out while working for one employer but what happens when you change your job? And thirdly, perhaps the key issue, there *is* no correct percentage: ideas about 10 per cent of the population being homosexual is entirely a product of heterosexist wishful thinking – and control. As lesbian and gay worker groups formed in local authorities, and in voluntary organizations, all these matters, as well as pertinent issues, such as what constitutes heterosexist harassment in the work place, began to be reopened for discussion, in the entirely new context of local government.

During the past decade, lesbians and gay men have found themselves, often for reasons they might not have chosen on a personal or theoretical plane, under pressure to develop a commonality of aim and interest. This has partly been due to the AIDS crisis, and partly to the right's exploitation of the attendant surge of heterosexism. Also, we did not want to be left out of the movement towards equal opportunities in employment practice (in the unions and under Labour administrations). However, lesbians, especially, did not want to drift into a ready alliance with gay men without careful thought. We were, for the most part, uneasy: years of experience had shown us that gay men had been largely uninfluenced by feminism. Any analyses from *them* of male power, and their own part within it, were still largely absent. As you will see from the pieces in this book, men hardly mention the problem. They may execute a swift genuflexion in the direction of feminism, or acknowledge the marginalization of lesbians to punctuate a passage on the masculinization of the 'gay movement' but there is little genuine evidence of our influence. Male brain death on the issues of patriarchy is not confined to heterosexual men.

Discussions about the constitution and effects of anti-lesbianism have always gone on in the Women's Liberation Movement, sometimes raging loud and productively, sometimes submerged and bitterly. Occasionally they have surfaced in brilliant and provocative collections of writings, mentioned in some of the lesbians' contributions here. At off-peak times debate has become more fragmented. Lesbians have to deal all the time with the sexism and heterosexism of straight men, the sexism of gay men and the anti-lesbianism of heterosexual women, including heterosexual feminists. This particularly painful and prevalent 'feminist' anti-lesbianism is a phenomenon which is also described in the book. In mapping the movements, rather than the Movement, of lesbian feminists over the last fifteen or so years, we can detect a strong exodus from GLF in the mid-seventies (described in many of the pieces here), a heightening of energy and activity in the Women's Liberation Movement until the mid-eighties, and then more recently a period of reflection and even withdrawal, which is partly due to the resistance of heterosexual feminists against challenging heterosexism. In recent campaigns for lesbian and gay rights, heterosexual women have again been absent: the reflective assumption of lesbian feminists that women's issues are our issues has almost never been repaid in kind by heterosexual women – even in the matter of lesbian custody.

It has been during this period of re-collection and regrouping – which is still to be documented – that some lesbians have moved back into projects alongside gay men, often (in fact, mainly) to ensure that gains around lesbian and gay rights *include* our interests and are *moulded* by our issues. Lesbians retain reservations about the alliance, for, whatever we may feel about our continued marginalization in the Women's Movement, we are, generally speaking, much more likely ultimately to identify as women than as 'gay'. And we by no means feel that sexism is a dead duck, or that gay men are non-sexist brothers.

We are now entering a period when the pressures to define our oppression, and the differences as it affects us as lesbians or gay men, are throwing up alliances which could prove highly productive, even though they may be frail or temporary, as they have sometimes been in the past. It is interesting that in this book, as in current campaigns with broad support (such as the Organisation for Lesbian and Gay Rights [OLGA]) we still have difficulty in defining clearly what our oppression is, or even in giving it a name. We have few theorists putting energy into an analysis which would help us move forward: those (mainly white) socialist and anti-sexist academics who have been fortunate to be working and teaching around the issues of sexuality in the universities and polytechnics during the mid-seventies to mid-eighties have either focused on sexism – with some notable and helpful redefinitions of gender asymmetry – or on post-Freudian notions of desire. Both these trains of enquiry are part of the intellectual structure we need, but they stop short of making connections that would push forward our notions of the driving forces behind *hetero*-sexism and its power both to separate *and* complement the genders.

Perhaps a more forceful commitment towards developing theories around heterosexism might have come from British radical (lesbian) feminists (even though they would not have seen alliances with gay men as productive) had they been appointed to academic posts in the same numbers that socialist feminists and socialist gay men were during the seventies. However, *their* ideas have consistently been represented as intellectually unsound, and unsuitable for an academic setting. Such women have had a consistently hard struggle to get published, let alone get paid jobs in their theoretical fields. Investigative work around oppressions other than heterosexism, notably racism, and more recently, disability, has been much more stringent and revolutionary, and popularised versions have begun to affect social policy, however slowly and however great the resistance from, for example, the current Labour leadership.

This book's strength will lie in its recollections of lesbian and gay themes and actions, and the way it sets out on a personal and practical level the methods in which lesbians have cared for each other, and the growing support network that has been developed by gay men. I had no intention that the book should include pieces by women which related in any detail the arena where most lesbian strength has been poured: the women's movement. This is because I did not feel that a book with and for gay men is the correct place for these matters to be laid open. Readers with knowledge of the women's movement will surely notice the gap, and it will make for a strange inbalance. In my view, this silence is representative of how many lesbian feminists, including myself, feel at the present time about our relation to gay men: we have things to contribute, we have a determination to make ourselves heard, but we also have much to hold back, for ourselves and for all women.

V

Susan: There have always been individual and specific working and support relationships between some lesbians and some gay men which have lasted the whole post-Wolfenden era – such as London Lesbian and Gay Switchboard, and befriending agencies, like Friend. And lesbians have in many cases given support to gay men's campaigns: there are many lesbians working, for example, as volunteers to the Terrence Higgins Trust. But after the major exodus from GLF into the Women's Liberation Movement, most lesbian feminists, myself included, were so disillusioned with gay men's lack of reciprocation over women's issues that we saw little need to consider *their* issues, and the heart went out of joint campaigning. Those women who remained in joint ventures continued to battle it out over sexism with their gay male colleagues, and often, too, suffered exhaustion in the process.

Meanwhile, however, women dealing with other oppressions, such as race and disability, often developed different forms of alliance with men, while retaining every bit as much a pro-woman, anti-sexist politics. It was their exclusion from the perceived 'mainstream' movement and events which led to particular mixed groupings and alliances, some of which are described in the book.

Bob and Susan: More specifically, being gay and being socialist was not enough of an impulse for us to get together to work on this book. We had both undergone similar major surgery for different life-threatening diseases, and working on the book together was part of getting our strength back.

So it has come about for us, as for many lesbians and many gay men we know, that it has been the sense of our *other* shared oppression-disability – that has given us the momentum to see this project through. We had been learning, in the intervening period of separatism (chosen by lesbians and imposed on gay men, and a period that has still by no means ended), about many other forms of oppression and our own parts in them, as oppressors and as survivors. We had been reflecting on hierarchies of oppression, differences between them, their relationships to exploitation, and about the pressures of priority for those who are continually on the front line and who, unlike the two of us, have no chance to 'pass' or rest from the struggle. We can't claim to have any special perspectives or to be particularly enlightened on the complexity of issues that have arisen. But the 'feel' of what we have absorbed, what we have been through ourselves and our changed attitude to our own lives and those around us, has made us all the more determined to ensure that accounts like those in this book are published. Accounts which, we hope, capture not only some of the main lesbian and gay actions and enterprises of the post-Wolfenden period, but, above all, the ideas and struggles which have informed them, ensuring their permanent transformation and radicalization.

Autumn 1987

2 Battling for Wolfenden

Allan Horsfall

I was born in 1927 in the village pub at Laneshaw Bridge on the very edge of the wild moorland which is the Brontë country and I spent my childhood and much of my adult life in the small mining and weaving towns of industrial Lancashire. It was in places like these that the pressures for social and legal conformity bore down most heavily on homosexuals. Whereas in the cities it *might* be possible – perhaps behind the façade of some 'gentlemen's club' – for homosexual men to be themselves, the small towns offered no such refuge.

There *might* be some corner of a bar, usually in the 'best' hotel, where small groups of gay men could gather to drink and talk – always quietly and sometimes in code – maybe of some visit to the wicked city or to some holiday resort where it was possible to congregate and communicate more openly because of the anonymity afforded by strange and distant surroundings. I cannot remember any similar arrangements for lesbians, no doubt due in part to the then prevalent disapproval of unaccompanied women in bars – unaccompanied by men, that is! The small groups of gay men gravitated to the better hotels because it was there that people felt least prone to the prying curiosity of others, but it was an arrangement which served to reinforce the prevailing misconception that homosexuality was something alien to the working class.

Those who – perhaps with no knowledge of or entrée to any gay coterie – found the social desolation of small-town life too daunting to contemplate, would sometimes leave their homes for good in order to savour the marginal benefits of life in a larger and more amorphous community. Others who, because of the stresses set up by guilt and frustration, found themselves driven to seek psychiatric help would often be advised to move to the cities for the same reason if, that is, they had the good fortune to be referred to an enlightened practitioner. But those who found themselves in the clutches of the more prejudiced doctors were usually consigned for a course of aversion therapy or subjected to some kind of chemical assault upon the personality.

Most cities had bars where gay men were tolerated – welcomed even – and these were often located in the commercial centres where most of the regular business was at lunchtime and where evening custom had to be sought in more unusual ways. It was a constantly shifting scene as first one and then another of these establishments fell foul of the authorities. Licensees would be 'leaned-on', managers would be dismissed, licences would be withdrawn or suspended. The huge Clifton Hotel in Blackpool was denied a public drinking licence for a long period during the busy holiday season simply for allowing homosexuals into one of its bars. For the same 'offence' the licensee of the Union Hotel in Manchester was actually *imprisoned* for twelve months after being told by the Recorder at Manchester Crown Court: 'Your conduct of the licensed premises amounted to an outrage of public decency. You exploited abnormality for personal gain and allowed this public house to become a canker in the heart of a great city.' This was as late as 1965.

Returning to my own story, I was brought up by my maternal grandparents who were dyed-in-the-wool Conservative publicans, fervent upholders of law and order and flag-waving Royalists to boot. But religion played little part in their lives and I was free from religious influence at home. Thus I grew up with a healthy respect for the rules of society, if not for those of God alone. I was undoubtedly the kind of person that Conservative Home Secretary R.A. Butler had in mind when, seeking to justify his government's failure to act on the Wolfenden Committee's homosexuality recommendations, he referred to 'those who take their ideas of what is right and wrong from the law'.

The 'age of innocence' for me did not accord with anything that Mary Whitehouse might mean by that expression. It ended not with the dawning awareness of sex, but with the later realization that my own sexual nature – of which I was aware (as A. E. Dyson once put it) 'as an irremovable Trojan horse within the gates' – was inevitably destined to involve me in a life of crime. It was not a pleasant future to contemplate at a tender age, but all my inculcated respect for the law never once caused me to consider whether a celibate existence might provide an acceptable alternative.

During three years in the RAF, I made only two gay friends. After demobilization one of them, a convert to Roman Catholicism, entered into training as a priest but had to withdraw after suffering what was described as a nervous breakdown. The other one married and was shortly afterwards found hanged.

When these separate pieces of sad news reached me they fitted all-of-a-piece with the overall bleakness of small-town gay life in the early fifties: a time which saw a new intensification of police action against gay men prompted, it was later claimed, by pressure upon the British government from an American ally obsessed by the imagined security risk posed by homosexuals.

People were aware of the danger in which they lived, but it was impossible to quantify it. Police attitudes varied not only between one force and another, but also between one Chief Constable and his successor. Multiple prosecutions were frequent and seemed to be a product of the towns rather than the cities. Dr R.W. Reid captured the atmosphere exactly in a letter in the *Spectator* in 1958:

> The pogroms continue, one in this neighbourhood having started with long and weary police court proceedings on the eve of Christmas, so that the festival may presumably be spent in contemplation of the Spring Assize.
>
> And this for a lad of seventeen. The pattern is much the same in all these cases. The police go round from house to house, bringing ruin in their train, always attacking the younger men first, extracting information with lengthy

questioning and specious promises of light sentences as they proceed from clue to clue i.e., from home to home, often up to twenty.

This time the age range is seventeen to forty, which is about average. Last time a man of thirty-seven dropped dead in the dock at Assize. Just because this happens in country places and at country assizes it all goes largely unreported.

If promises of light sentences, along with other inducements and threats, failed to produce the evidence which the police required, it was not unknown for some of the suspects to be offered immunity from prosecution in exchange for their testimony against the others. I know of one man who was convicted for a single private act which had take place *ten years* previously.

Had it been conceivable to produce a gay man's survival guide at that time it would have urged him never to reveal his name or address, never to discuss how he earned his living or where he worked, never to take anybody to his home or give anybody his telephone number and never to write letters, whether affectionate or not, to anybody with whom he was sexually involved or even to anybody he knew to be gay.

Many gay men, of course, did some or all of these things and remained untouched by the law. But their untroubled survival was due to good luck rather than wise behaviour. Others lived strictly by the code. There could hardly have been a less satisfactory basis for a social or sexual existence, but it was soundly rooted in a practical awareness of the risks, a point to be pondered by those who cannot understand how 'cottaging' came to be institutionalized in the British homosexual sub-culture.

Differing factors sparked-off the police witch-hunts which always struck the first victim without warning. Many people took the fatalistic attitude which had been common during the wartime blitz – that the bomb would only hit you if your name was on it – and simply got on with life as best they could. There was nothing else to be done apart from ending it all, which many did – particularly those facing prosecution or blackmail. But even that desperate remedy was a crime and a botched suicide attempt could result in some poor wretch facing two charges instead of one.

It never seemed to occur to anybody in the working class that things could ever be different. It was known that there were places abroad where homosexuals were tolerated, where rich people spent some of their time and which offered them permanent refuge if they were fortunate enough to see the writing on the wall as the law closed in on them. But the idea that the British law could ever be changed was dismissed as absurd. Even when the Wolfenden Committee recommended partial decriminalization in 1957 nobody believed that it would ever happen. Any working-class homosexual who expressed the view that change was possible was regarded as deluded and any who proposed assisting the process of change was thought of as recklessly insane.

And so it was to be when I first became openly associated with the law reform cause. I say 'cause' because it was to be many years before it could be described as a movement and even more before it became the Gay Movement.

Any gay man who became voluntarily and publicly involved in this protracted struggle before 1960 and who claims that he did so without trepidation is, almost certainly, a liar. I was by no means certain that I could fend off the enemy – in the shape not only of the law, but also the whole rag-bag of reactionary forces which were uniting to defend it. I was quite unsure whether I might be completely overwhelmed and I was certainly in no fit state to find myself fighting on two fronts at once.

It was therefore with considerable dismay that I realized that some of my gay acquaintances were distancing themselves from me. It was as though they regarded me as a marked man. If I joined a group of people drinking at a bar one or two of them would drift away. If I was drinking with a group I would see somebody who would normally have joined it enter and order and sit elsewhere.

Those who remained my friends missed no opportunity to remind me of the folly of rocking the boat and the wisdom of letting sleeping dogs lie. The man I was living with was treated in the same way. Someone he had known for years asked him, please, if he saw them in a bar would he kindly not speak to them there. I even found myself suggesting to him that it might be better if we were seen more often drinking separately rather than together.

The Wolfenden Committee had been given its task as the result of considerable disquiet when the police had been foolish enough to include some well-known names in one of their regular purges. This case had also served to reinforce the public perception of homosexuality as a perversion of the upper classes and this may well have accounted for some of the difficulties which I was to encounter in the Labour Party. I had joined it in 1956, not because I had suddenly seen the blinding light of socialism but rather in revulsion against Eden's armed intervention in Suez and in appreciation of Gaitskell's spirited stand against it.

In June 1958 I had offered my support to A.E. Dyson who was putting together a Homosexual Law Reform Society (HLRS) which was based in London. I was to remain a supporter (it did not have members) through all the years of its existence, although sometimes a critical one. I suspect there were times when they regarded me as more of an irritant than an asset. At the behest of the Society I had written to my local paper, the *Nelson Leader*, generally supporting law reform but more specifically in answer to a somewhat dotty commentary about the Wolfenden proposals by their medical correspondent. There were many letters to the press to follow that one and if I quote some here it is because there was a long period when that activity seemed to be the only immediate way to advance the reform because of the absence of any grassroots campaigning organization and the hostility of the political parties.

1958 was the only year in which Labour secured complete control of the Nelson Borough Council – every alderman and every councillor on the authority, a Labour man or woman. I was one of the new intake and my election also entitled me to a seat on the party's local executive committee. I decided to try to get a resolution in favour of homosexual law reform passed by them as a move towards reshaping national policy. Surprisingly, perhaps even perversely, much of the early pressure for reform had come from the political right. The Wolfenden Committee had been set up initially to review only the laws on prostitution and it was only after sustained urging by the late Robert (later Lord) Boothby that the government somewhat begrudgingly agreed to add homosexual offences to its terms of reference.

The *Spectator* was then pushing harder for reform than the other political journals and even after the inquiry on the first two occasions when votes were taken in the House of Commons, people now regarded as hard right placed themselves on the side of the reformers – Margaret Thatcher, Enoch Powell, Sir Keith Joseph and also Nicholas Ridley, who not only voted for change but was also a sponsor of Humphry Berkeley's defeated reform Bill of 1965. As time went on the *New Statesman* overtook the *Spectator* in the amount of space devoted to the issue and more Labour MPs moved into the reform camp, but it was depressing to find the party itself so possessed by hostility towards the homosexual cause when it should by then have been occupying an ascending place within its thinking.

I suppose the party's attitude should not have come as a surprise. They saw the condition as a product of the public schools from where it was carried into the decadence of those upper echelons of society to which they were so implacably opposed. This misconception was able to maintain its grip despite the awesome discovery that this shadow stalked even within the party's own ranks. The wayward propensities of the late Tom Driberg MP were well known throughout and beyond the Parliamentary party, long before Driberg himself (after his elevation to the peerage) decided to tell all that was printable. The easy-going tolerance of Driberg concealed the essential hypocrisy of the party which was only revealed when misfortune struck one of the gay brothers, who would then find himself without either support or even sympathy.

When W.T. Field, a Labour MP, was fined a small sum in 1953 simply on the basis of police evidence that he had smiled at some sailors in a public convenience, he disappeared from public life completely. A decade later, and even more worrying, was the party's complete lack of reaction to the killing of George Brinham.

Brinham was a member of the Executive of the Amalgamated Society of Woodworkers and had been chairman of the Labour Party from 1959 to 1960. He was forty-six years old when in 1962 he met a violent end at the hands of a sixteen-year-old cellarman he had befriended. At the Old Bailey the youth was acquitted of both murder and manslaughter and was discharged. The judge said: 'A statement by the lad shows clearly that this man had attempted to make homosexual advances . . . . That is as clear a provocation as it is possible to have.'

Brinham had met the youth at Charing Cross. They had been for a coffee and then for a drive, visited Brinham's flat and drunk a couple of brown ales. They then went to a cinema and followed that with an hour in a cartoon show, then to a pub for a couple of pints before returning to the flat.

What happened there was revealed to the nation by a drooling *News of the World* to whom the youth had sold his story and who presented it 'in his own words':

> . . . he'd made this pass at me you see. He put his arms round me and said give us a kiss. It made me feel sick. Disgusted. I just wanted to get out of his flat. But he tried to grab hold of me and press me against the bookcase. I put my hands behind my back, like a lever, to push myself forward. Then I felt this decanter. Heavy cut class it was. Empty. I hit him with it and he just stood there looking at me, then came forward. I hit him again. And again. It took less than a couple of seconds.
>
> He sort of staggered into the hall, then went down. And he was bleeding all over the place. Now if I hadn't done a bit of slaughtering as well, pigs and things, this blood might have panicked me. Made me vomit or something . . . . I got him under his armpits and dragged him back into the room. It didn't make me feel funny or anything touching him like that after I'd felled him. I thought if he doesn't die he's not going to report this to the police after what he tried to do to me (*News of the World*, 27 January 1963).

Brinham's body was not found until the following week. The youth had stolen a car to get to the Midlands where he had told his mother who had in turn told the police, who then spent days frantically searching for a flat to fit the vague description given to them.

No attempt at indecency had even been alleged and I
thought then, as I think now, that it would not have been
unreasonable, even in 1963, to expect that somebody, from
among the many colleagues who had known Brinham and
served with him, might have stood up and said that it was a
hell of a price to pay for trying to steal a kiss.

But all was silence.

With the Party in this mood I expected trouble and I was
not mistaken. After much lobbying and manoeuvreing I
managed, at the second attempt, to get a pro-Wolfenden
resolution through the Clover Hill ward committee, but the
alarm bells were soon sounding at the town hall and in the
Labour Party offices. My resolution was the only one down
for consideration by the Executive of the Nelson party and
the meeting was clearly packed with people who had not
attended for years in order to block its progress. Instead of
outright defeat, I was put down by a procedural manoeuvre
to the effect that the resolution should not be discussed.

Maybe there were some lessons which could be passed on
to a wider audience? Brief mention of homosexuality in a
new Liberal journal had led to claims that this had lost
Liberal votes at Inverness. I wrote:

> Sir: The annual conference of the Scottish Liberal Party is
> not the only place where attempts are made to hamper free
> discussion about homosexual law reform and it may be of
> some help to the increasing number of people who look for
> early progress on this reform if some of the devices
> commonly used to secure suppression were more widely
> known.
>
> The most popular seems to be the contention that these
> sexual matters are not really political issues at all, but are
> questions for the individual conscience which are
> traditionally dealt with in the House, if at all, by a private
> member. In answer to this it is appropriate to draw
> attention to the method by which the Street Offences Bill
> was enacted and then go on to ask how the dictates of the
> individual conscience, which is inclined towards a greater
> tolerance of homosexuality, are to be made effective, in a
> matter involving legislation, except through political
> action.

The next move is likely to be a corollary to the above, maintaining that this is a non-party matter which cuts clean across party lines. This is perfectly respectable when used by a party spokesman commenting upon a matter which his party has not considered, but when it is used to prevent discussion within a party it becomes a very shabby get-out indeed.

Next comes the 'vote-loser' dodge from the expediency-before-principle-every-time boys and finally (Lord help us!) the claim that the matter is not one which can be discussed in mixed company (*Guardian*, 18 May 1960).

All these arguments had been used against me in the Nelson party. Nobody had actually said that it would frighten away new industry and, looking back, I feel only surprise.

When I finally set down my experiences within the party for *New Left Review* in an article called 'Wolfenden in the Wilderness', the editor inserted a preface to the piece:

... Labour has not only fudged the larger issues. It's as if the Party's political imagination and grasp are paralysed. It no longer seems to know where our discontents are, or how to give them voice .... It has lost that sense of 'being in tune' that every successful radical party *must* have .... Has it forgotten that people act and vote politically not because of election pleas but out of discontent and anger caused by injustice, inequality, the abuse of power and privilege? (*New Left Review* 12, December 1961).

A relocation of my employment caused me to say a sad farewell to Nelson and to decline an invitation to stand for re-election to the Council. I had no appetite for repeating this futile exercise in some other local Labour party, so I decided to seek some other way of making progress.

Fate, with more than a little help from the National Coal Board, had brought me in 1963 to work in Tyldesley, a God-forsaken hole on a worked-out corner of the south Lancashire coalfield. The move had torn me from my political and other involvements and, with time on my hands, I began to put pressure on the HLRS in London urging them to give the campaign a provincial dimension.

Some of the urgency to form a northern committee was personal. It had been five long years since that first hesitant letter to the *Nelson Leader* and my only contact with anybody else in the campaign had been through protracted correspondence with the successive secretaries of the London organization. I needed somebody around who would give me a bit of comfort and support.

The witch-hunts were starting up again, including one in Bolton where ten men faced charges in respect of private behaviour. This led to imprisonment, loss of employment, and ultimately, a suicide. It was in connection with this case that I got my first indication that police confidence in the law they were enforcing was possibly beginning to crack. I had written to the *Bolton Evening News* condemning the prosecution and ending with the somewhat dramatic question, 'Is there nobody in your town with the dignity and guts to speak out against this senseless cruelty?'

The immediate consequence was publication of letters from a prominent businessman and Liberal parliamentary candidate and from a Canon of the Church of England both supporting a change in the law, followed by another letter from me. The paper's deputy editor, who assured me that he loathed homosexuals, told me later that it was at this stage when he received a visit from some senior local policemen. They had asked if the fact that he had published four consecutive letters all calling for a change in the law really reflected the views of local people. He told me that in fairness he had felt obliged to tell them he had received other letters so violently opposed to the idea that he had returned them all to the senders with a request that they should be rewritten in more moderate terms. Presumably this news sent the police away feeling less disturbed than when they arrived, although the other letters, if they were rewritten, were certainly never published.

The atmosphere in Parliament was becoming thick with talk of compromise. Desmond Donnelly MP produced a Bill which would have repealed the Labouchere Amendment which had first criminalized all male homosexual acts in 1885, but would have left buggery punishable by life imprisonment. Leo Abse MP sought to introduce a Bill which would have reduced the maximum sentence for homosexual offences and would have required that no charges for private consensual behaviour could be brought without the consent of the Director of Public Prosecutions.

I condemned the move towards compromise in a letter which the *Guardian* published on 26 February 1962, but was saddened three years later to find the *Guardian* itself moving into the compromise game with an astonishing leading article in its editorial:

> The Wolfenden Committee made a distinction between crime and sin, and considered that only those sins should rank as crimes which injured someone other than the sinners or which constituted an offence against public decency. A sexual act committed in public clearly offends against public decency. But it was argued by the sole dissentient in the Wolfenden Committee, Mr Adair, that not only the act itself but also 'the presence in a district of adult male lovers living openly and notoriously under the approval of the law is bound to have a regrettable and pernicious effect on the young people of the community'. This is not a negligible point.
>
> Could it perhaps be met by adding a proviso to the effect that the parties concerned would forfeit the defence that they had acted in private if their conduct was such as to advertise their relations to the public at large? That is not to say, of course, that such public conduct would constitute an offence. It would, if proved, merely negate the defence that the sexual acts were private – and they would also have to be proved (*Guardian*, 27 May 1965).

This fatally-flawed freedom formula, every bit as well-intentioned as the Abse and Donnelly efforts, fortunately sank without trace.

The first tangible move towards a North-Western Homosexual Law Reform Committee was made at a meeting held at 4 Moxley Road, Manchester 8 on 4 June 1964. It was the home of Stanley Rowe who had written to me inviting me to join a small group which had been meeting for private discussion under the title of 'Homosexual Law Reform Society – Manchester' – an appendage of the London Society. Rowe was a youth club leader who did social work within the Jewish community. He and his wife had hosted speakers from London. He had been under pressure for nearly a year from both them and me to expand the Manchester group, but he appeared to be hopelessly over-committed in his other work.

Of the eight people at that meeting, I imagine less than half were gay. It was decided to re-establish the group on a wider basis and to work towards a large public meeting in the north, though in the event it was to be two years before this took place. I found myself secretary of an Advisory Committee charged with organizing a semi-public meeting to formally launch the new group under the title 'North-Western Homosexual Law Reform Committee'. This took place on 7 October 1964 at Church House, Deansgate, Manchester. This venue was facilitated by the late Colin Harvey who was senior social worker for the Manchester Diocesan Board for Social Responsibility and who was to become first vice-chair and then chair of the new Committee.

Attendance was by a fairly open invitation process involving the twenty-five or so supporters of the London Society who were resident in the area, together with representatives of a large number of social work agencies in the north. I addressed the meeting first, followed by Antony Grey, Colin Harvey and then Rev. Bernard Dodd, a methodist minister who became the first chair. A paper was circulated for signature by all those who wished to be enrolled as supporters.

The many charges that the Campaign for Homosexual Equality suffered because it was too rigidly structured could never have been levelled at this, its predecessor, which had hardly any structure at all. The process of imposing a constitution upon this loosely-knit set-up came much later and was, I am sorry to report, a very messy business indeed with many raised voices – including mine – and much metaphorical bloodshed.

While the mailing list was predominantly non-gay, the active attendance at policy-making meetings was the reverse. But these open meetings were soon proving to be too nebulous to form an effective controlling body and when the then Bishop of Middleton – a vice-president whose Board Room we used free of charge for our meetings – urged that decisions should be made by an identifiable committee, we agreed. An immediate consequence was that half the people who used to come to meetings were never seen again!

However odd it may now seem, in the very first years of the committee, an unwritten rule required that questions about individuals' sexual orientation were never asked. If this information was available it was because it had been volunteered. There were no self-identified lesbians on the pre-reform committee, but it did have the support of two dedicated women, one a medical social worker and the other an author who spent months seeking out and interviewing every personnel officer on the huge Trafford Park industrial estate soliciting pledges of non-discrimination against homosexual workers.

The launch meeting had ended without resolving the problem of an address for the new organization and left me, as its new secretary, in some difficulty. The Church of England, which continued to support us in many ways, was nevertheless keenly aware that its reactionary wing would certainly rebel if we were allowed to use church premises for our postal address and none of the social work agencies with which we were in touch felt able to help.

We were drifting, apparently inexorably, towards some sort of Box Number arrangement which I felt, and I was not alone, would be very bad for the image. My landlord, if asked, would certainly have refused, so I delivered a pre-emptive strike and ordered the notepaper to be printed with my own address.

Three Robert Street, Atherton was one of a block of well-maintained miners' cottges which the Coal Board eventually sold to the council for peanuts over the heads of its incredulous tenants who would have eagerly bought, but were given no option.

The first 10,000 leaflets which we circulated in 1964 bearing that address attracted a lot of press attention and my workmates soon informed me that the Coal Board's Estates Manager was more than a little aggrieved that he had not been consulted. They urged that I should visit him to sort the thing out, but I said that I had not contravened my tenancy agreement and that if he wanted to see me (I worked in his department, not ten yards from his office), he would have to send for me. He never did, nor did he ever mention it on the many occasions when we met on other matters and shortly afterwards he sanctioned my promotion. I suspect he was a closet liberal who felt he had to put on a show of annoyance because it was expected of him.

The calmness with which the local mining community accepted the campaign eventually enabled me to reassure the still-nervous NUM-sponsored MPs in a long letter, concluding: 'If the miners' MPs can produce a shred of evidence to show that the mining community is particularly or even mildly hostile to this reform I should like to hear it. I know of none' (*New Statesman*, 26 February 1966).

In 1964 I had been involved in a great deal of liaison work with the London Society. Relations between the two organizations were equivocal from the beginning. London seemed to embrace us or reject us according to the mood of the moment which was influenced in part by what we were doing, and in part by which faction of their committee happened to turn up for any particular meeting. They had taken the view that any new organization was necessarily going to corner a proportion of finite financial support which had hitherto been at their exclusive disposal, and as a consequence weaken them. It never seemed to occur to them that there was a vast reservoir of people who remained unlocated and untapped either for their money or their energy. Long discussed proposals for a link-up between the two bodies came to nothing. Their legal man advised against any formal association and we decided against any financial arrangements.

But at an administrative level we got along well enough. Their dedicated and competent secretary Antony Grey (A.E.G. Wright) was always helpful to me and I in turn spoke at a number of meetings and debates for him when he was snowed under with work. Indeed, before 1967 more of my time than I would have wished had been spent giving talks of various kinds (for I truly hate public speaking), from small parish meetings in country vicarages to full-blown university debates. But invitations never came from any political groups, with the single exception of the Marxist Society at Lancaster University, so I eventually wrote individual letters to a large number of local Labour parties in the north asking them to receive a speaker on homosexual law reform. The response was abysmal. None replied except my own (Atherton) party which declined the offer with the observation, 'There is little we can do locally'.

The long-planned public meeting finally came in November 1966 in Manchester's Holdsworth Hall. It was the only provincial public meeting during the ten-year campaign between Wolfenden and the 1967 Sexual Offences Act and was matched by a single earlier one in London. Anxiety about this move was forcefully expressed by some members of the Executive of the London Society who took the view that sympathetic MPs would withdraw their support for the reform if it became apparent that some of the demand for it was coming from homosexuals themselves! The persisting edginess among NUM-sponsored MPs was undoubtedly further soothed by the presence among the speakers of one of their number – the late Alan Fitch, MP for Wigan.

The exercise also served to quieten the *Manchester Evening News* which had by then taken to reproducing one of its vituperative anti-reform editorials in glossy leaflet-form for wider distribution and retention – a remarkable thing for a newspaper to do and something which I have never encountered before or since either in Manchester or anywhere else.

But by then the reform was just around the corner. By the time it came our support was coming overwhelmingly from gay people and it seemed the obvious thing to re-establish the Law Reform Committee as an organization working for the further extension of gay rights. It became first the Committee, then later the Campaign, for Homosexual Equality and most of what followed has been, or will be, recorded elsewhere. I continued as secretary until 1970 when an illness forced me to move back from the front line, as it were, and I became chair and later president of CHE.

My active involvement with the gay issue spanned twenty years. It was an anxious and exhausting but ultimately rewarding experience. It came as no surprise to me that it took ten years after Wolfenden to achieve the recommended reform. That it took twenty-eight years to wring a commitment to gay rights out of the Labour Party was both a surprise and a disappointment.

No examination of the Labour Party's attitude towards homosexuals would be complete without reference to the Bermondsey by-election of February 1983. The Labour candidate was Peter Tatchell, a 31-year-old (non-Militant Tendency) left winger who was not only gay, but who also had a ten-year history of active involvement in the gay movement. The by-election was caused by the resignation from Parliament of Labour chief whip Robert (now Lord) Mellish. Mellish had tried hard to prevent Tatchell becoming the Labour candidate and he threw his weight and considerable local influence behind an independent 'Real Bermondsey Labour' candidate, John O'Grady.

O'Grady, ex-Labour leader of Southwark Council, ran a viciously anti-gay campaign directed personally at Tatchell. Mellish, who had voted for homosexual reform during the Parliamentary debates of 1965 and 1966, found no difficulty in going along with O'Grady and his support for him was but one example among many others of people who were prepared to suspend their otherwise positive attitude towards gay rights in order to secure Tatchell's replacement by somebody of more orthodox political ideas or, if that was not possible, to secure his defeat, which they eventually did by a substantial majority.

The failure of the Labour leadership to condemn the scurrilous campaign mounted by O'Grady who, against all the rules, was still a member of the party, was quite remarkable. It was as though the party was condoning the crucifixion of Tatchell by its silence – just as that earlier silence had condoned the killing of George Brinham.

It was this behaviour of the party leadership which signalled to the press that Tatchell was fair game for the vultures of Fleet Street. Political commentator Walter Terry, seeking to defend the disgraceful and absolutely indefensible press campaign against Tatchell, said on television: 'It was the Labour Party who did it and caused the trouble. It was Bob Mellish stirring it up like mad. It stemmed from the House of Commons, the shadow Cabinet and Walworth Road.' It was a sorry story and I hope – without a great deal of conviction – that we shall never hear its like again.

How long will it take to secure the Parliamentary action

which will be necessary to remove the remaining legal discrimination against gay men and to give both to them and to lesbians statutory protection against harassment and victimization in connection with employment, housing, child-custody, inheritance, hospital-visiting and (quite conceivably) health-care? Many people believe that the achievement of a two-thirds majority in support of gay rights at the Labour Party conference in 1986 will require the inclusion of a commitment to further reform in Labour's election manifesto, but this is not the case. A two-thirds conference majority only obliges the committee drawing-up the manifesto to *consider* an item for inclusion and a programme prepared at a time when public attitudes towards homosexuals are hardening might well omit any reference to gay rights.

And even if a commitment *is* included it is likely to be nothing more than a pledge to allow time for a private member's Bill which – in the event of a Labour victory – would mean that reform was dependent upon the uncertainties of a free vote, with homophobic Labour MPs being left free to vote with opponents from the political right in order to block progress. That would not be good enough. In any case, the rule about the need to confine legislation on 'moral issues' to private members' Bills is only called in aid when the proposed legislation is of the liberating kind.

Governments have been eager enough to legislate in this area when the trend was towards repression. A good example was the Street Offences Act of 1959. This placed new restrictions upon the freedom of prostitutes and was enacted through a Government Bill only eighteen months after publication of the Wolfenden Report – upon which it was based – while Wolfenden's other recommendations about homosexual offences had to wait ten years until the time was ripe for a private member to act.

But there have been occasions when governments have been prepared to take action in order to humanise the law, although, perhaps surprisingly, in recent times that good example seems only to have been set by the Conservatives. It was they who decriminalized suicide in 1961, thus ending the wretched spectacle of failed suicides being dragged through the courts. Even more amazingly, it was they who abolished hanging for over five-sixths of murderers through the Homicide Act of 1957. In a sense they were doing the right thing for the wrong reasons, since the purpose of that Government Bill was to hold back for a little longer the tide which was flowing ever more powerfully in favour of the complete abolition of capital punishment.

That complete abolition was eventually achieved during a period of Labour Government, but, even though the Labour Party conference had first passed a resolution calling for the abolition of capital punishment as long ago as 1934, the government itself was not prepared to introduce a Bill, despite the earlier Tory example, and the task was left to a private member in 1965. That member was the late Sydney Silverman, a Labour MP who had fought long and hard for abolition both inside and outside Parliament. Although the Conservative Government in 1957 had not been delivering all that Silverman desired, he was generous in his tribute to them: '... at long last the Government have taken their courage in both hands ... without waiting for public opinion, without a General Election, without a mandate and without worrying what the man in the pub or club will think about it.'

It would be nice to have Silverman's words engraved on a little brass plate and fixed on the desk of the next Labour Home Secretary in order to give courage to *that* government whenever they are agonizing about whether to do what is expedient or to do what is right.

Particularly when they get round to thinking about lesbian and gay rights.

3 Scotland: against the odds

Ian Dunn

Me? A war baby. I was conceived near a Gloucestershire aerodrome in the summer of 1942 and born on May Day, 1943.

My family was prosperous in that especially Glasgow middle-class fashion. There were links to wealth on the male side with shipping, steel and engineering; and on the female side with property and manufacturing (Beatties Biscuits). It was well into 1946 before I saw my father, when he was demobbed from North Africa. The following year my only sister was born and we moved to Bearsden, a posh dormitory town just outside the city boundary.

My first conscious memories, then, are mellow and of a world full of hope and high expectations. I was growing up right at the end of a vigorous period for the mercantile middle class, and Glasgow was still dubbed the 'second city of the Empire'. But those hopes were never realized. There were family migrations – to South Africa and Australia – and a loss of confidence.

My early politics were Scottish Unionist; Labour was the big bad demon in our family. My granny, Sybil Watson, was the President of the Woodside (Hillhead) Conservative and Unionist Association. Glasgow was pulling itself out of the Victorian past in the fifties, with massive plans for demolition of the old tenements and an enormous municipal house-building programme. I watched without pleasure the building up of Drumchapel and Easterhouse and – in the sixties – the soulless tower blocks of Hutchesontown Gorbals. The Glasgow middle class was clustered in Kelvinside and parts of the southside. Society was very obviously class divided and divided, too, in other alienating ways – women from men; leisure from work.

I was not 'good' at school. I still wince when I remember my (unwanted) pant-wetting standing in front of the class and my voice, *damn it*, refusing to break. I was crimson with shame when I first heard my voice on tape at fifteen: so *that's* why they taunted me and called me *Miss* Dunn! Throughout adolescence I had to carry around the personal, mute burden of virginity which was not lifted until I was nineteen on a sunbaked beach near Prestwick in 1962.

People like me had a godawful time in the fifties. There were the Montagu and Wildeblood trials and the brouhaha surrounding someone called Wolfenden. Americans like Senator McCarthy put the fear of death into me. When, in 1958, our much-liked scoutmaster was hastily dismissed because he had 'struck a boy', I realised that 'they' (adult authority) were lying to me: he must have touched the boy in a different sort of way.

I do not want to dwell on what is not such an exceptional story, except to say that the anger that was gradually fighting its way out – elbowing out a profound sense of hopelessness – was given an enormous shove at my coming-out party in 1964. It was the kind of occasion when the eldest son of good Glasgow parentage was presented at a sumptuous dinner-dance to those he was expected to marry into, and to do well for. I kicked against this muzzling but was not yet ready to jump the walls of middle-class respectability.

It was not just me who was awakening in the sixties. On night shift at the Prestwick Airport control tower, on duty for the Meteorological Office, I was listening to the English language broadcasts from Prague; closer to home, Labour lost Hamilton to the Scottish National Party in a by-election in 1967; the Sexual Offences Act was passed – and it deliberately excluded Scotland. I was finally stung into action.

But where was the action to be organized? Ian Christie (*Gay Scotland*, January/February 1987) has described features of the still illegal gay male scene in Scotland in the late sixties:

The usual routine on a Friday or Saturday night was to
drink in one of the gay pubs until the closing time of 10
o'clock, then to traipse to a gay café such as Crawfords in
Frederick Street until 11 pm and then proceed with a
bottle to a party. There we danced, drank, gossiped, joked
and we entertained each other until five or six in the
morning... Perhaps we were more closetted, but in our
closets we asserted ourselves more defiantly in drag and
outrageous campery. Effeminacy was 'in' and the sight of
the modern leather-clad macho clone would have made most
of us run a mile – except those of us who were into rough
trade. We sometimes forget, I think, that the original
Stonewall rioters were drag queens. Certainly, we didn't
have commercial discos, but we had far more parties in each
others' houses and flats. It was nothing for one hundred
people to crowd into one small apartment in Edinburgh or
in Glasgow, word having gone round the cafés and pubs
like wildfire.

Once you had made up your mind to thole* the outrageous
camp-and-bitchery and were willing to accept a camp name
and 'bow down' to the 'Mother' or 'Duchess' of a particular
coterie, *then* you were launched. But, as Ian Christie
continues, there were problems with the outside world:

On one memorable occasion a Glasgow party was raided by
the police. An Edinburgh group arrived by car outside the
house just in time to see sixty of their friends being loaded
into Black Marias. Next day they appeared, six of them in
drag, before the local magistrate who charged them with
breach of the peace. The *Daily Express* had a field day with
names and addresses and photographs of the drag queens
coming out of court. Unfortunately, several of our number
lost their jobs as a result of this exposure.

It was bloody hard to talk about changing the world when
fellow queers (we did not say 'gay' then) were trying to gild
the cage and insulate themselves from outside realities.
Nonetheless, I thought that it would be useful to set up a
branch of the HLRS in Scotland. By that time I was under

---

* 'thole' is a Scottish word meaning endure.

the influence of two very different men – Antony Grey in England and Frank Kameny in the USA. Tony Grey was keen to see an organization off the ground but reluctant to have it as part of the HLRS. At that time the only branch of the HLRS was the North-Western Homosexual Law Reform Committee and it was proving to be an awkward off-shoot – far too pushy for the well-mannered London executive committee!

The crucial influence proved to be Frank Kameny's. A footnote in Donald West's then pioneering paperback, *Homosexuality*, had given the address of the Mattachine Society in Washington DC. More than anyone else, Frank brought me out ... from 3000 miles away. His letters, preserved in the Scottish Gay Archive in Edinburgh, invigorated and astonished me. In 1968 at a meeting of the (US) East Coast Homophile Organizations (ECHO) the rallying cry of 'Gay is Good' was adopted. I was electrified – and also terrified. Frank sent me a badge; I hid it. I was not ready – yet.

There were quieter local influences. Contact with the North-Western Homosexual Law Reform Committee brought me in touch with Allan Horsfall and Colin Harvey. Colin had been a social worker attached to the Church of England Liverpool Diocese before he moved to Glasgow with his wife, Elizabeth, at the end of 1968. A group of us met, at first, in the drawing-room of my parents' home in Buckingham Street, Glasgow. There were six of us at what must have been the very first organized gay business meeting in Scotland on 7 February 1969. I had access at work to duplicating facilities and to a telephone, both of which proved to be organizationally invaluable for us in those days before photocopiers and STD telephones. We decided to set up a separate Scottish organization called the Scottish Minorities Group (SMG). Twenty-five people – nineteen men and six women – attended the founding meeting of SMG on 9 May 1969 at the Chaplaincy Centre of Glasgow University.

The name Scottish Minorities Group is now thought to be quaintly out of date and the concept of gay men/lesbians as a minority is discredited. Part of me still warms to the old name (SMG became the Scottish Homosexual Rights Group

in 1978) because the minority concept was very helpful in
some negotiations for advances. It proved useful in other
ways too: most lesbians and gay men before Stonewall/GLF
were highly reluctant to come out and so welcomed the title.
And, whatever the actual title, we certainly made a big
splash in Scotland after 1970.

We acquired meeting places in both Edinburgh (23
George Street) and Glasgow (214 Clyde Street). We began to
organize social events as well as meetings and from 1971 we
organized the Cobweb disco, Scotland's first gay disco. Local
groups were set up outside Edinburgh and Glasgow – in
Aberdeen, Dundee, Falkirk, Paisley, St Andrews and Fort
William. In 1973, the first national forums were held to
bring together people from all over Scotland. We were able
to raise thousands of pounds and canny-like, invested our
surplus in property which has ensured our long-term
survival.

Lesbians and gay men in the pre-SMG period had led
entirely separate social lives. SMG, however, was mixed.
Lesbians were welcomed into SMG by gay men for a host of
rather mixed reasons. Some men were glad of the presence of
women, because women legitimized their own involvement;
women 'de-queered' SMG. I never subscribed to this view
but it was widely held in the early days. Most others wanted
lesbians to join because we believed that, as homosexuals,
we had a lot in common to fight against, especially the
hard-drinking, woman-battering males we found ourselves
surrounded by. Women got a raw deal, and we gay men were
on their side. This can now be seen as a simplistic outlook,
one which was innocent of, or ignorant about, sexism.

SMG tried to rework the best of Scottish radicalism and
deliberately did not push ahead with an all-out attack on
capitalism and society, in the way that the Gay Liberation
Front tried to do. GLF was, in fact, only active in Edinburgh
for three years, fading away in 1974. The reformist outlook
was characteristic of SMG. SMG wanted to make life more
bearable, more equal with heterosexuals. Actually, we rarely
discussed what that equality meant and the discussion was
often truncated with a shrug and a laughing remark, 'Well,
we are all better than straights anyway.' The limitations of
this outlook were not immediately apparent. We were by far

and away the most radical thing happening on the personal-is-political front in Scotland at that juncture and what we were saying and doing was astonishing in the eyes of the Scottish establishment.

I wrote scores of articles in 1971 and 1972 and made an historic appearance on Scottish Television on a programme hosted by George Reid (later to become a Scottish National Party MP) when I declared to a large audience that I was homosexual and proud of it. An assistant Chief Constable sitting next to me was seen quite literally jumping away from me.

At the same time I was in touch with Andrew Lumsden and in a small way I helped to get the first British homosexual newspaper – *Gay News* – off the ground. In Edinburgh we held teach-ins, theatre events and dances, dances, dances. In the summer of 1971 I went to the States and stayed for three months on a $99 Greyhound bus pass. I looked at, learned and loved lesbian and gay liberation. I very nearly did not come home and by the end of the summer clocked up my thousandth sexual experience – an immensely sobering thought in these days of AIDS. The main lesson, for me, was the passion and pleasure of the successful Gay Community Centres in New York and Los Angeles. But I did come back to Scotland and threw myself into the fund raising for Centres in Edinburgh and in Glasgow.

It had always been one of the main aims of SMG to set up centres. We were almost zealots about this. Being much more internationally minded than the English organizations, we had learned not only from the States but also from the Netherlands. The Dutch had regrouped in the fifties and, as the Scots and the Dutch are often temperamentally rather alike, we felt that this could be repeated in Scotland. We saved our bawbees (halfpennies) and by the end of 1974 had raised £3,000. We borrowed a matching sum from one of SMG's founders and bought 60 Broughton Street, Edinburgh, outright. It was to be our Information Centre. One of the parts of the UK where all male homosexual activity was still outlawed was the first to have such a building, wholly owned by open, campaigning homosexuals.

The strength of the Scottish movement for gay rights was

confirmed by the fact that the International Gay Rights Congress was held in Edinburgh in December 1974. There had been an international organization for homosexual rights with members from Scandinavia, Holland and France which had met occasionally from the thirties through to 1955. Ours, however, was the first such international meeting since Stonewall and we were demanding not *homosexual* rights, but *gay* rights. It had been largely organized by Derek Ogg, then Senior President of Edinburgh University Students' Representative Council, and myself with funding from the university gaysoc. The arrival of 400 delegates was a spectacular coming out.

With the Congress, the opening of the Information Centre, plans laid for even better premises in Glasgow, my first serious relationship with another man – Dr Michael Coulson, head of the Sanskrit department at Edinburgh University – and the purchase of my first house – a flat above the Centre – a chapter in my personal history of struggle for gay rights had closed.

Postscript

As the movement grew and expanded, there were to be hermit days for me in the late seventies: Michael's suicide was a considerable shock and made me wary about immersing myself in another close relationship.

I became involved in straight politics – first in the short-lived Scottish Labour Party; then in the 'British' Labour Party. I have a worry that straight politics sucks out your energies and spits you out if you are found wanting – or if you are outspoken like me.

There have been more rewards in my gay politics. After the Congress in 1974, the international links were maintained and developed through the establishment of the International Lesbian and Gay Association. I have also seen the Centre at Broughton Street go from strength to strength. It is now home to a café, a gay accessories shop, the Merry Mac Fun Co-operative theatre company, a bisexual phoneline and *Gay Scotland* magazine. It has also in its time helped generate the Edinburgh Switchboard and the Open

Gaze bookshop (forerunner of Lavender Menace, then to become today's West and Wilde). In 1985–6 we spent £23,000 – with no help sought from the council – on re-equipping the Centre. Since the late seventies the migration of young lesbians and gay men to the metropolis of London has slowed down. Some of that is due to the uneven effects of the economic recession, or perhaps the fear of AIDS. But some is certainly due to the growth of the Scottish gay community – to which I am proud to have been able to contribute.

4 Memoirs of an anti-heroine

Elizabeth Wilson

These days I seldom take the road that runs along the top of Regent's Park between Camden Town and Maida Vale. But whenever I do, the ghost of a former self waits to greet me, standing on a corner in the defiant gaiety of a striped trouser suit and a hat from the camp sixties emporium Biba – a huge fuchsia cartwheel, its floppy brim shadowing a deadpan face with black-circled eyes and pale lips – a fellow-traveller who lived in a different London. For London is so large that a slightly altered geography maps one period onto another, and to wander unexpectedly into a once familiar district can be to walk into the past.

In a flat just off that main road north of the Park I remember parties where hectic scenes of rivalry were played out. Our hosts, a married couple, were a gay man and a lesbian. They organized a little coterie around themselves, entertaining us in a room with black walls and a harpsichord. He told the Tarot cards with obsessional and compelling attention to detail, while she regaled us with wild tales of pick-ups in the British Museum Reading Room. Their flat was a staging post on the run from my home in Islington to friends in Warwick Avenue, Paddington, and the Gateways Club in Chelsea – we all used to drive there in a group.

The wife had an affair with a woman with whom I was also entangled, and as we drove home late at night, my lover (the woman I actually lived with, that is) and I used to glance up at the lighted windows of the flat with a mournful pang. But that was at a slightly later period.

A year or so earlier I had a passing fancy for another woman in the coterie, and I used to take the Bakerloo line tube out to Maida Vale. Once, as I waited even longer than usual on a platform at the interchange, a man engaged me in conversation about my school days. Gradually the discussion worked itself round to school discipline, corporal punishment, but, my mind on my romance, I was only half-listening. When he asked me if I got the cane, if they pulled my knickers down, however, I retreated in appalled embarrassment from this unseemly monologue, feeling all the same that I must somehow have colluded, or even that some propensity of my own and not mere absent-mindedness had made me so unaware. As it was, I moved off in a huff, but he followed me as I boarded the train, and I remained stickily aware of his meaningful, conniving gaze from the other end of the carriage until I jumped the train at Little Venice.

Another time I took a cab from the Gateways. This time, the driver's friendly small talk began with a discussion of fancy dress parties and ended with a desperate plea for used underwear ('I suppose you think I'm kinky').

I did not exactly take offence at these slightly mad, obsessed encounters, did not think of them as an intrusion of a hateful masculine sexuality, as a form of verbal sexual assault, as male violence. These fantasies which burst out into the public domain, a shared secret at least, seemed to me to mark the parameters of that freed sexuality of the period, a period in which sex and madness lay close together, and in which a new romanticism of lust and deviance replaced the old romanticism of adultery and star-crossed lovers. I was a lesbian – a deviant also; were they not my brothers, mirror images of me, outlaws like me. Already in the late fifties a vogue for Jacobean tragedy had foreshadowed this attraction towards a rawer, uglier sex. Incest was one theme but most 'modern' perhaps, most in tune with the ambience of the early sixties, was Thomas Middleton's *The Changeling*. The giddy heroine's obsessive love-hatred for her loathsome, creepy, evil servant, de Flores, prefigured the sinister side of modern love, and could be relived in contemporary themes of forbidden lust and the compulsion of ugliness and pornography.

So these phantom desires spoken by strangers, squalid in one way, or amusing, as I chose to anecdotalize them, in another way spoke for the times, when to dare to speak the unprintable was to break taboos. The sixties was all about showing, displaying, saying it, as much as about doing it.

Perhaps of all the slogans of the early seventies, the gay slogan, 'We are the people our parents warned us against', spoke most urgently to me. For what I was doing in the sixties – from the moment I first gingerly descended the steps of the Gateways Club in 1960 to the strains of Elvis Presley's 'Only the Lonely', to my final encounter with the bouncer exactly ten years later, when I got banned for polluting the place with gay liberation leaflets – was trying to be the people my mother had warned me against. Any chance encounter, therefore, that ran against the norms of bourgeois discourse, and particularly any that ran against the prescribed role for women, was to be welcomed. These men who spoke of their desires might seem sordid or comic; but at the same time, bearers of inadmissable longings to which they frankly owned up, they appeared as witnesses, like myself, to a deeper and perhaps uglier truth than the truth of the public world above the labyrinthine map I was trying to explore. So my London of the sixties was not a different geographical location, but was rather a different mental state, or a geological map, a layered territory, a zone beneath, in which rules were abrogated and anything could happen, the underside of the world of respectability and nine-to-five.

The desire to explore that labyrinth of inchoate desires propelled me in two opposite directions and invaded my work as well. I worked on the fringes of psychoanalysis, in the child guidance movement. As defined by my colleagues, my work was to help women to be better mothers – not an aim with which I had much sympathy, or for which I was appropriately equipped. What I'd wanted from psycho-analysis was to understand myself, not police other women. The psychoanalytic movement – at least as I experienced it, as it filtered through the social work of the period, was conservative, banal. It stereotyped women, elevated feminity and motherhood to the status of spiritual imperatives, and by the early sixties this ideology had become slightly mad itself, preserving a drawing-room of illusions in the face of the advancing tide of social change.

The aims of the child guidance movement were ambitious, humanistic, well-intended: to improve family life, to relieve the sufferings of disturbed children, to promote an ideal of child-centredness. But its middle-class assumptions and its support for male privilege warped it fatally. Also, the circularity of its belief system, so that criticism and dissent themselves automatically proved the pathology of the dissident. That used to enrage me, and the seamlessness of the culture seemed like gross complacency, as the fifties lingered on into the sixties in the discreet consulting rooms. I could not accommodate myself – yet I stayed there for a long time, feeling trapped but ever beckoned on by the promise of self-understanding, of a thread through the labyrinth. So I lived in secrecy and rebellion. With savage social gestures I lashed out verbally at the status quo, out of hours. At work I was silent, a demure little girl in my mini-skirts (although they signalled an ambivalent message too) and my concealed but total alienation resulted only in lack of spontaneity. I had a secret: lesbianism – which was to save me from the dismal, spinsterly respectability of my colleagues.

In retrospect I see a lot of lesbianism in the dedicated, conservative circles of psychiatric social work in the sixties. No one ever hinted, of course, but there were those women living in contented couples, others whose looks and personalities displayed an awkward mingling of the masculine and feminine; mannish gestures clashing with a smooth dress and seamless french pleat hairdo, or a lacy jumper with a short crop, a tightness of manner, a lingering maternal concern for other women, hints of depression, loneliness, thwarted love. In the knowledge of my 'free' life outside work, I perceived these women as wholly other, dismissed them as the negative of myself. That now seems so naïve. No doubt they were less repressed than I realized, perhaps thought of *me* as the one who wasn't quite aware, who was playing a game or deceiving myself. I was closer than I would admit to them, and for that reason felt even more hostile to the whole social work ethos, felt trapped, marked by its introspective interrogation which pathologized and reified sex. I did not understand that overt lesbianism might coexist with conservative views and middle-class values; too readily did I equate lesbianism with a general bohemian way of life. Similarly I'd believed the teachers at my girls' school were blighted spinsters in their sober garb until, years later, a fellow feminist who'd attended the same school a few years after me revealed that there'd been a monumental lesbian scandal – the teachers I'd stereotyped as sexless turned out to have been raving it up all along, and to have known very well why they wore tailored suits and flat-heeled shoes.

But I imagined I was *totally* different – smart, trendy, knowing, where they were dowdy and inhibited, these umarried women. But I was different only in linking my sexuality with a particular political standpoint, and I don't know where that idea came from – Simone de Beauvoir perhaps.

So I lived a double life, in which my womanliness was a masquerade, inhabiting a space between the open rejection of society and an underworld that bordered on prostitution. There, just beyond my experience it lay, a real underworld that I observed with fascination, without ever letting it get too close to me. Years later, it was no surprise to recognize in the waiting-room at Holloway Prison two women, strippers, who had once frequented the Gateways. With their blonde mink, bleached hair and pale boots soft as kidgloves, they stood out in the shabby crowd of waiting visitors. So the worlds did touch, theirs and mine, through alternative politics, for now – this was 1972 – I was visiting an alleged member of the Angry Brigade, they some friend on a drugs rap.

The sense of a decade doesn't necessarily match the actual dates, and it's mere change that my years at the Gateways happened to coincide exactly with the sixties. In any case, the 'Gates' wasn't really a very sixties place – more late forties or early fifties – a drinking club in a slight time warp, left over from an earlier period.

The early sixties, from 1960 to 1963, seem in memory to have more in common with the late fifties than with the late sixties, an earlier break having come in 1956, when the leaden clouds of the early fifties had started to lift and life opened out, protest movements began. 'Kinky' was an 'in' word then, yet those brief years seemed to have a fresh innocence that was lost by the mid-decade. The fifties had seemed to sinful, so *old*. In my twenty-first birthday photograph I look older by years than I do in my late twenties; so young, my dark lips, vaselined lids and tightly-waved hair, heavy black evening dress and pearl necklace lend me a poignantly sophisticated melancholy. But by the time I was nearing thirty my hair was cropped in gamine style and I was wearing high-waisted Kate Greenaway dresses, Peter Pan collars, flat shoes and white stockings. The fact that clothes altered so much did mean something; with the advent of the mass-market designer, Mary Quant, who catered for the youth market, clothes became childish, light-hearted, *fun*, of a piece with the boom and consumerism.

It was a period of political frustration, though, the early sixties, with the Tories and Harold Macmillan caught in class stagnation, while CND got locked into the power struggles of the Labour Party. Until the Profumo scandal seethed to the surface. I was working at a hospital near the Old Bailey, at the time of the trial round which the Profumo affair hinged, and every day I saw the crowds pressed round the entrance for a glimpse of the call girls and pimps and famous persons – prurient, hating, inquisitive crowds.

The Profumo affair was neither quite of the fifties, nor of the sixties, or rather it partook of both. It was both the end of the repressed, drinking club, sex-for-hire world of fifties bohemia, where even adultery could take you close to the margins, and it was the beginning of the satirical sixties, the iconoclasm and end to deference, just as the assassination of President Kennedy seemed to inaugurate an era of crazy murders, sometimes political, always fantastic, and it was gradually borne in on me that anything could happen to anybody, no one was ever really safe.

It was crazy in another way – there was money, things to buy, fun to be had. The property boom: in 1966 my lover and I co-purchased a house in gentrifying Islington. I was able to do this because an uncle had left me £4000. I sat on a *chaise longue* in the dolls-house front room, bursting with childish glee at the windfall that had enabled me to buck the system. We had made this huge purchase so easily – at a period when an unmarried woman could *not* get a mortgage. We did inquire. One estate agent squeezed my shoulder and said, 'Don't worry, my dear, with a nest egg like that and such an attractive girl, you'll be married in no time.'

In our new house we entertained a colleague of my lover. I cooked a leg of lamb. 'How delicious,' said the visitor, author of a classic sociological text on the modern family, 'what a pity you're not married.'

I wasn't married, didn't live under the protection of a man. In my childhood with my divorced mother I had experienced that absence and felt my mother's marginality, her stubborn will to survive spiritually if not socially. I did not expect a man to look after me, did not want it, had rejected it. But although my lover *did* look after me our relationship was largely invisible.

'When are you going to get married?' from relations and friends. No one objected openly to my 'single' state – but there was always that absence of affirmation. I was hell-bent on pleasure, skating on the surface of the social whirl. I was shielded from the raw edge of society's discrimination against women generally and lesbians in particular, and so I perhaps underestimated the real social disapproval, and, determined not to be marginalized, refused to admit that I could not prevent others from marginalizing me.

Just as, of course, I marginalized those other women, the spinsters, the social workers and teachers, whose lack of a chic style I despised. A double standard as well as a double life.

What were the sixties anyway? Far from being the era of joy and promiscuity, as so often retrospectively described, they seethed with angst and madness. The bright young things, like me, stood on the edge of a volcano and peered in, maybe giggling, maybe excited, but horror was not far beneath the surface. Others may have a different memory – Angela Carter, for example, writes of the sixties with unfailing affection – but for me the childish aspects of the time were always more of the *Brideshead Revisted* kind, grown-ups playing at childhood, and the later sixties dripped with decadence.

In 1967 we went on, after the Gateways had shut for the

night, to strange basements off the Tottenham Court Road, where silent movies flickered along the walls, crowds decked in portable outrage openly smoked joints and rock music throbbed in your cunt. The opening out of sexuality that occurred, though, was never more than the inverse of the tight-arse fifties, psychedelic ecstacy was maybe a kind of emotional diarrhoea.

A confusion of sensations, a confusion of being, a sense of things boiling up, a great froth of sinister energy bubbling into the culture, spreading across its surface, and the people your parents warned you against appeared through the smoke and the strobe lights with all the tacky drama of a drag queen.

I think the Tories have got it all wrong. They shouldn't blame the sixties, they should be grateful to them – to the fermenting individualism, to the crazy joy of the consumer world, to the greed for love and for money that prefigured the 'post-modernism' of the eighties, the surreal dress rehearsal of cultural happenings and art protest for the real thing of now.

Yet, at the beginning of the decade (or in 1959) Adam Faith had a hit – 'Whaddya want if you don't want money? Whaddya want if you don't want love?' Like many others I wanted authenticity, and both the pull of psychoanalysis and the pull of hedonism were part of the search for it. But it was so hard to disentangle authenticity from pose. I enjoyed, was mad about, dress and dressing up, but then wasn't that just the same old 'womanliness as a masquerade'? I posed as an aesthete, a dandy, yet weren't my efforts to study, to write, to *know* about art and music the sincerest things about me, the things I really wanted? Or was that mere pretension too?

To be middle class and white gave me more freedom than many women and certainly than most lesbians. And paradoxically, the loosening up that did take place at that time, the image of young, free, untrammelled women, was in a way more consistent with lesbianism than with female heterosexuality. We had no children, so we avoided the constraints to which the heterosexual girls fell victim, and which in turn generated women's liberation. We were never confined to the home, while economic privilege lifted us clear of the intense oppression faced by many working-class

lesbians. Yet the psychological oppression was also real –
there were enormous tensions, unresolved problems. It was
exciting to enact defiance, but it was difficult too. I was an
anti-heroine, consciously the bad girl, yet in a mode that
society often refused to recognize as bad, converting me
repeatedly into a sad, mad or sick girl, a girl without
pleasures because the pleasures I sought society would not
recognize. Sex with women wasn't 'real' sex, love with
women, in the words of one psychoanalyst, was 'more than
love, but really less than love'.

And the sixties was more than love, but less than love, I
think.

5 A community of interests

Keith Birch

We believed everything would change, even ourselves. Days
and nights were an exhilarating turmoil of ideas, actions
and experiments, about politics, sex and our whole lives.
For a few years in the early seventies, the Gay Liberation
Front provided the focus for a new experience of sexual
politics. This experience seems today to be a glorious
memory, or sometimes a mad nightmare, but one that is
now difficult to make real in our very changed climate.
Many of the ideas remain valid. Some have been partially
fulfilled, though in ways very different from those we
imagined. Others have been dashed or discarded in the wake
of 'Victorian values' and AIDS in the mid-eighties. But we
should not lose sight of the importance of that moment or
take for granted the changes that are so recent.

GLF brought together politics which had been flowering
in the social movements of the sixties and other political
ideas which had laid dormant for many years. The
immediate inspirations were the Civil Rights and Women's
Liberation Movements, combined with the style of the
counter-culture. To this was added a variety of ideas
borrowed from socialist and libertarian tradition.

The particular emphasis that GLF gave to this brew came
from the experience of being homosexual in a hostile
society. For lesbians and gay men as individuals it meant
coming out and taking pride in being gay, making the
personal political, and trying to live out our ideals. It meant,
too, challenging the roles of the heterosexual nuclear family
and the ideal of monogamy.

This complex development of our politics meant that challenges were thrown out in all directions – to 'straight' society; to the state and various institutions; to the left; and not least to the ways of existence that the gay male community had carved out for itself.

It is difficult to describe the impact that GLF had without referring to my own experience of those years. For me, meeting with the flowering GLF in 1971 felt like an accident of fate. There was no sense in which it was a natural progression of what my life had been before. I was eighteen having recently left school in a small Midlands, working-class community. My politics were a confusion of socialist ideals and sixties counter-culture, which had even had its effects in Stoke. Practice, however, had been limited to contacts with the Young Socialists and reading *International Times*. Sexuality meant very little – or perhaps everything. I recognized that I desired men but had never met anyone who I realized to be gay. I never even had the impulse to initiate such a meeting or knew the means by which it might occur.

The move to London had not been a consciously positive step, more a dive into the anonymity that a large city seemed to promise. But the sight of a GLF dance advertised in *IT* held a fatal attraction.

An awestruck evening at St Pancras Town Hall, when I was too fearful to speak with anyone, acted as the catalyst. Within a few days I had ventured to the weekly GLF meeting in Covent Garden, attended by hundreds of people. In the space of another few weeks I had set sail on my first affair and had joined the youth group, a consciousness-raising group and the commune group. My whole life was soon taken over by the movement. My relationships were made through it and eventually I was living in a GLF commune.

Involvement in GLF changed many lives radically, and had a very wide influence on the way in which being gay could be lived and was perceived by society. The people who came to GLF were overwhelmingly male, white, young and appeared independent of family and other restrictions. They were students, people new to the city and those who had dropped-out; also people dissatisfied with the lesbian and gay subcultures and the political and social movements which ignored our sexualities and experience. Whatever its base, GLF felt enormously diverse in culture and ideas. Anyone joined in, with no apparent hierarchy or rules, though, of course, this could be exploited by the experienced and self-confident who could speak in public and expound their ideas. But even I was co-chairing one of the weekly meetings attended by hundreds of people within a couple of months. The mass democracy of GLF certainly threw people into new situations and involved them in ways the socialist groups I had worked with, did not.

The ideology espoused by GLF was indeed revolutionary especially for gay people. What had been a secretive and isolated lifestyle became one of the most visible and aggressive in making a public statement about itself. GLF's sexual politics, following the Women's Movement, presented a challenge to what formed the public debate about politics. It also confronted the ways in which the left had lost sight of the arena of personal relationships. Like the Women's Movement, GLF raised the question of power between the sexes and in sexual relationships. We opened up to scrutiny the conduct of personal relationships and everyday life. Sexism and heterosexism, words so current today, were new concepts for debate. The notion of the personal being political informed both the theory and practice of GLF and was perhaps both its strength and weakness, as the commune experience testifies.

It was with this notion of personal and political development that a number of us came together to form the commune group. We held meetings to discuss what we wanted out of living communally as a group of gay men. The members reflected the make-up of GLF. Only one or two women ever became long-standing members of the commune group and though there were people of diverse nationality, there was only one Black member. There were no spoken rules as to who joined the initial discussion group, though a process of self-selection and exclusion inevitably took place. After some months of meeting, the chance came of somewhere to live and so a number of us took this leap into new territory.

For more than two years the commune moved round several, inadequate homes across London, some four or five of us surviving the whole process and always at least a group of eight or more living together. There were other gay communes during this time, such as the 'radical feminists' (gay men) who more exuberantly kicked over the traces. The gay male radical feminists adopted a style of radical drag and confrontation in rejecting traditional male roles and power. Their commune in Notting Hill seemed to offer a much more challenging lifestyle – one that I remember admiring and at the same time felt intimidated by. But for all of us it often appeared that we were trying to defy gravity in overturning the accepted conventions.

The ideal of the commune brought together two of the central features of GLF, consciousness-raising and coming out. Both were to be lived out to the full!

'Consciousness-raising', while sounding like a term from the personal growth groups in the USA, had much more to do with building a collective sense of identity. Lesbians and gay men had often been isolated in their oppression and possible guilt, rarely getting support from others and having no positive models. These groups in GLF operated as an intimate forum for the exchange of personal histories and feelings, bringing out a shared experience. This forged a greater personal strength and developed a sense of solidarity amongst us. New members coming along to GLF were all encouraged to become part of such groups.

While some may have gone along the path of therapy groups, most concentrated on this building of social awareness, of ourselves as lesbians and gay men.

The concept of coming out entailed the basic political stand that GLF demanded and depended upon. It brought together the positive self-affirmation of our sexuality as individuals and as a political act on which could be built the whole edifice of the movement. It meant a rejection of self-oppression and of the internalization of heterosexual values. For the commune it meant living openly together as gay men, a statement that there were alternative lifestyles to be followed.

By the combined forces of ideology and necessity, the commune arrived at a system of making everyday life possible. Every space was communal, including the sleeping area of wall-to-wall-mattresses. Rotas and mutual responsibility were the practical means of organizing living. We had a house fund which we paid into and from which we paid the rent and bills and bought all the food. Rotas for shopping, cooking and cleaning immediately appeared necessary as practical means for getting things done with some fairness. Shortage of money often meant bulk buying of cheap food – and rotting sacks of sprouts and three-course meals based on carrots for each course testified to our lack of resources and occasional poor planning. Simple things like washing-up remained a source of unending argument but got done eventually, though sometimes with severely depleted stocks after much crockery smashing.

Initially many members were in paid employment but as time progressed more joined who were not, and others found too great a conflict between our lifestyle and their job to continue with the latter. Paid employment also meant people had very different resources to put into the commune of both time and money and this was always a source of tension, never entirely resolved. Conflicts might arise about responsibility to the collective good when we could not pay bills; conflicts between the failure to pay into the kitty compared to the loss of day-to-day commitment that an outside job meant.

Our belief in personal and political change through this process of living together led us to hope that the differences we had, in background or objectives, or on the level of whether we actually liked one another, could be overcome. We had weekly formal sessions to iron out problems and discuss future plans. This was combined with intense house discussions where we talked about how we were experiencing the commune and our feelings towards one another. To be honest, perhaps we were never honest. At times the tension was so great, especially around the formal sessions themselves, that everyone dreaded the house meetings. The commitment to the ideal prevented us from asking whether we really liked or understood one another: 'Are these really the people I want to share so much of my life so closely with?' There had of course been the subtle process of excluding people whom an unspoken consensus felt would not fit in.

There was the involvement with GLF which provided a

considerable communality of goals. The practicalities of everyday life also pressed us together along with the excitement of taking part in such an experiment. All this provided a strong momentum which kept us together for so long.

Day-to-day practice was often at odds with how we felt we should behave. GLF strongly rejected monogamous role-playing relationships. The emphasis was on developing sexual friendships and overcoming the dependency and jealousy associated with couples. There was much less of the debate about sexual practices and the expression of desire which has dominated recent times. The communal bedroom was one expression of breaking down barriers, one which was always the first to be commented upon by visitors. In fact, there were several couples in the commune and there was, after some initial attempts to extend friendships sexually, relatively little sexual contact amongst us outside of this. I was in one of these couples and perhaps gave the least, having almost no other sexual involvement during all that period. Being part of a couple in a commune committed to breaking down personal barriers was a contradiction but not one which I ever overcame. Making love in a communal bedroom never ignited any spark that would lead to communal sex! The closeness or the tensions between lovers, of course, had their effects on the life of the commune as a whole and they were played out in this open forum. Rather surprisingly, I was rarely challenged by the commune members as a whole for my very conventional behaviour on this score.

But sex and sexual practice were probably the areas of life that were confronted the least by us collectively, though to the outside world it might have appeared to be the very basis for us being together.

Much of our energy was directed into the activities of GLF. As a semi-official commune and crash pad, we had a never-ending stream of people passing through. Those on holiday, people on the run, people in need of help or those just interested in the idea. This was a source of positive input as well as regular crises. Relationships could blossom or police raids follow. It is hard to disentangle the life of the commune from GLF because it touched on so much. The weekly meeting of GLF and its action groups led on to the more public face of our activities. Demonstrations, dances or communes were all part of our politics. Any event, or simply wearing a lesbian or gay badge in the street, was a political statement of our existence and identity.

GLF had almost as many confrontations with the gay community as it did with the wider world. We criticized mainstream male gay culture for its secretiveness, timidity and acceptance of the status quo. We were often excluded from pubs after the weekly meetings in Notting Hill, as much by the gay ones as the rest, in the test of wills about what was acceptable gay behaviour. We also had demonstrations through the 'gay male ghetto' of Earls Court on a route which took us to the most famous gay pubs, chanting slogans about coming out to a shocked and unwilling clientele. I still remember the closed doors and emptying streets that our appearance caused. GLF never managed to bridge the gap with the mainstream gay and lesbian communities even though its growing confidence and awareness helped make possible the wider changes that started to take place during the seventies.

Relations with the socialist left in those years were also limited and tense. It was easy to dismiss the left as heterosexual and male, and much of the left easily dismissed us in return. GLF as a whole was perhaps more influenced by libertarian and counter-cultural thinking than a socialist one in speaking of revolutionary change. But we had borrowed many of our concepts and ideals from socialism even if only a minority of GLF was explicitly socialist. We shared a critique of exploitation and oppression; identified the bourgeois state and institutions as a source of this oppression and believed in mass, popular action by the oppressed to achieve 'liberation'. Common cause could therefore be made with the left on occasions such as in opposition to the Tory government's attack on trade union rights, though on major demonstrations we were met with some discomfort and disbelief by many of the other marchers and put at the back by the stewards, a not unfamiliar occurrence in following years.

Central to our politics was direct action against organizations identified as being anti-gay. This ranged from the medical profession, the media, education and the law.

Action was taken against the medical profession and the Harley Street practices, identified as the home of medical and psychiatric abuses against lesbians and gay men which classified homosexuality as a sickness. There were actions against bookshops selling anti-gay material and against organizations such as the Festival of Light which was launching an anti-gay crusade. While there was often much anger, there was also imagination used in confronting these 'enemies'. Demonstrations against the highly-hyped sex guide *All You Ever Wanted to Know About Sex* involved the street theatre group in a very vivid and bloody 'abortion-by-coathanger' scene in a Charing Cross Road bookshop following advice to women contained in the book. A major Festival of Light rally was infiltrated and dis-organized, while the rally itself was disrupted with non-violent and humorous happenings every few minutes by groups amongst the audience. GLF's confrontational politics often had humour, however serious the point being made. We also made everyday events into political spectacles. Dances were major political events around the staid town halls of London. Gay-days around the main parks were a cross between picnics and carnivals where we made our existence 'public'.

While this may seem flippant and superficial, it was an important aspect of the energy that flowed through GLF gaining confidence and getting noticed. There were more serious activities: the establishment of self-help groups which were forerunners of the present switchboards and counselling groups.

The police also for a time wanted to believe that there were links between groups such as GLF and the Angry Brigade who had set off a series of bombs during that period in 1972. Communes seemed to be a particular target, and we did not escape police attention or their night-time raids.

The whole experience was intense, almost claustrophobic and left us politically and emotionally exhausted towards the end of both the commune and GLF. We had changed, the world had changed a little and we went off in our different directions with new involvements and lives to lead. I was still with the same lover and we continued to live together, sharing a flat with other friends.

Gay groups and politics remained central to my life, although the overwhelming coherence that GLF had provided fragmented for a time. Daily life, relationships, sex and politics were no longer so immediately mixed together to make sense of my hopes and ideals. But GLF had made possible many developments in the following few years. The expansion of the commercial lesbian and gay scenes was based on a much more confident and visible lifestyle. We also saw the formation of lesbian and gay groups in many of the socialist parties which began to take sexual politics more seriously. And there was the growth of self-help groups, switchboards, papers and pressure groups ... in all, positive new ways to understand and live being lesbian and gay that we are still exploring.

6 Coming to terms

John Phillips

I attended my first Gay Liberation Front meeting sometime about the end of 1970. There must have been about 150 people present, crammed into a lecture room at the London School of Economics. It was a varied group, more men than women, but predominantly like myself within the twenty to thirty age-group. There appeared to be an emphasis on the so-called counter-culture style or the beginning of it – longer hair, jeans and sneakers – in contrast to the Carnaby Street style found in gay pubs and clubs. There was nobody I knew or even recognized, and that I found surprising after five or six years on the scene. Where did these people come from or, for that matter, where did they go to?

I felt that many people, like myself, were attending their first meeting, not sure what to expect and hoping not to have to say or do anything. The atmosphere, however, was relaxed and friendly. A group of four, two men and two women, appeared responsible for what little procedure existed. They gave their views and comments, as did many other people in the room, on a whole range of subjects – police harassment and entrapment, the importance of Gay Pride, the wearing of GLF badges (which many in the room were doing) and the need to express our homosexuality in public.

My first sexual experience had taken place when I was sixteen years of age. He was the other office boy in the insurance company I worked for somewhere in the city. Mutual masturbation, with very little caressing and strictly no kissing continued for almost two years. As we both lived with our respective families, it was a case of doing it wherever we could be alone: the print room at the office; changing rooms at the local swimming baths; or cubicles in public toilets on faraway District Line stations. Strange how in another context it could have been construed as romantic or even erotic – two eastenders having it away! However, the truth was that we shared no emotions other than disgust and guilt after the physical release, not because of the act itself but because of the lack of feeling that accompanied it. We always parted company as quickly as possible to resume conversation in work the next day as if nothing had happened. He went on to get married and raise a family. I took what seemed a gigantic leap at the time into the semi-public world of the practising homosexual.

It was a world that appeared to ignore class differences and to offer emotional comfort and warmth. There was an abundance of roles and signals to be learned. Butch and bitch were everyday jargon to denote sexual roles. She and her were applied to all. Shirley Bassey and Danny La Rue were living legends. Signet rings on little fingers and white socks were signs of one's homosexuality – but only to other homosexual men. The so-called sexual revolution had yet to occur and affairs and boyfriends were of the utmost importance. Although illicit sex took place in lavatories and parks, the mimicking of heterosexual relationships seemed to be the practice of the time.

Within a short period I felt absorbed into my new lifestyle. I left home in East London to share a flat in Victoria with new found friends. I started a new job, had affairs and was taken to the theatre and ballet; places I had never visited before. The cockney accent began to disappear and I saw *The Sound of Music* four times. There were a few gay pubs (some still in existence today), a few after-hours coffee bars and, it seemed, a party every weekend. There was one all-night coffee bar-cum-disco in a basement in Soho called La Douce where it was possible to dance. But any form of caressing or touch-dancing was prohibited by the management on instructions from the local police force. I was delighted, however, to be moving together with somebody of my own sex in a semi-public environment.

Heady days indeed, or so it seemed at the time. Things

came together – the Beatles; love and peace slogans; liberal legislative changes legalizing abortion and homosexuality (albeit with restrictions); the repeal of capital punishment. There was the growth of various radical groups, the use of soft drugs and, for someone of my age, a feeling of momentous change. It seemed, however, to have little impact on the gay community. The number of gay pubs had increased but the owners of these places appeared happy with their lot – profits – and were unwilling to make any major changes. Two men kissing in these places would almost certainly lead to expulsion for an indefinite period. The predominant feeling appeared to be that the male gay community should be grateful that such places existed, regardless of any restrictions that might be imposed. It was this inability of the gay scene to break out of its isolation in terms of the changes that were appearing in other parts of society that made it appear outdated and introverted. At twenty-four years of age I felt the need to break away from the stereotypical gay male image that I began to feel trapped in.

GLF appeared to catch the mood of the time perfectly: the growth of the Women's Liberation Movement and the recognition of sexism; actions taken by Black people against racism; the growth of youth culture as expressed in the anti-Vietnam demonstrations, music and clothes. I became aware that GLF was offering gay men and women the opportunity to become part of that growing radical climate as open and proud homosexuals.

I attended my first public demonstration which was organized by the TUC against Ted Heath's government's plans to restrict the powers of trade unions. It was decided that we would join in as gay workers and trade unionists opposed to the restrictions and to march under the GLF banner. Over 100,000 were estimated to have attended that day and we were the last group to leave Hyde Park Corner, a point noted in a particularly nasty cartoon by Jak in the *Evening Standard* the following day. There were between twenty and thirty GLFers arm in arm and we were determined to make our presence felt. Chanting and singing mostly gay slogans we made our way through central London. Marching down the Haymarket I became aware of the ever-increasing amount of noise that we were making and, looking behind, I realized our numbers had increased to nearly two hundred. Gay men and women, sympathizers from other groups and onlookers from the pavement had joined us. We were criticized by many in the TUC for marching under the GLF banner but it was imperative to make the point that our homosexuality was as important as our alliance with the trades union movement.

Later, I joined the street theatre group, one of the most vocal and public of all the groups within GLF. The first event I attended was a short scenario depicting gay oppression which we performed up and down the Portobello Road Market. Besides the usual curiosity and amusement from onlookers, we were moved on several times by the police and pelted with rotten fruit from unsympathetic stallowners. This appeared naïve compared to some of the street theatre's actions later – the zapping of Mary Whitehouse's Festival of Light rally in Central Hall by very well-disguised male and female nuns; or impromptu performances against the Miss World contests at the Albert Hall, now firmly established at the annual Alternative Miss World contests.

The use of men in drag, or radical drag as it was known, began to play a large part in GLF's activities. The drag was obvious, sometimes combined with beard or moustache, and was meant to shock. We were acting out the 'freak' labels that society attached to us. The members of the gay male community who were most oppressed and ridiculed were transvestites or those thought to be excessively effeminate. They were attacked not only by straights but also by many other gay men. My only experience of drag was a demonstration I attended aimed at a bar in the Imperial College in Kensington which operated a male-only policy. Five men and five women, all in convincing drag, turned up and demanded to be served. The aim was to see whether they would serve men dressed as women and vice versa. They did neither. Chaos followed as fire hydrants and the occasional dart were aimed in our direction. Fortunately nobody was injured before the police arrived and we were thrown out.

Although GLF emphatically refused to endorse any form of leadership or structure within the movement, the amount it achieved in its relatively short lifespan still impresses me. It seemed there was a demonstration every week covering a wide spectrum of grievances. The street theatre group would combine with the anti-psychiatry group to protest at psychiatrists labelling us mentally ill, and especially against the use of the controversial Electro-Convulsive Therapy (ECT) for the so-called 'cure' of homosexuality. Publishers of books and other sections of the media hostile to the gay community were also subject to very well-arranged publicity-seeking confrontations. Other events included a mass sit-down in a pub in Notting Hill Gate which refused to serve GLFers and the leafleting of the lesbian Gateways Club in Chelsea. The latter resulted in ten men and women being arrested, held overnight at the police station and later charged with affray. They, along with others arrested on other demonstrations, were supported by as many GLFers as could attend the relevant court case.

At the beginning, when participating in some of these events, I felt embarrassed and lacked the courage to become really involved. Later, however, things became easier after I became aware that I was still to a certain extent ashamed to express my homosexuality in public. I was helped in this respect by the collective influence of other people within GLF. Demonstrating and taking action generated an atmosphere where people supported one another and increased their involvement in the movement.

Equally as important was the alternative social network provided by GLF. Discos were held on a regular basis, usually in rented rooms above pubs, and, less frequently, the larger Come Together dances were held in town halls in various parts of London. These dances sometimes attracted as many as 700 people. Mostly male and young, they were obviously not to everyone's taste with their emphasis on loud psychedelic music. Their popularity was perhaps a measure of the general apathy that many felt about the pub/club scene as it existed at the time. It also proved to critics that almost overnight GLF could create a non-commercial alternative social setting. These events also helped provide the small amount of money needed for the renting of meeting halls or the printing of Come Together, the monthly newspaper.

GLF was criticized by many gay male critics, both those not involved in the movement at all or members of the more conservative groups such as the Campaign for Homosexual Equality. They saw its actions as being far too radical and blatant. This kind of action, they felt, would turn what little sympathy existed in society firmly against us. As I was told by one friend outside of the movement, 'I do not want a bunch of freaks with painted faces and dresses to represent me and gay society as a whole.'

Another major criticism, even by some within the movement, was its pursuance of a Marxist political ideology. These critics argued that this was taking precedence over the struggle for basic gay rights and was a manipulation by the few over the majority. As for myself, I found that the Marxist approach to sexual politics helped me to understand why so much prejudice existed against the gay community. I began to understand more deeply how the fight against sexism and the growth of the Women's Movement was as important as the work of GLF. I became aware of the workings of other groups and realized how our struggle had, to a certain extent, copied theirs. The Black Power Movement in the States, with its emphasis on creating a new form of identity and pride through history, culture and the 'Black is beautiful' slogan, had been particularly influential on me.

I was made aware that homosexuals, along with Jews and socialists, had been marched into the gas chambers in Nazi Germany. On the other hand, I was also aware that, at the time of being involved in the movement, gays were held in detention camps in Castro's Cuba and that homosexuality, according to the authorities, did not exist in Mao's China. Although I could understand the Marxist philosophy that the family unit and the inferior role of women suits the capitalist economic structure, replacing it with a worldwide communal environment in which genderless children were raised seemed utopian and unrealistic.

Towards the end of 1972 GLF in London began to decline, especially in terms of the central caucus meetings. One of the most important reasons was the split that occurred when women members left, mainly to join the Women's Liberation Movement. Also at the same time smaller GLF groups were being organized in other parts of London and major towns around the country. Fragmentation away from the central meetings also occurred with a breaking away of various groups such as the Under 21s and some of the religious groups. Although at this stage there was a central office in the Kings Cross area (later the Lesbian and Gay Switchboard office), the anarchic lack of leadership and organization failed to keep the various groups together under the GLF banner.

Before its decline, however, I began to become less involved. I began to recognize and understand what I saw as the self-defeating nature and structure of the movement. I did feel a sense of partial liberation achieved through both individual acts and actions taken collectively with other members. But by the acceptance and pride in my own sexuality the movement became surprisingly irrelevant. The emphasis on waving the flag had mellowed to the point of becoming just another part of one's life. I felt that as long as I remained open and proud I was now able to become a person to whom homosexuality was part and parcel of my whole being.

Three months after attending my last meeting here in London I left to live and work in New York where I stayed for seven years. My only involvement with the gay movement there was to march in the annual gay parades commemorating the anniversary of the Stonewall riots of June 1969. These were spectacular events with as many as 50,000 men and women marching with costumes, floats and, sometimes the occasional horse or elephant. Even though I was unaware of any political actions by gay organizations, these parades were clear signals of the importance achieved earlier by groups such as GLF. On my return to London I was surprised to find how, like gay politics, much of American gay male lifestyles and fashions had also crossed the Atlantic. There appeared to be a similar emphasis on open sexuality, although much of that seemed to be enjoyed outside Britain.

After a year of being back I received a letter from a friend in New York telling me he had contracted AIDS. I had heard rumours of such a disease from other friends but I was not aware of its full implications until he died six months later in a hospital in Chicago. Later I was to learn of three other friends who were suffering from the disease. With one of them I had shared a fifteen-year friendship. His, and the other, deaths had a profound effect on me and other mutual friends. It seemed to be about the same time that the press here started its (for the most part) barbaric and homophobic coverage of AIDS. I read and watched everything on the subject. Something or somebody had to explain why these people were no longer here. I could not accept that death could result from two people making love, regardless of their sexuality. Drug addicts, prostitutes and male homosexuals were, I was told, the main victims. Gay men were, it was claimed, promiscuous and could have as many as 2,000 sexual encounters in a year. It was moralistic and obviously meant to shock. The terms used were to describe culprits rather than sufferers. I felt deeply a mixture of guilt and anguish for these friends, their lovers, their families and their whole circle of acquaintances.

I felt the pressure was back on again and, in 1985, attended my first Gay Pride march here in London in about ten years. Strange how I felt a little anxious, just like the old days. Nevertheless, the march was a wonderful morale booster. More people marched that year than ever before. Many were, like myself, old GLFers, some wearing the original badge and all of us knowing that it was time to be out marching again. We marched behind Body Positive, the self-help group for people who are HIV-positive; chanting all the way. Tom Robinson roused many of us, yet again, to a chorus of 'Glad To Be Gay!' With all that shit going on outside, it was good to feel that support from all the others in Jubilee Gardens and to express a pride in our homosexuality whatever the situation.

I have since joined the Terrence Higgins Trust as a volunteer. Their response to AIDS has been light years ahead of the government's. Besides the money and time it spends on telephone helplines and health education, it also provides moral and financial support for sufferers, their friends and relatives. I am involved mostly in fund raising, which can range from bucket rattling at pubs to leafleting or selling posters at the various galas and benefits held to raise money for the Trust. The response I have experienced has always been positive and it is reassuring that so many are

aware and willing to do something to help tackle this
massive problem. It is important that, as homosexuals, we
regain ground lost in terms of increased bigotry until such
time as AIDS is seen for what it is – a disease that can affect
all humans, a threat to everyone, regardless of their
sexuality. We gay men have taken and will continue to take
the initiative, but our concern is not only for ourselves but
for the whole society in which we live. It is through such
mutual support that we can and will fight the major
problems that confront us.

7 Separatism: a look back at anger

Janet Dixon

Separatism is to feminism what fundamentalism is to Christianity. It is the centre, the beating heart, the essence. The dogma is of absolutes, the lifestyle is of attempted purity and the zealot is subject to continuous derision. My involvement with separatism lasted five years, but in a very real sense it will never leave me.

Separatism is not acquired politics. Clearly, you cannot inherit a taste for it by coming from a separatist family, nor by living in a separatist neighbourhood. Equally, you cannot read about its history and be moved to sympathy by those revelations. Separatism is an exhausting act of faith, and because of insistent pressure on you to repent, it requires almost daily reaffirmation. The faith is in the belief that women, left to themselves, would make the world a beautiful place to live. It claims for all women a far greater potential in terms of powers and skills than any woman has ever demonstrated. Women are seen as the source of compassion, love and harmony. It was ironic that as we deified womanhood, we unleashed more anger, suspicion and even, I think, hatred – woman for woman – than any issue had aroused since feminism began.

So what caused this anger and mistrust? Why were heterosexual feminists outraged and repelled by us and all we stood for? Why did socialist feminists accuse us, at best, of being hedonistic female chauvinists, and at worst, Fascists? Why were lesbians angered when we questioned the sense of working with gay men in order to counter gay oppression?

It had, in part, to do with the nature of separatism being highly offensive to those who held traditional broad left views. Prior to this time, the early seventies, there was no real precedent for autonomous women's groups organizing around a woman-only issue. The definition of socialism which I can grasp most readily, because it is so simple, is the one given by George Bernard Shaw in 1928: 'Socialism is an opinion as to how the income of the country should be distributed.' I include it here because at no point was it ever put to me in such bald and comprehensible terms. We saw the goal of feminist socialists as raising the status of women and to include them in the share-out. In any case, however crude my understanding of it, socialism to its everlasting credit, is about including everyone. Separatism is anathema to this. We saw socialism as yet another squabbling position in male politics. We thought that the women in socialism would never be seen by their men as anything except an 'uppity' lump stuck on their side. Not only were we not interested in how socialism was realized, we didn't believe it would make the slightest difference to the position of women even if it were. We didn't want an equal slice of a male cake, we wanted the men and their cake out of our lives.

Gay oppression is class oppression: the people can't be free until the women are free. We saw this as a lot of sloganizing nonsense. This class dumping on that class, this class more oppressed than that class. As far as we were concerned, if you removed the architects and managers of the system then the whole thing would collapse, and who, we asked, in the massive majority of cases were they, if not men?

Separatism is shamelessly exclusive. The rules are simple: whatever your race or class, provided you are a woman, you are a potential separatist. Whatever your race or class, if you are a man you are irredeemably the enemy. The separatist position was clear. It was not that men held the power, but that men were the power. Something inherent in maleness necessitates its expression in systems of oppressive hierarchies. Competitiveness, aggression, brutality and maleness are all one in the same. That Y chromosome, that mutated afterthought, was the cause of it all.

In the winter of 1970 I attended the second national conference of the Women's Liberation Movement, held in a grim out-of-season holiday camp at Skegness. I was, to put it mildly, wet behind the ears, politically. In my first year in a London art school my two major preoccupations were whether you really could see William Turner's late canvasses as a precursor to French Impressionism, and how the hell I could afford to clothe myself in the right gear to make a stunning impact on my new friends at the Gateways. I went to the conference armed only with a general feeling of being pissed off that men seemed to have it all their own way. Along with taking LSD and deciding after some very unpleasant attempts never to fuck again, attending Skegness was one of the most powerful and formative experiences of that part of my life.

On the Saturday morning we shuffled into the camp's concert hall for a 'plenary session'. As I took my seat it dawned on me. Amongst the couple of hundred or so there, were some twenty or thirty men. Not only that, on the stage was a long table, and yes you've guessed it, among the dignitaries were several men. We sat through some very boring speeches which attempted to make the thoughts of Mao, Marx and Lenin exciting and accessible to a bunch of dumb women, and then broke for coffee. In the camp canteen I looked for the woman who had encouraged me to come to what, by the minute, I was beginning to feel was a god-forsaken hole. I wanted to know why she thought I would be the least bit interested in all that drivel I had just had to sit through. It turned out she was just as fed up as me, and we were not the only ones. A group of us hastily slung together a plan and went back into the concert hall in an effort to oust the ruling junta.

The bravest of us raised her hand and asked by what authority the Maoist Women's Liberation Front had commandeered the stage, and seen fit to hand out reams of papers as proposed discussion documents. The famous stuff hit the fan. After trading what were to become stereotypical insults about bourgeois middle-class women and hard left male domination, a very large number of us walked out and from then on abandoned the formal conference altogether. I spent the rest of the weekend in small discussion groups with women from all over the country with a wide variety of ideas and opinions. I was excited and happy and enthused with the thought of becoming more involved in both the WLM and GLF. As a codicil to this I should tell you that at the same time in another part of the camp, the National Union of Miners were holding some sort of conference themselves. On the Saturday evening they were having a social and were to watch a striptease. Some of us decided to get into the social and talk to the men. As it turned out, productive discussion proved impossible. Abuse followed insult and eventually the police were called. The gutter press version went something like, 'Libbers storm miners' social'. If only we had.

In the early seventies I was active in both the Women's Movement and in Gay Liberation Front; more of GLF later. Of those very early times in the Women's Movement, I am left with a memory of two distinct feelings. The first is one of a self-conscious confusion, the second of discomfort at being a lesbian.

The first arose because even though I myself and the women I was involved with, called ourselves feminist, I wasn't really clear what we were doing about it. I went to national and regional conferences and attended all sorts of local workshops. I went to Grosvenor Square and abused 'American Imperialists', I got thumped about a bit on Troops Out demos, and I dutifully handed out time and money in support of 'the miner's wives'. Although I was convinced of the correctness of all these issues, I harboured unspoken doubts about their relevance to me, and I couldn't help wondering if the sight of our banners on the demos was always welcome.

As for my discomfort at being a lesbian, now that was much more painful. The public reaction to the reawakening of feminism was to dismiss us all as bra-burning lesbians. The reaction of WLM was strenuously to deny this 'insult'. Heterosexual feminists argued that we had to be taken seriously as women, and if the media got away with the label of lesbians, then 'the women out there' would be alienated. But wait a minute, I thought, hadn't I been a woman out there? In any case, if the business of women's liberation was what we were about, then shouldn't that mean all women, even those of us with embarrassing sexual habits? I was told that what I did in my bedroom was a private matter. I was made to feel that wanting to have it openly discussed was just exhibitionist boat-rocking.

As the seventies wore on the numbers of lesbians in the WLM increased dramatically, the rumbles of discontent turned into roars. Lesbians put their weight behind issues such as child care, abortion, race, battered wives and rape. In return we wanted the skeleton of sexuality wrenched from the closet and flesh put on its bones. The WLM had begun to come of age. We had stopped trailing around after the men in the left, contorting ourselves in the hope of receiving some grudging crumbs of approval. We had our own campaigns and set of demands, and what's more, amongst them was a woman's right to define her own sexuality.

The inclusion of this demand, in the context of feminism, may seem now to be obvious, but the struggle to make sexuality a respectable platform was an acrimonious one. At national conferences such as Acton and Edinburgh, the lesbians in general, and the separatists in particular, were accused of being elitist, divisive, of tearing the women's movement apart, and taking energy away from 'the real struggle'. Even at lesbian conferences such as Canterbury, Nottingham and Bristol, separatists were castigated for being smug extremists. In both these settings, women who had been toiling in their communities came to conference to exchange ideas and information, and to gain strength by being together. Because of the in-house nature of separatism, we saw the conferences as opportunities to disseminate our beliefs to huge numbers of women.

As you can see, I am once making great claims on behalf of separatism. Were separatists really responsible for making lesbianism, eventually, respectable inside the WLM? Wouldn't it have happened anyway? (Some might even say sooner!) Did separatists really lift feminism from under the coat-tails of the male left and establish autonomous women's political activity? Wouldn't heterosexual women have tired in the end, of explaining why Marx ignored women and how rape was the result of capitalist oppression, and found less contrived answers? I don't think so. You only have to read what women in emerging feminist groups and movements are writing, to see that these patterns repeat themselves time and again. But, of course, the question of just how much in terms of autonomy can be attributed to separatism can never be definitively answered. Nevertheless it is my belief that without us, feminism would never have been more than a caucus of the broad left. Separatism was right there in the middle, influencing all women, and, despite themselves, even those who were most vociferous in their resistance to our ideas. What separatists did was to reduce the very complex set of circumstances which combine to oppress women, to a single uncluttered issue. That is the stark injustice of the total humiliation of women on all levels, by men. Separatism was the source of this theme and the means by which it spilled into every area of feminist activity.

To make the language of separatism less cumbersome, I want to call this central theme, pure separatism and the effects that pure separatism has caused, graduated separatism. Let me return to my own experiences to illustrate the relationship between pure and graduated separatism.

At the same time as I was being bundled in and out of police vans for telling the troops in Northern Ireland exactly where they should go, I was also attending GLF meetings. I just can't remember when I found the time to wash my hair and iron creases into my flares. The weekly meetings, held on Thursdays, were megalithic in proportion. Upwards of four and even five hundred people attended. We hired halls at the London School of Economics, the Middle Earth Club in Covent Garden, and the church hall of All Saints in Notting Hill. Of the hundreds who went, we were lucky if twenty-five of those were women. With the best will in the world, and there was initially a lot of it, lesbians found it hard to make their voices heard. Inevitably the inequality in numbers was reflected in the priority given to issues. Against the backdrop of queer bashing and police harassment, the more disguised problems associated with lesbianism, fared badly. Even in the smaller specific groups, women often felt that they were struggling against thinly-disguised misogyny.

Gay men who had been shown a stiff cock in a public lavatory by a policeman, and were then promptly arrested for showing an interest, weren't slow to remind us that, thanks to Queen Victoria, lesbianism was not illegal. The fact that none of the lesbians I knew wanted to pick up a woman in a public toilet underpinned those very basic differences in the sexuality of gay women and men, at that time, which eventually led to the split.

There were those men, lots of them, who quite simply ignored us, viewing our presence, I'm sure, as an intrusion. There were those men who made strained efforts to submerge their mistrust, dislike and fear of us. And there were those men who encouraged us to reprimand them for sexist thoughts and deeds. In the end, once again, women were servicing men, women were raising the consciousness of men, women were giving their energy to men.

We, the lesbians, began to abandon the GLF dream. We gave up expecting GLF to solve our problems because we could see that it was essentially a movement built around the freedom to choose and practise your own sexuality. Further, in terms of heterosexism, whatever your sexuality, if you are a woman you are always second best. Gay men, under pressure, could return to the closet and regain all the privileges of being male. Where could lesbians go?

We became increasingly angry and frustrated, feeling more and more that to work politically with men, whatever their sexuality, was simply a debilitating exercise. In 1972, a group of us, finally exhausted by our tokenist existence, announced at one of the mega-meetings, our intention to leave GLF and work politically only with women.

This decision, inspired by pure separatism, was graduated separatism. Not all of the women who took that decision were separatist by any means, but the fact that we had rejected men was not a gesture of feminism alone. After all feminism alone does not exclude men. Some of the men in GLF had called themselves feminist, as had the Mao-ist men at Skegness. Graduated separatism on the other hand draws a line beyond which men cannot go.

Pure separatism involves a woman taking steps to remove men from her life. She must live with women, be a mother ony to girl children. Male culture in all its manifestations is shunned. She must abandon all relationships with men, lovers, fathers and brothers. Sexually she is either celibate or lesbian. Politically and socially, her contact is confined to women. The music she listens to must be composed and played by women, the books she reads must have a woman author. Her morality is not dictated by patriarchal norms, but rather guided by the belief that women's needs are her sole concern. To steal from men is not theft, it is reclamation.

Graduated separatism, the acceptable face of separatism, can be seen as the ripples which pass outwards from this. Graduated separatist spaces, women-only spaces, can be moved into by all women. You do not have to be a separatist or even a lesbian to enjoy the benefits of graduated separatism. It has meant that women's groups of all kinds, even those outside mainstream feminism, can now quite legitimately organize around women-only issues. Having said this though, it is what goes on in the woman-only space, which defines it as graduated separatism or not. Groups of women working or socializing together are not automatically separatist. Of course, there are many precedents for women-only societies. The Women's Institute is devoted to the service of husband and family, a convent of nuns to the service of a male god: their very existence depends on this element of male service. Can you imagine how how long a convent of sisters devoted to the worship of Hecate would have survived?

Women-only groups are active in local and national politics, at work, in job training and skills courses, in youth work, in sport. The existence of Greenham Common, women's refuges, rape crisis centres, health care projects; women-only workshops at mixed events, and lesbian-only bars at gay gatherings: all these and more are examples of how the energy of pure separatism has filtered through to affect the lives of many women, including those who have no interest in politics of any kind, let alone separatism. Graduated separatism creates a space where women and girls can be free from the burden of men and their persistent sexism long enough to gain confidence and a skill, which would otherwise have been impossible.

Had separatism confined itself to a political context, then however violent the discussion, its impact and effects would not have been a fraction of what they are. Those of us who 'became' separatist in the early seventies carried our politics into our lifestyle in a way that, to us, obviated our beliefs and put teeth into our thrashing gums. To our zealous eyes, hypocrisy was everywhere. A white anti-rascist was only a guilt-ridden ex-colonial WASP. A car-driving, home-owning, polytechnic lecturer with a fake northern accent, was a bleating guilty liberal, not a socialist. Equally, a feminist who left a meeting, went home and jumped into bed with hubbie or boyfriend, was no better than a member of the fifth column. It was easy enough to demand racial equality, fair distribution of the wealth of the world, or equal rights for women: none of those would happen tomorrow, and none of them involved more than the most superficial cosmetic surgery to make yourself credible. Dialectic, however moving and seductive, was just words. To us, lesbianism and feminism were synonymous, either one without the other was untenable. A non-feminist lesbian was just a failed heterosexual. A non-lesbian feminist was just a male apologist. We demanded proof of intent, and that could only be achieved through living a separatist lifestyle. That was the revolution here and now.

On leaving GLF in 1972 I didn't realize that I was now a separatist; those of us who were didn't use the word. We called ourselves proudly the extremists, the vanguard, but it wasn't until we read the American CLIT papers in 1973 that we knew we had a name other than men-haters. In her SCUM (Society for Cutting Up Men) manifesto, Valerie Solanus outlined a matriarchal utopia with men as a slave class. This was not what I wanted. For me, men had to disappear altogether. I didn't want a geographical solution – a women's farm or island or country. I didn't want, either, a sexual apartheid or to use violence or magic. All these solutions were current and much discussed. But I accepted what G.K. Chesterton had put so well in 1911: 'A woman putting up her fists at a man is a woman putting herself in the one position which does not frighten him.'

The first stage in the process of making men disappear was to ignore them totally. One by one the men in our mixed household left or were thrown out. We stopped going to GLF, and to mixed gay discos and on mixed demos. We sold all our male records, stopped reading the newspaper and watching the telly. When I wrote letters home I addressed them to my mother only. I sat alone in the canteen at college, I stopped drinking in pubs and chatty male bus conductors and shop assistants were met with blank stares. To ignore men was to cut the umbilical cord once and for all, to deny them their very lifeforce. Men could only wield power if we, the women, let them. Without our minds and bodies to leech from, men would eventually shrivel and die. William Golding's book *Lord of the Flies* was to me an apt exercise in male self-disclosure, chronicling as it does what happens when the civilizing female influence is removed from the life of the male. Without women men revert to animals, without men women could heal and restore to harmony a world raped and ravaged. We further argued that this mass withdrawal of support from men had to happen quickly if the world were not to be destroyed by pollution or holocaust. We couldn't wait around for the magic day when the men turned to us and said, 'OK girls, now it's your turn.' Anyway we didn't have to wait, we didn't have to persuade, we had simply to stop conspiring in our oppression. In *A Room of One's Own*, Virginia Woolf describes how,

> 'Women have served all these centuries as looking glasses possessing the magic and delicious power of reflecting the figure of man at twice its natural size.... if she begins to tell the truth, the figure in the looking glass shrinks; his fitness for life is diminished ... The looking-glass vision is of supreme importance because it charges the vitality; it stimulates the nervous system. Take it away and the man may die.

Without the telly, the pub, and most gay social life, I had time to read and study. I experienced a personal Renaissance. Layer after layer of male confusion cleared away from my eyes. I had almost daily visions of a cathartic kind, with the total and even religious intensity of those experienced by Paul on the road to Damascus – an unfortunate comparison! You could not properly take account of my experience of separatism without acknowledging my feelings of being swept away by this sort of fervour. It had all been lies, everything men had ever told us! I reconstructed my life and all other women's in the light of male distortion and women's stolen potential. Nothing men had said or written was to be trusted. I read women authors voraciously, and when you consider this was in pre-Women's Press and Virago days, it meant I read a strange variety of subjects: history, travel, witchcraft, politics, poetry, theology, philosophy, even Victorian novelettes on the evils of alcohol inspired by the Temperance League. When, in 1974 an American friend brought me over from the States a copy of Elizabeth Gould-Davis's *The First Sex*, I had a scholar's confirmation of my conclusions.

The squat we lived in was falling down, but like Patience and Sara, we tackled our problems with a pioneering spirit. We saw it as an opportunity to demystify the male worlds of plumbing, electricity and carpentry. We read and experimented until we could stride into builders' suppliers and ask for one-way cistern inlet valves, 1.5 mm triplecore insulated or three-inch steel angle brackets, just as though we had been born knowing all about it, like men! I stopped wearing Tampax (cotton wool pricks), and I stopped eating meat in case the chunk of sizzling corpse I was about to sit down to had come from a male animal.

At first it was men who were not allowed into the house and although this position resulted in a lot of criticism and ridicule, most feminists had some sympathy so long as we didn't seriously advocate separatism for all women. But of course this was inevitably what we did do. It happened initially because at that time separatists were few in number, and across the country we all knew each other more or less. As a result of the huge curiosity our stance aroused, we had to continuously explain and defend our politics. We had literally hundreds of almost identical conversations. These were often emotional and traumatizing, and left us exhausted. We would often find out later that these conversations had been reported in a distorted way. All sorts of rumours spread about what went on in our house. We had, 'shaved our heads so as not to be sex objects, and boarded up our windows so that men in the street couldn't see in'. We also 'drowned male kittens, beat up the man who came to read the meter, and held covens where we stuck pins in male voodoo dollies'. We were easy targets for ridicule, and because we were angered and hurt by all of this, we withdrew further into ourselves, and stopped having contact with heterosexual women almost entirely. At one point a group of us decided that the best way to stop being hassled about separatism was to publish instalments of the CLIT papers in the weekly newsletter, which was mailed to women all over London and beyond. We thought that if women wanted to know about separatism they could read this, and then leave us in peace. It didn't work, and by about the third instalment the outcry was such that we abandoned it.

Over the next few years the numbers of separatists grew. Women began to leave the cities and to establish women's houses in the countryside and in Scotland and Wales. We had contact with women from America, France and Scandinavia. I began to read pieces about separatism written by women who I didn't know. All this meant that I no longer felt personally responsible for separatism. Sometimes many weeks went by without me having to defend my politics. I had time to think about where I was going and what I had become. I look back on 1975 as a year of the most painful self-scrutiny. I had made so many enemies. Had the means justified the end? In the winter of 1975 the council evicted us from our squat and those of us who formed the nucleus of that original women's house were dispersed around the country. I felt very stuck. I was trapped by a set of dictates I had imposed on myself and others, and my aggressive public image doggedly intruded itself into my personal relationships. I was frustrated by my ghetto, sickened by my reputation. I needed a fresh start. I had to let go of separatism.

In the spring of 1976 I decided to act on a need I had felt for a very long time. I wanted a child. By June, after one attempt at conception, I was pregnant. (This, in the days before widespread artificial insemination, meant a public climb down from separatism.) My separatist friends said I was selling out, and taking on the role of mother was just doing what the patriarchy had trained me for. In any case they would never sanction sex with a man for whatever reason, not to mention taking the risk of giving birth to a male child. Women who I had attacked for bringing up boy children wanted to know if it had been an immaculate conception or simply parthenogenesis, and what was I going to do with it if it were a boy? Although I did what I could to try to conceive a girl, I couldn't be sure that I had. In any event both sets of protagonists were right. My aggressive five-year ego trip along the path of separatism was over. I had to face the music, I had to face myself.

By the autumn of 1976, halfway through my pregnancy, I fell asleep one afternoon and had a very powerful dream. In it I saw my child's body inside my own, but it wasn't curled up like a foetus. It wasn't a baby either, it was a child of about three, and what's more it was a boy with a shock of fair hair. When I woke up I was almost as amazed by the fair hair as I was by the sex, because both his 'father' and I are very dark. In the spring of 1977 I did indeed give birth to a boy who later grew that shock of fair hair.

So, what do I feel about separatism now, ten years on, and the mother of sons? How can I claim any loyalty to separatism after what has happened to me? Well, most obviously I have learnt that what is good for me cannot necessarily be applied to everyone, although I still tend to dish out unsolicited advice. But, more importantly, I have learnt not to see any stage of my life as the final one. Politics, sexuality or whatever, must be a framework to build on, not a rigid cage which restricts change.

All women who come to separatism do so as a reaction to the brutality and institutionalized sexism of men. The rage and sense of injustice, for a separatist, is not powerfully enough voiced anywhere else. But let me make the point here that separatism and man-hating are different things. A man-hater is someone (and it can be another man) inspired by revenge. A separatist, by definition, lives separately from men, although hatred of men does occur. The man-hater is locked into the initial stage of separation, where repressed hurt and previously unarticulated anger are explored. Many man-haters, in my experience, come fresh from a traumatic relationship with a man, or a recent realization about men. The overwhelming need to return the hurt, although this seems to be a necessary stage, can become the overriding passion. It can lead a woman into almost daily aggressive confrontations with men in order to sustain high levels of hatred. In some separatist spaces time and energy were spent in endless discussion on the evils of men. Here is the first uncomfortable contradiction of separatism. Whereas separatism should result in women devoting all their time and energy to women, in fact and probably inevitably, men manage to exhaust us even in their absence.

If my withdrawal from separatism had in part to do with feeling unhappy with a surfeit of hatred, which is mentally and spiritually very depleting, it had also to do with how you go about communicating feelings of being cleansed and enlightened. In contact with other women the separatist becomes more and more impatient with women who to them seem stubbornly bogged down in male values. As I have already said, it can reach the point where you have virtually no contact except with other separatists. This is an unreal place to be, because if you can't talk to other women, yet you believe all women must in the end come to separatism, then either those women have to be born separatist or they have to come to it through isolation, pain and struggle. The process of separatism growing into a global force would thus take a very long time. In this sense, separatism doesn't address itself to the business of making life better for all women, and is then restricted in large part to acting as a channel for the energy of women once they have become embittered by heterosexism.

Finally, I think the issue which more than any other led me to break with pure separatism, was women's compassion. In defining the source of women's oppression being pro-male sexism rather than capitalism, separatism shifted the emphasis of the whole of feminism. But, having done this, separatism went on to offer only one solution, an all-women world. Here separatism dissolves, at best, into romantic/cosmic/evolutionary answers, or at worst into violence and male genocide. Separatism, despite any protestations to the contrary, came up against the age old problem of how to transpose the idea onto the material world.

However men are 'are gotten rid of' many women would be immeasurably hurt in the process. For separatists to impose their solution on all women, even if it was viewed as being 'for her own good', you cannot escape the fact that you are simply replacing male domination with female. Women have massive amounts of love invested in fathers, lovers and sons, and many of these women despise the systems their own men may be helping to sustain. Haven't women always so been torn? But to insist that women somehow amputate their love and compassion is to ask them to destroy the very thing which in my view favourably distinguishes us from men. Patriarchy has shown women that there is no such thing as peace, there are just gaps in the wars. To me, we were not offering anything different. If we were to solve our problem by disposing of our enemy, we would set a very disgusting precedent in terms of separatist problem-solving.

Graduated separatism accepts pure separatism's definition of the problem, but not the solution. Apart from anything else it is self-defeating to nurture girl children, to teach them self-respect and self-defence, and then have to watch them go to war with men and boys whose ideas are left unchallenged. Having said this, I don't mean that it is the job of women to re-educate men. Once a woman has decided what and who she wants to be, it is for the men in her life, if there are any, to re-educate themselves to take account of her.

Because I lived away from men for so long, part of me is now permanently closed to them. I can honestly say that I feel at least equal to them, often above them; and I don't enter any relations with them that aren't on my terms. I don't need men to make me feel secure, to be a mother, to frame my morals, to pay my bills, to organize my life, to give me self-esteem. I do not want matriarchy to replace patriarchy as an interim measure because I retain unshakeable faith in women's ability to organize, to be caring and to be, just in so many ways, superior to men. Eventually men could probably be readmitted to positions of influence, provided they had somehow overcome their taste for violence, greed, rape and power for its own sake.

Although this may sound harsh and unreasonable, experience has made it hard for me to trust women who have never been through some form of separatist reaction. If, as a woman, you can see clearly what men have done to us, how can you stay calm? If you don't explore your anger how can you stop internalizing it and shed the costume of the victim? So long as heterosexism continues, it will continue to spawn separatism. My hope is that we could develop the kind of separatism which doesn't make women, both on the inside and the outside of it, feel attacked, vilified, stuck and lonely. To feel compassion for men without having been a separatist is dangerous. It is a love which has been kept in ignorance: haven't women been kept uninformed for long enough?

8 Faltering from the closet

Terry Sanderson

Rotherham – what a dump! It's the sort of place where the pigeons fly backwards because they don't want to get muck in their eyes. Someone once told me that even breathing the air was the equivalent of smoking twenty cigarettes a day. It's a mean place for anyone to live, but particularly bad for gay people.

I grew up in a small mining village on the outskirts of Rotherham during the fifties and sixties. It was all pits and steelworks in those days and there was a resultant machismo about the place. Men were men and women knew their places. Homosexuals were unheard of.

I was quite effeminate in my youth, but no one mentioned this fact to me. I was just thought of as 'spoiled' or 'like a daft lass' rather than being gay. I suppose it was considered such a terrible thing to say about anyone that it had become a totally taboo concept – even for your worst enemy. I was well into my teens before I even knew there was a word to describe these secret feelings I had, let alone that they had been legislated against. But when I did find out I was profoundly relieved to know that all these troubling fantasies which had been playing twice nightly in my head were, in fact, shared by others.

But where were these others? How could I find these rarities who wanted what I wanted? According to the Sunday papers of the time there was a 'twilight world' somewhere where gay vicars and school teachers and scout masters 'assaulted' their youthful charges. It didn't sound very pleasant, but I was still anxious to find it.

During my sheltered youth I had two fleeting experiences which gave me some indication that I was not alone. The first happened at the local cinema. I was in the habit of going in there each Sunday with my (straight) friend Kenny to see the horror double-bill. We were both sixteen. On one occasion a man sat next to me and after a preliminary bit of footsie, he invited me to slip my hand into his pants. I was most happy to oblige. All this happened in total silence with Kenny sitting on the other side of me, totally unaware that my life was changing. At long last it was happening and I was receiving confirmation that the exotic and rare species, The Homosexual, existed somewhere else other than in my imagination.

My second gay encounter was quite soon afterwards. In my first job I was required to wear a suit. My mother insisted on accompanying me to the tailor to ensure that I got something sensible. She knew that I was perfectly capable of having the whole thing made in black leatherette if left to my own devices. The man who measured me – he had red hair, I remember – lingered over my inside leg and when he realized I wasn't going to object, gave me a comprehensive fondling. I was thrilled, of course, but this was tempered somewhat by the knowledge that my mother was standing in full view, three feet away, leafing through a pattern book.

Then I got a job in a camera shop in the High Street. It became apparent very soon that I had not been employed because of my skills as a salesman. It turned out the manager of the shop, Mr Farrer, was gay and it wasn't long before there was a different kind of developing in the darkroom. This, as far as I was concerned, was the great romance of the century. Regrettably, he did not feel the same way. Whilst I was mooning about singing 'I'm in love with a wonderful guy', he was entertaining just about half the gay population of the town.

However, this job revealed to me the big, wide, illegal world of the homosexual. I came to realize that the twilight world actually existed unseen, but in parallel, with everyone else's world. The manager of the local department store used to come to the shop regularly, so did the butcher from three doors up. Mr Farrer seemed to know so many people, and the reason he knew them was because they were all gay.

What a revelation! But this was too soon in my own development for me to be able to grasp the opportunity and eventually the shop closed down and Mr Farrer moved on.

It was in 1972, when I was twenty-five, that I decided that something had to be done. These occasional chance encounters could not in any way be said to constitute a satisfactory emotional life. It was around that time that I spotted an advertisement for CHE (Campaign for Homosexual Equality) in the personal column of the *Sunday Times*. So I wrote off. Back came the reply. To my disappointment I realized that the nearest group was in Manchester, which was too far away to be useful.

'Isn't there somewhere nearer?' I asked.

'No,' they replied, 'so why don't you start something?'
They put me in touch with a few other people in nearby Sheffield and we arranged to have a tentative first meeting in someone's flat. It was a fraught time. We were all very wary of each other, not really knowing that we wanted, what was possible or even what gay people could do together besides have sex. In Sheffield (Britain's fourth largest city) the only gay facility at the time was an upstairs bar in a pub called The King William. To get to this bar you had to pass through a billiard room full of jeering straight men. It amazed me to think that even though the gay bar had been situated up those dark stairs for many years, the straight men downstairs managed to keep up the impetus so that no queen should pass without an insult. Indeed, the only people willing to endure this ordeal on a regular basis were the screaming queens who had already decided that the best way to cope was to flaunt it.

It took another year before the group felt confident enough to organize its first semi-open event – a disco. We hired the Cemetery Road Vestry Hall, organized a bar and some records and the show was on the road. For one lovely evening – one very important evening for the gay people of Sheffield – Cemetery Road Vestry Hall was paradise. We had a convener of the group who was energetic, out, and determined to make CHE a dynamic group. His name was Dave Brown and he eventually went on to establish one of the first clubs in the country to be licensed as an openly gay establishment. I was amazed that someone should have such big ambitions for a group like ours, but the ideas were getting through and soon my own expectations increased.

After the success of Cemetery Road the group hired the City Hall for another disco and soon the whole thing became a regular event which still occurs today. Indeed, over the years it developed into one of the largest regular gay events in the country. One of the best aspects of it was that gay men and lesbians were represented in almost equal numbers. The concept of a 'gay community' was born in Sheffield through those discos. Suddenly there was somewhere where you could 'be' in peace, where plots could be hatched, messages got across and, best of all, where romance could be safely experienced.

Having made such progress in Sheffield, I felt it was time to move back to home ground, so I set up a CHE group in Rotherham. It was soon clear that this was an entirely different kettle of fish. Gone was the anonymity of the big city, gone was the support of the hundreds of people who were prepared to get involved, as they were in Sheffield with its university and other cosmopolitan influences. What I now faced was a small town with a strongly macho bias and an inbuilt resistance to change. However, fired with enthusiasm from the successes in Sheffield, we opened for business in a church hall rented to us by a sympathetic vicar.

The group was slow to get off the ground, despite an encouraging article about the group in the *Rotherham Advertiser*. Prospective members seemed reluctant to present themselves. After all, the only tradition of homosexuality in the town was in the cottages, and stories in the local papers about court cases for 'gross indecency' indicated that they were well patronized.

By this time – the early seventies – homosexuality was no longer a taboo subject. The Gay Liberation Front and CHE had laid the foundations. The subject was occasionally aired on TV or in the press and *Gay News* had hit the streets. But there was still a strong feeling among the citizens of Rotherham that the whole thing didn't really concern them. It happened somewhere else.

After about a year, and with a paid-up membership of about fifteen men and five women, we decided that we would try to organize our own disco at the town hall

Assembly Rooms. We would try to do for Rotherham what Checkers discos had done for Sheffield. But the local councillors in Rotherham lacked the political sophistication of their neighbouring big-city colleagues and they turned down our application to hire the room. I was angry as hell at the time and disappointed, too, for this was a strongly Labour-controlled council, but looking back now I realize that this was the best thing that could have happened to the group, for now we could present ourselves to the people of Rotherham as a genuine minority with a grievance.

The local press and radio picked up the story and carried it week after week – for a couple of years the gay struggle was big news for the folks back home. The citizens of Rotherham were, at last, being confronted with the topic in their own town, in a way that was difficult for them to ignore. They were forced into formulating an opinion.

It was at this point – a year or so into our campaign – that I realized that my efforts were not always appreciated by the other members of the group. Many of them were feeling distinctly insecure at having taken the first step out of the closet and they kept the escape route in sight at all times. This was a dilemma which was never really resolved. I was arguing that gay people have nothing to be ashamed of and yet my troops remained invisible as though they needed convincing too. CHE was a campaigning group, but it was also supposed to be a support and social outlet. I wasn't fully aware at the time of just what profound personal changes were taking place in the lives of some of the members. Those who were nervous and struggling with their own feelings did not want to expose their gayness in the way that I had done. I understood this. I had, quite deliberately, burned my bridges – there was no returning to the closet for me. I was fighting my own terrors in public, but others wanted to do it more gently. And so I became the single, visible manifestation of homosexuality in South Yorkshire. Whenever the papers wanted a quote they came to me, when the local radio wanted an interview I was the spokesperson.

For three years it went on. A sympathetic local media helped us harass and embarrass the silly burghers as they repeatedly refused to let us use the Assembly Rooms. Then they also turned down our application to have *Gay News* in the library, which provided us with further ammunition and an unexpected new member.

One of the councillors on the libraries committee took a copy of *Gay News* home to study so that he couldn't be accused of being uninformed when the time came for him to vote for its rejection. Whilst *GN* was in this councillor's house, his twenty-year-old son read it and saw the contact number for the CHE group. Within a week he was a member, within a fortnight he'd come out at home and within three weeks his father was at the CHE group wanting to know what the hell was going on. But we had at least one vote in our favour when the application was considered.

I had been very naïve when we started out in Rotherham and it came as a shock to me to realize that not everyone can see the justness of a just cause. I had been hurt by the crude insults, deliberate distortions and sheer venom that had been directed at us. It brought home to me that even tinpot local councillors will ruthlessly exploit irrational prejudice if there is political mileage in it. I also had a rather childish trust in the police until the day they turned up on my doorstep to question me about a murder. It was then that I discovered that they had been keeping our group under surveillance and noting down the registration numbers of cars parked outside the meeting place. My rather innocent trust crumbled when I realized that as far as the police were concerned, I was little better than a criminal on whom they must keep tabs. It frightened me to think that my name and address and those of the other members were on police files for no other reason than that we were gay. We were referred to as 'sinister' and this made me see how little impact we had made upon the establishment and how much further we needed to go.

All around me, as this was going on, dramatic personal transformations were taking place. More and more people contacted the group; very few actually joined, but an awful lot were metamorphosed by it. Some needed only to know that we existed – that was enough for them to throw themselves wholeheartedly into the gay life. Others were diffident, unable to cope or come to terms with their sexuality. Some found the conflict too intense and retired back to the closet, perhaps for ever. There had never been any doubt in my own mind. The prospect of a heterosexual involvement on any level was simply out of the question for me.

Coming out was the key issue then as it is now. I remember the first TV documentary I saw about gays – the participants appeared only in silhouette and questions were couched in hushed and tragic tones. Many of the older people found it difficult to throw off the 'criminal' associations which had carried over from the fifties and sixties. Many long-standing personal crises were brought to a head because of the existence of CHE. A sizeable reservoir of homosexuality, which had been held in abeyance, suddenly stirred in the town. I was astonished, for instance, at the number of married men and women who contacted us. So many of them had married simply because they had no idea that homosexuals could have *relationships*. Many of them had had sex with other gays, but few of them had accepted that you could make a way of life out of it. Then suddenly there was this group of people who asserted that not only could you commit yourself to a member of your own sex, they were actually doing it.

Reactions from people were not generally hostile. Except for a few stereotyped responses from the wilder churches – Pastor David Powell of the Rotherham Pentecostal Church actually banned gays from his services – and a few jibes from the local National Front, we were always treated politely, listened to with interest and generally well received. This surprised me somewhat. I was always waiting for the day when I would be beaten up, but it never came. And then when the invitations to speak to the Housewives' Register and Parish Council started rolling in, I realized that CHE had been noted as a part of the life of the town and it had a lot of potential friends.

Rather belatedly the local Labour Party got its act together and, along with the Trades Council, passed resolutions condemning its own councillors. But still the council wouldn't move over the issue of hiring rooms to us.

It was after the third year of struggle that we decided to go militant. We arranged a disco at the Assembly Rooms under a false name and invited two hundred gays to come along.

They did. The local papers got wind in advance of what was happening and I was petrified that the police would come bursting in to arrest us all. But the disco passed pleasantly and our point was made. The following morning the local paper headlined 'Gays Lead Council a Lively Dance', which made the mayor very angry indeed. Then the local government ombudsman put his boot into the council by issuing a report which said that CHE had been treated unjustly. The local vicar and local MP Stan Crowther added their names to a petition of local worthies calling for the council to change its mind. Under all this pressure, the council simply had to relent and change its policy.

No one should get the impression from this that Rotherham had taken the gay community to its bosom. Things didn't change all that dramatically. I went along to the surgery of Rother Valley MP Peter Hardy, who was resident in one of the safest Labour seats in the country, and despite all that had gone before he was able to say, 'This has nothing to do with the people around here – it all happens in London'. As far as he was concerned, homosexuality did not exist north of Hampstead (or perhaps south of it, either) and despite the fact that its local manifestation was sitting in front of him he would not be convinced.

But lots of things were falling into place for me. I had come out relentlessly to my family, my friends, colleagues and everyone else who came into my life. At every step I was told not to do it because I was bound to suffer from the kind of prejudice I was always talking about. It didn't happen though. I was never assaulted, never kicked out of my home or sacked, even though I seemed to be inviting it.

I was, for my final seven years in Rotherham, working at a hospital for the mentally handicapped. This was supposed to be a 'sensitive' job and if I came out I would automatically be adjudged a danger to the patients and given the elbow. In actual fact, I got nothing but support, encouragement and – dare I say it? – love from my colleagues. They must have been sick and tired of my harping about gay rights, but by the time I had decided to move to London in order to set up home with the man of my dreams, my workmates organized a leaving party which was a touching celebration of the relationship between Keith and myself. About thirty of us gathered in a hotel in Rotherham - all people I'd worked with including the cleaner and the consultant, and those who had them brought along their own partners, girlfriends, boyfriends and husbands and wives. They toasted Keith and me (Keith had come up for the day to join in) and bought us a slow cooker for our new home. I wept buckets, but it wasn't until later that I realized what had happened. These people - ordinary working-class folk like me - had come together to celebrate a gay relationship and to wish it success and happiness.

What I had been fighting for for all these years - the right for gay people to live their lives openly with dignity and respect - was actually happening, and in the most unlikely of places.

I could not have had a better send off, and I realized that the public battles had played only a marginal part in it. The slogan 'the personal is political' made perfect sense to me. I could see that only by changing our own personal worlds will we change the world at large. The happiness we are all seeking isn't granted by politicians, although I accept they can create circumstances that make the achievement of happiness very difficult. At that time, of course, unemployment was not the major issue it is today, neither did we have the burden of AIDS, but I still maintain that the most important changes we can make are the ones inside our own heads.

9 The importance of being lesbian

Eilís Mhara

This piece is about coming out in Dublin in the early seventies. It is a personal, highly subjective account which seeks to relate my experience as an Irish lesbian, my involvement in political action at that time and my subsequent emigration to England in the mid-seventies. I would like to thank the following women for their support and encouragement as I was writing this piece: Anne Collins, Linda Stepulvage, Tricia Darragh and Lisa Hunt.

In 1973, I was living in Dublin in a teeny bedsit with three other women. It was the kind of rabbit warren in which you could not swing a cat and there were thousands of them in the city. Our beds touched but we never did. Arm-in-arming for Saturday shopping was permissible but the finer more subtle expressions of love between women were channelled into food, presents and a particular kind of teasing that conveyed the messages of knowing each other on different levels in ways which neutralized the intensity.

We got up every morning and went to our routine, boring and badly-paid jobs, some of us hoping, some of us dreading the advent of Mr Right: he who would relieve us from, God forbid, the tedium of having to rely on each other for company, comfort, support and stimulation. We went dancing on Saturday nights with a kind of patient horror, anticipating the humiliation which accompanied these expeditions. I often stood and just watched the women, the mascara-ed, the pansticked, the lacquered and the lonely, line the walls and wait to be asked to dance. We were not allowed to dance with each other. If you did, you risked verbal or physical abuse, derision and expulsion. Women policed each other, stopping rebellious acts with cold and disapproving stares.

Apart from the occasional drunken foray into heterosexual foreplay, we remained within the girls together fold in all other areas of our social and domestic lives. I was working as a tele-ad girl with the Irish Press Group. I sat day in day out with headphones over my ears, '*Irish Press*, can I help you?' nearly losing my job once because the owner of the newspaper, Vivian De Valera, thought I was too forward on the telephone ... my manner was not subservient enough.

It was in that office on the fourth floor that I heard and felt the city of Dublin roar and shudder with the explosion of three massive bombs which ripped through the heart of the city and its people. It's a day I will never forget as the death toll rose and office workers were told to give blood or go home. I did both. People were crying in shock and smoke billowing above Pearse, Talbot and Parnell streets marking the spots where a few hours earlier, country women and men had hurried past to catch trains home for the weekend. We all knew that this carnage was the work of Unionist Fascists bent on teaching the Republic a lesson – stay out of our affairs.

Six months prior to this horrendous attack, I had come out. During the lead-up to my emergence as a fully-fledged lesbian, I suffered unspeakably as I steered myself through a minefield of heavily internalized Catholic dogma. At night I tossed and turned to dreams of such emotional intensity that I went to work as tired as I was the day before. The urgency of coming out was precipitated by contact with the 'real thing'. I was part of a small group of women who met regularly above a shabby public house in Baggot Street to talk feminism and discuss the current state of Irish politics. Sitting in this seamy room one evening waiting for the meeting to begin, I was startled by my friend exclaiming, 'My God, there's a man coming up the stairs.' I looked over the bannister and saw two women, one holding the other by the hand. My stomach contracted and my heart went into a somersault. I spent the rest of the evening pretending rivetted attention on the discussion while all the time practising ways of looking at the two women without them catching me. It was deliciously terrifying. I wanted to follow them home, ask them a million questions. Instead I kept silent, but inside I was singing in a very loud voice. Over the weeks that followed I noticed more of them. I could not use the word though; its power caught in the back of my throat and held me, voiceless. The urgency of coming out was building and I felt like a firecracker about to go off. The anticipation and joyous feelings were continually offset by my fear of great social ostracization, loneliness, exposure, ethical confusion and the permanent threat of moral damnation.

On the streets, in meetings and in work, I began to dread women's perceptiveness and intuition for fear they would penetrate my three-dimensional protection, silence, an accepted assumed heterosexuality and aloofness. It was not to work for long. My hetero-dithering, which might have continued indefinitely, was abruptly ended one day over lunch with a good friend. At one point during the meal, she reached over to me, put her hand on mine, looked me straight in the eye and said, 'I think you are a lesbian.' As I bit through the clingwrap on my sandwich, I gulped, and summoning indifference said, 'Oh why do you think that Brenda?' Every intonation in my voice was struggling to disguise the yes, yes, yesses that were bubbling under the surface. 'It's just the way you are when you are with the lesbians in the group.' She had hit a note of such deep truth in me that I just sat looking at her. And, of course, it was true. I was a lesbian dammit. I had known it for a long time, ever since I had confided to my Mum at age fifteen that I fancied the other girls at school, the 'it's just a phase,' syndrome. I had instantly buried the intense feelings hoping that with time they would decompose or reform and grow into normal healthy heterosexual longings. Of course, they did not and now when I wake up in the morning and thank God that I'm a lesbian, I remember to thank myself as well. Brenda's direct statement pushed me to act, to move and to go to where my energy had always been.

Coming home to the lesbian in me, my joys and fears were of a different nature from those posed by continually having to straddle the mutually hostile worlds of lesbianism and heterosexuality. All my senses were heightened and I dwelt in a sort of kaleidoscopic twilight zone of longing, terror, political affirmation, sexual discovery. Overnight, almost, I became a voyeur. I sat in cafés or stood in bus queues observing the phenomenon of heterosexuality. From the unsafe distance of my perversion I could, at last, allow my real reactions to emerge. I was me and it was both frightening and exciting, like driving very fast round a precipitous bend with someone now and again taking my hands off the wheel and forcing me to trust. One of those times when you wish that varieties of public screaming were a permitted social outlet without the perpetrator risking, at best, hospitalization and, at worst, incarceration.

Now when I look back on that part of my life, I want to make a film and call it *The Loneliness of the Long Distance Latent Lesbian*. And I had been lonely. There were other lonely women too. Especially isolated were lesbians living in the country in Ireland. Without the safety of numbers and the resources, however limited, that Dublin provided, many women were too frightened to come out. They fled to Dublin or England or came out in very small numbers and lived in closeted fearfulness of exposure, job loss and increasing isolation. In my own backyard, friends who could not cope with their own homophobia deserted me . . . I became the kind of woman that my friends, mother, sisters and other friends warned them about. A couple of years after coming out, I met a heterosexual woman with whom I had been particularly close before I had blasted our cosy set up out of the water. I watched her shuffle, wriggle and avert her eyes while we made stilted conversation about our lives. She carefully avoided the personal for fear she might learn more about me . . . a lesbian, a woman who loved other women. After all, I might trigger off some of those well-repressed feelings in her and what would she do with them? They were not the sort you could put out in a black bin bag and hope they would be gone in the morning.

To this day, I still marvel at the fact that, in a country where even the most seasoned and recalcitrant dyke can be made to feel truly perverted in a very short space of time, women found, and still do find, the courage to step into the breach of difference and come out.

During those early seventies, despite the avalanche of heterosexism that constantly slid in our direction, including the virulent expressions of women-hating propounded by Father Church, a group of us waged our own war at the patriarchal system. The overt and crudest manifestations of Irish misogyny were our first target and we vented our rage and flexed our lesbian muscles in a myriad of dangerous and daring ways.

The Forty Foot at Sandycove was our first port of call. A bastion of male privilege on the rocky Dublin shoreline, so called because of the water depth. A beautiful non-tidal cove where Dublin's finest flaunted themselves at an indifferent sea while their wives, children and girlfriends sat half a mile away on what was an excuse for a beach amidst the polluted debris of the capital and not a wave to be seen. The only movement was an occasional flock of intrepid sea gulls foraging through the mess. A huge sign at the entrance to the Forty Foot, 'Men Only', barred all Irishwomen from what was legally part of their national heritage. We were resolved this nonsense had to stop. A number of previous attempts to penetrate this male club had been unsuccessful, with the raiding parties being driven back by irate men. Agreeing that precision timing and strategic planning was essential to our success we assembled a group of twenty indomitable dykes. A co-ordinated land, sea and air attack appealed since the element of surprise would considerably affect the outcome and would probably produce the most dramatic results. This plan was no sloppily organized affair, aware as we were of the lengths to which threatened men will go to protect their most prized territory. However, the extraordinary pleasure of seeing a bunch of terrified men running in all directions and in complete disarray spurred us into action.

At precisely two thirty on that fateful Saturday, two sinewy dykes climbed into an old-fashioned rowing boat in a small Dublin harbour and began their arduous row towards the Forty Foot and victory. Back on terra firma, fifteen others bundled into an assortment of cars and drove slowly towards the unsuspecting target. With fine timing we arrived, parking under cover of some distance so as not to arouse suspicion. Reaching the 'Men Only' sign, we laughed loudly and one of the women painted a massive women's symbol at the entrance, a sort of ritual 'open sesame'. We ran in the rest of the way and lo and behold, what a sight met our eyes. Naked men of unbelievable varieties were standing, sitting or lying all round the cove. Their bodies, although all different, had a sort of common denominator ugliness which only a group of undressed men can produce. As we came into view, hairy male legs moving like pistons beat a hasty retreat to the nearest available nook where they crouched and huddled in speechless terror. Others, clutching large and not so large towels to their exposed crotches, stood rooted to the spot appalled. All were transfixed by this group of laughing and exultant lesbians as they walked resolutely towards the rocky promontory stripping off their clothes with Amazonian brazenness.

On cue, the rowing boat appeared from around the coastal bend and in it two topless dykes roaring and cheering were urging their little craft into the cove. Suddenly, they both jumped up, pulled off their remaining cotton restrictions and plunged straight into the water. It was a gorgeous sight. On the diving board armed with umbrellas, a bevy of beauties in fashionable bathing attire dropped one by one into the cove ... splish, splosh. Some of the men had run for their lives by now. Others too mesmerized and trapped in their nakedness stood aghast watching their male sanctuary being defiled by a bunch of lunatic lesbians. As remaining male stragglers dragged their shocked bodies out and past the 'Men Only' sign, the women relaxed and, for the first time in over a quarter of a century, Irish women's bodies felt the pleasure of sea and hot rocks in the Forty Foot at Sandycove.

The sweet taste of this victory lingered a long time on the lips of Dublin dykes. On the broader political front, Irish women were also fighting. Equal pay claims were brought and lost by several groups of working women, bakers, confectioners and factory workers. Women who could carry a child under each arm on a day's shopping trip were told they were not strong enough to do men's work; that lifting and lugging were better left to the lads after all. In the kitchens women bakers seethed as they watched their male colleagues lift dough trays into the ovens, the lifting warranting a third more pay than the women. Other more stout-hearted women resorted to testing the powers of the newer European legislation. But to no avail. Ireland was told to pull its equal pay socks up or else. At the same time, the fathers at home were given years to implement the law and still the women suffered and raged.

Irish Women United formed in the early seventies, a radical counter to the government sop, the Council for the Status of Women. This was a liberal middle-class reformist cop-out guaranteed to give the right women a step up in the power stakes as well as provide appeasement for male consciences which were getting a bit ragged at the edges from the constant battering of Irish feminists. Many of the smaller radical politically active women's groups reformed under the Irish Women United umbrella. Disaffected women from the male-dominated left, women from single issue campaign groups like Contraceptive Action Programme (CAP) came together. Acknowledging and dealing positively with political differences was vital to our continuance and effectiveness as we struggled and worked on fundamental issues of feminism and socialism, the emphasis of our commitment being governed to a large extent by our differing political histories. Classically, the majority of the women I met and worked with in Dublin in those days were lesbians. Irish Women United targeted rape and all other forms of violence against women, contraception, equal pay, political censorship, union rights for women, etc. We campaigned, picketed, called public meetings, organized actions, held conferences, disrupted government meetings, created opportunities for educationals and talks, embarrassed government ministers and challenged the church. We linked ourselves in solidarity to other nationalist struggles. Visiting women from other countries struggling under the yoke of imperialism spoke to and advised us. I remember one meeting six months after the CIA had murdered Allende. Irish women cried as they heard from two Chilean women of the horrors being committed in post-Allende Chile.

Abortion and divorce were two other issues of grave concern to Irish feminists but the climate was too hot politically and our numbers too small to effect change in those areas at that time. Given that the sanctity of the Irish family is rigidly built into the Irish constitution, it was going to take years to break down and change the incredible legislative and political barriers.

Nationalist and feminist women in Northern Ireland were organizing around basic issues of survival. The early and mid-seventies were a time of 'no warning' bombs and sectarian killings were escalating. Women prisoners in Armagh had political status until 1975 but lost it in the following year and the numbers in Armagh rose dramati-cally during the late seventies. Campaigns to secure decent housing, health and employment brought women together to organize. The Women's Movement in Northern Ireland developed out of the twin oppression of class and imperialism. During those years, especially in the early part of the seventies, political contact between women from the North and the Republic was limited. This stemmed largely from a lack of political analysis and clarity in relation to nationalism and feminism on the part of Southern feminists.

Women's Aid Centres were set up in Dublin and other major cities as I was preparing to leave Ireland. The Dublin Rape Crisis Centre came into being a year or two after I had left. Many of these organizations were self-financing and depended heavily on donation, feminist patronage and solidarity from other better-resourced groups. Just shortly before I departed, I attended a small inaugural meeting on the quayside in Dublin. It was the first meeting of the Irish Republican Socialist Party of which Bernadette Devlin was a founder member. Some weeks after this Party launch, one key member was shot and a major split created the Irish National Liberation Army.

In describing some of the political action Irish women took, I hope to reach those English feminists who think, erroneously, that feminism got its name from them. Feminism has lived in the bellies of Irish women for hundreds of years. You might even say we are gut feminists.

I remember one particular conference held in Dublin in Ballyfermot, around 1973. They were called Women's Liberation Conferences in those days. Ballyfermot is a high-rise architectural nightmare on the outskirts of Dublin, a working-class ghetto sufficiently distant from the bourgeois elegance of the city centre as to pose no threat to the burgeoning middle class, absorbed as they were then in the mild stirrings of environmentalism, as Georgian Dublin vanished up its own pastiched arsehole. About one hundred women attended the conference but local women were conspicuously absent, forbidden to attend by their husbands who feared the power of women's words, their wives' innate feminism and the possibility of lesbian contagion. Nell McCafferty, Bernadette Devlin and other notables vented their feminist spleen at an appreciative audience. We were reminded of the artful political ruse of a band of women who, flouting the Republic's law on contraception, returned from Northern Ireland by train having procured hundreds of contraceptives. On reaching the Customs post and the point of confiscation, the women flung packet after packet at red-faced customs men, while alerted press and other media looked on gleefully. Thereafter the event was known as the Pill Train.

We heard from the few local women who did attend how they took the law into their own hands and arranged regular supplies of contraceptives from the North. The Pill Train aroused much publicity and it proved extremely effective in forcing the issue of contraception into the front line of public consciousness. Along with other actions it became the springboard towards legislative change in Ireland.

As the conference afternoon wore on, two Gardai were noticed at the back of the hall standing, ears bent listening to the speeches. Little did they know that shortly after the conference their services would be required in the lounge of a local public house by a group of frustrated dykes and an infuriated publican. Needing a well-earned drink after the afternoon's work, ten or twelve dykes repaired to a nearby bar. In those days, if you were a woman or recognizably so, it was wellnigh impossible to procure a pint of beer in a public house. The logic of this defied Irish women who were forced to deduce that the spectacle of women wielding pints must offend male sensibilities at a very deep level, especially those who equated pint-downing by women with lesbian leisure. After all, if we were allowed to wield pints what else might we wield and where would it all end?

Not being averse to a challenge and imbued with extra
fervour from the conference, the women, all dykes, ordered
fifteen hot whiskies. Upon completion of the hot whisky
order the women planned to ask for fifteen pints thereby
coercing a reluctant publican to serve women pints. It was
not possible to resell or rebottle hot whiskies. As soon as
the pint order was lodged it was brusquely refused. The
women remained firm that unless the entire order was
completed they would not pay for the hot whiskies. At this
point a puce publican, determined to make the scene a battle-
ground of the sexes, threatened the women with the law.
The challenge was accepted and amidst cheers from a group
of semi-inebriated local husbands, the offended owner
headed out the door in search of a couple of friendly Gardai.
He found them quickly enough and returned to the pub.
What he had not bargained for was the fact that these two
Gardai had been listening to well-articulated feminist
rhetoric all afternoon and were still reeling from the effects.
They took one look at the group of adamant women and
ordered the publican to complete the round. It was the
women's turn to cheer while the surrounding men scowled
and muttered obscenities.

In 1976 with the Tories gaining votes I left my friends, my
lover, my job and my political life in Ireland. I came to
England – Ipswich – to study for the social workers'
qualification, a CQSW in Community Work, believing that I
could work with women in the ways I wanted, provided I
had the necessary qualifications. With the required piece of
paper in my hands, I planned to return home to work. At the
time of qualifying, however, I realized that I had the choice
of working for the Eastern Health Board or the Catholic
Church (the two are interchangeable). I reluctantly decided
to stay and came to London knowing one lesbian. My
natural instinct once I reached the rather intimidating
environment of London was to seek out other lesbians.
Having been wintered out on the heterosexual plains of
Ipswich I longed for the company of other dykes. Finding
this rare breed was to prove a long, uphill struggle. I learned,
too, that English lesbian feminists expected you to become
one of them . . . you either assimilated or you disintegrated.
Over the years I was to meet Irish women who, unable to

stand the barrages of racism, distorted and changed their accents in order to pass. Hundreds of us were isolated from each other. Those who could not stand it returned home worn out by the virulence of anti-Irish racism which they experienced from English people. Many Irish women, including myself, who had come to England for the first time were truly shocked by the levels of anti-Irish racism directed at us. We simply did not know the extent to which English people are taught to despise us. For those of us who focused our energies on lesbian and feminists issues we were to find ourselves marginalized and isolated in English feminist groups, amongst women whose racism mirrored the population at large. These women ran and organized all the groups and I remember often being approached as if I were a rare species of animal. Not to be trusted or even understood but to be treated with caution and sometimes indulged.

It took time to translate the political terms and conditions being imposed on me by my colonialist sisters, heavily disguised as they were under a veneer of, 'Of course we know the issues are different for Irish women'. Behind this superficial and meaningless acknowledgment lay the galling assumption that Irish women had come to England to learn about 'real' feminism. Seldom in my experience did English women demonstrate the slightest interest in learning from us, from our struggles and from our political experiences. After all, we did all want abortion on demand and rape in marriage was a central issue for concerned Irish women. Meanwhile in Ireland, at that time, women were being arrested and harassed for reading *Spare Rib* and the war in the North was raging on with ever-increasing numbers of Republican women being imprisoned without trial. These facts escaped the attention of our radical sisters and thereby so did we.

It was a strange land to find myself in and one in which I observed many phenomena. One of these was the worship of the superstar. These tended to be white, middle-class academic English women who expounded on the latest dogmas of feminist political theory with a vigour reminiscent of evangelism. Women who lacerated young feminist apprentices at conferences if they made the mistake of admitting confusion or heretical leanings. Women who talked from their heads while their guts and hearts ached for tenderness. Women who through their racism, collusion and a profound lack of political intelligence, made my sisters and me completely invisible. Women who had long since stopped listening except to their own ossified ramblings. Women whose respect for and understanding of difference extended only to the marginal realm of their lesbian sexual partner.

Slowly I began to stumble across other disaffected Irish women and I felt like a traveller finding a friendly inn after a long, cold journey. What a relief to be among women who approached me positively and whose language and way of being I shared. Of course, we had many political differences but the twin oppressions of being Irish lesbians and immigrants brought us together and gave us a strong framework upon which to build our own movement and within which to begin articulating our anger at English feminism.

In my experience I was acutely aware that Irish lesbians had been active within the English women's movement for many years. Attempts by Irish women, lesbian and heterosexual, to voice our oppression and to struggle for support were largely ignored. As an Irish lesbian, I was expected to denounce my Irishness in favour of acceptability as a token English dyke. Feminist organizations and the media appeared almost impenetrable to us. Coverage of Irish women's issues was considered dangerous and potentially lethal to rising circulation figures. So English women went on being under-educated with nothing to counteract the filth and lies and daily racism of the English media. Lack of political motivation to change on the part of English feminists and increasing racism, combined with determination and effective networking of Irish women, resulted in our permanent separation from the mainstream of English feminism. It was untenable for us to continue to support and put energy into a political movement which in no ways respected or reflected our separate identity and struggle as Irish women.

Over a period of years and with a fierce amount of energy and commitment from Irish women in London and other parts of the country, our dedication to build a political organization of Irish women began to pay off. Work to develop and accumulate resources, to create effective ways of bringing Irish women together was slow and unsupported. We were actively thwarted by English women who flung accusations at us. An arsenal of political treacheries was employed to impede our progress, from the medium-range one of accusing us of lacking the right political perspective, to the more insidious long-range ones of accusing us of divisiveness, bringing men into feminism by speaking about the war in Ireland and, even on one occasion, attempting to show an exhibition – the famous, 'Bin Lids and Barricades'. The final salvo was that of jumping on the bandwagon, a wagon we were informed which was already jam-packed with Black and Jewish women: women whose political history among white gentile English women, in some ways, paralleled our own. It should be noted that Black and Jewish women consistently supported our struggle towards political autonomy. British imperialism in Ireland, whilst an erratically popular issue for the left, albeit as a practice ground for the more exciting nationalist struggles further afield, was certainly not a serious issue for concerned English feminists. This situation had only marginally changed but now Irish women no longer look, with the same expectation, to English women for support and solidarity.

In the spring of 1987, as I write this piece, a very different political climate prevails. The Tories are about to enter their third term of office having driven a knife through the heart of much of the more advanced social legislation of the past few decades. Fascism, racism, anti-Semitism and attacks on lesbians and gay men are on the increase and gaining ground year by year. Because of the continuous pressure exerted by Irish, Black and other women over the years, some English Women's Movement has died and that if they want must wake up to the fact that the middle-class, gentile English Women's Movement had died and that if they want to go on referring to us as ethnic minorities then they will have to include themselves as a separate group. If this does not happen then sooner or later we can all dig a hole and get in. For those white English women who are still in doubt, hear this ... we are all over here because you have all been over there.

With several well-attended Irish women's conferences behind us, a well-resourced and staffed Irish Women's Centre, many autonomous groups and campaigns operating all over London and in other parts of England, I will say with strength and pride that Irish women, whether heterosexual or lesbian, from Anne Devlin to Bernadette, remain the 'unmanageable revolutionaires' they/we have always been.

10 Living on the fringes — in more ways than one

Yik Hui

How do I begin describing myself so that anyone could understand where my politics were coming from? My experience in England has led me to the conclusion that most people are unable to see me whole. That is – if you're a lesbian you're white, and if you're Chinese you're exotic, passive, inscrutable, and the whole pack of racist stereotypes which I'm sure you could fill a page with without any help from me. As a result, I have spent many early years in this country perfecting what I call my chameleon act: fitting into whatever environment I found myself in; making myself, my Chinese self, invisible in order to avoid hostility. However, I had already begun the process, long before coming over, of minimizing and dismissing my cultural identity.

I am a product of the British legacy of colonialism: the reason why I ended up here, why I stayed, and why I still have one foot out the door. Both sides of my family left rural south China for Malaya to get away from the grinding poverty, encouraged by the British to fill their need for cheap labour in their colonies. My paternal grandfather started his working life as a water carrier – selling water house to house; by the time I arrived my father's family had 'made it'. On my mother's side, my grandfather and his family emigrated when he was offered a job as interpreter in the law courts. My mother had a Chinese education, returning to China for part of it. She saw at first hand the imperialist arrogance of the British in her mother country, aptly illustrated by the signs in the parks which baldly stated 'no dogs or Chinese allowed'. She was involved in some of the student protests against them during that period; but at the end of the day she still felt that an English education was a necessary tool for survival for her children. As immigrants in a British colony, the way to get on was through an English education. The price they paid was my cultural heritage. At school we were taught an obscenely distorted history of my people, as well as that of all the other exploited colonies. The recurring message drummed into our young minds was of the 'civilizing influence' of the British Empire and the superiority in values, behaviour and culture of the British. Never mind the exploitation and atrocities wreaked on whole countries in order that the British could plunder and fill their coffers from our raw materials and the sweat of our cheap labour.

The British also used the well-worn principle of divide and rule to run the country – keeping the Chinese and Indian settlers in Malaya from joining the Civil Service and administration which ran the country while nurturing the traditional ruling class to one day take over. Consequently, both the Indians and Chinese were confirmed in their immigrant status, discouraged from having a stake in our adopted country. Among my contemporaries at home – mostly middle class but not all – three quarters of them have emigrated: to Australia, Canada, USA and Britain. And as race relations worsen at home (the roots of which British colonialism planted) the drift away continues.

With this background of 'westernisation' it was considered natural to come over to England to complete my education. It was therefore a shock to face such hostile and patronising attitudes when I arrived. I had been fed on a diet of Enid Blyton and her boarding school series, so I was eager – even excited – to be joining one when I came over to take my 'A' levels in the late sixties: I was not at all prepared for the harsh realities of English middle-class racism. I was bewildered and numbed by it.

My only support at the time came from a Nigerian girl and a Ugandan Asian girl who were also in my class and shared my deep sense of alienation from our environment. We all had a similar colonial background and were desperate to 'fit in' and be accepted – so we never talked of racism directly. We had all been brought up to invest our hopes and future in the 'western way of life' and were learning to develop thick skins against the blatant institutionalized and individual racism we faced every day. The only outlet through which we dared to express our distress was sharing our fantasies of burning down our school!

It took me a long time even to begin to look at what I was going through. In the intervening years I allowed myself to be gradually undermined and finally succeeded in losing most outward traces of my cultural identity. I lost my accent very quickly and my style of speech which betrayed a cross-fertilization of three cultures – Chinese, Malay and Indian. I learnt to sit formally at table and to eat three inedible courses of stodge with an incomprehensible array of surplus cutlery; to whisper when I spoke as I was considered 'too loud'; and to stop gesturing with my hands or to touch in conversation, as people inevitably shrank away from me. I did draw the line at giving up the spices I cooked with even though for years I continued to receive remarks about my stinking of garlic, yuk, with monotonous regularity. By and large, though, I attempted to imitate the ways of the English.

However – although these contortions saved me from the worse excesses of daily racism, my face kept giving me away. I was endlessly patronized on my 'amazingly good English' at dinner parties and told in buses and in the streets to 'go back where you came from, chink'. In my early years here, I had a small group of friends from home who were also studying or nursing. They buttressed me to some degree from the isolation I felt. But, one by one they left, for home or elsewhere. I stayed.

I came across feminist politics while I was at college in London in the mid-seventies. I was mostly bored by the degree course I was doing and spent more and more of my time skiving off to extra-mural classes in Women's Studies, which were just beginning to happen, and devouring feminist books. Out of one of my women's courses I attended, a consciousness-raising group was formed. There were about six of us and we were eager to talk about – for the first time – the reality of our lives as women. It sounds *passé* now, but it was breaking new ground for all of us; putting into words the taboos in our lives – sex, sexuality, relating to men – and the bonus, our new found enjoyment of each other's company without men.

I was still at the time in a relationship with a man I had lived with for four years and was emotionally dependent on, in more ways than one given my immigrant status in this country. But we were moving in different directions and it had been clear for some while that we stayed together out of habit. As I explored more of the inadequacies of my relationship with him through my group, and made friends independently from him, he began to feel more and more threatened by my increasing feminism. The inevitable happened. But it was not painless: he had been, after all, my main emotional support through my middle years in this country, however flawed. But I was now finding a whole new community I felt more comfortable with.

Going to my first feminist conference in the late seventies: the thrill of seeing so many women together, and, even more so, seeing so many lesbians openly showing their affections for each other. The atmosphere was electric, it all seemed so natural, effortless: the joyous relating, the sensuality, the emotional sparks flying everywhere and the encouragement to participate in workshops ... so different from the male structures of chairman, standing orders and platform speeches. It felt like coming home, in a way.

I had never been politically active before in any organized way. With my friends from home we had discussed Third World politics and our growing awareness of exploitation globally. At college I had been thoroughly disgusted with the male egos that dominated the left-wing student politics. I had peripherally helped out at anti-apartheid offices, even gone on CND Easter Marches when I first came over, but it was always on the sidelines. Their structures and attitudes alienated me from participating more fully.

The Women's Movement changed all that. For the next few years I threw myself into a whirlwind of activities – involving myself in a Women's Aid refuge, women's centres, campaigns, demonstrations and conferences. I felt part of a movement. At first it all seemed so simple: the discussions, the unfolding of new ideas, the boundless energy we seemed to generate in each other, the solidarity we felt in working towards tearing down patriarchal structures and attitudes.

In those early days it seemed the sky was the limit! We were naïve, the cracks began to show. The political infighting between radical, revolutionary, socialist, separatist – women tearing each other apart at conferences and in our magazines and newsletters. Much later issues of race and class began to be addressed more seriously, after years of being ignored or side-stepped.

I mostly stood on the sidelines, watching the heavy-weights raging at each other. My own political education was rooted in the more down-to-earth practical realities of the day-to-day running of a refuge for women who had suffered domestic violence. It was there my consciousness of class, race and sexuality grew, as heated arguments took place, in weekly collective meetings between the residents of the refuge, workers and support group. We challenged and supported each other through the stresses of daily living, where women, who were at a particularly vulnerable point in their lives, had to make hard choices about their future and gain the strength to struggle through and survive.

But I was still invisible as a Chinese woman. Something was still missing. The feminist and, increasingly, the lesbian community had become my haven in this country. It was hard to acknowledge their continuing denial of my Chinese identity. Their understanding of racism was that it was about Afro-Caribbean people and maybe people from the Indian sub-continent. I didn't feature on the agenda. I remember many occasions when friends would reassure me that I was like them, there weren't any differences. I had *become* totally invisible. I was accepted – but only on their terms. Around that time I wrote a piece in a journal which I co-wrote with a friend. It was in 1980, and I would like to share some of it with you. It is revealing in how clear I was and yet I managed to stop short of naming it as racism.

Coming out as a person
I suppose I have been thinking rather a lot lately about my reluctance to stick a label on myself politically – as a lesbian. What really am I? Am I simply a lesbian? Why do I baulk at it? Because I feel strongly that I am *much more* than that ... perhaps many more nameless things, but valuable to me nonetheless. And I insist on their

recognition. I refuse to be fragmented, yet I feel so. I don't feel whole, and labels just make it so much more difficult for me to understand myself.

Sure, being a lesbian is intricately woven into the web of my identity. But so is that part of me that feels alien in this country, lonely behind my wall of defences, inarticulate in my deepest pain. These are also part of my inner core.

So when women talk of coming out as a lesbian, I want to ask – can I come as a person first? If I cannot come out soon – much of me will die, and only I will know enough to mourn its passing.

You may ask – but why didn't you say? We would have wanted to know. But would you really? You made assumptions which made those parts of me invisible, that shamed it into retreat, that said, 'You're really like us. We don't see any difference.'

But I am you know – I *am* alien, other, under this façade. I have learnt over the years to talk your way, behave your way, and even to think and feel your way. Speechless – in order to be acceptable. To hack to death all that didn't fit in. It hurts me now to realize how much I numbed myself from the searing pains of those years. And now, so many scars have grown over where it hurts that I'm not sure I'm clear anymore about what I've lost.

The part of me that is a lesbian has always had a lot of support and nurturing from friends around. It was recognized as valid. My other self – my Chinese self – has not had such understanding. That part of me feels negative and trodden over, wiped out. I want to reclaim it – so I can stop being a casualty of this war that has no name.

It was another two years before I was able to break through the painful years of silence and begin the fragile, tentative process of making myself whole again. It was the emergence of the Chinese Lesbian Group which allowed me to start this process of healing and accepting myself.

Three of us met at the Lesbian Sex and Sexual Practice Conference in London in 1983. Although it felt like a miraculous coincidence for us at the time, it was more that we were all ready to grapple with this issue in our lives. The rest of the conference was humming with the anticipated controversy over sado-masochism, and with the anger of women with disabilities over non-accessibility to the venue and to the discussion papers. Meanwhile a momentous event took place in the lobby. Three of us exchanged telephone numbers and the Chinese Lesbian Group was formed.

Two of us had already previously met, but we were nervous and shy and wary of each other. Making overtures towards another who mirrored our own disquieting and long-buried Chinese identity was both a fearful and exciting prospect, and neither of us quite got up the nerve to take the initiative. However, with three of us we felt we could start a group! The early days of the group were both strange and oddly familiar. Sharing our experiences allowed parts of ourselves to surface which were both painful and joyous. It felt fragile at first, but it was as if I had finally come up for air after nearly drowning in a pool of lies. There were occasions when we would get hysterical with delight at uncovering yet another layer of our much maligned identity, and find the words to talk about it.

We also discovered the richness and variety of our backgrounds and a growing understanding of our shared roots. All of us are living in a diaspora twice removed – that is, our ancestors were already immigrants when we were born, and we, or our families, have repeated it again, going this time to the country of our past colonial masters. Between us, our ancestors have travelled through three continents for us to arrive here. This group is my family in this country now, it is my anchor in an insecure world and it has expanded and grown in confidence.

With our increasing clarity of the racism we faced daily, we made tentative overtures to involve ourselves in Black women's activities. The response to us was and still is ambivalent. On an individual level I have been supported and validated by many lesbians of Afro-Caribbean and Indian sub-continent descent. However, as a political issue, it has so far not been properly thrashed out. Are Chinese people included in the political term 'Black'? Are Chinese people's experiences of racism different from but similar to what is experienced by those from other backgrounds? Over the last few years I have actively participated in various

Black women's activities. But I still have twinges of un-certainty about my place within the wider Black women's struggle. There are differing levels of acceptance at different occasions. However, I do feel optimistic that our growing understanding of our diverse cultures and histories, which exposes the myths and stereotypes we have been force-fed by the British for too many generations, will forge an increasingly powerful alliance in our struggle against racism in this country.

Equally, the lesbian and gay movement needs to make far more serious and energetic efforts to rid itself of racist assumptions in its political agenda. The recent political activities of Haringey Black Action has succeeded in raising the profile of Black lesbians and gay men. We can no longer accept marginalization. We are here to stay.

11 Oi! What about us?

Kirsten Hearn

I was born in South London in 1955, the fourth child and a twin. The history of my birth is unclear because NHS records have now been lost, so doctors in later years could only guess at the cause of my disability which became evident a few week after I was born. I was partially sighted and doctors talked about scarred retinas. My twin brother appeared by the age of about ten to have some hearing loss.

I have strong memories of feeling different from a very early age. These were compounded by my recollections of a series of visits to Moorfields Eye Hospital and at least one incarceration there when I was about four. My mother soon began to drum into me the notion that I was different because of my eyesight, and therefore that I should not expect too much out of life. By the age of five I was given glasses which had no effect, serving only to restrict my field of vision, since I could only really see to read with one eye. Reading was difficult for me, especially when it involved looking at the chalkboard, and I soon found myself being classed as 'thick'. This was the second disappointment for my mother, who prided herself on her own intelligence and wanted her children to succeed academically, because she felt it would be the only way we could be successful in life, there being no money at home.

Despite this, my parents found the wherewithal to send me to a cheap fee-paying dayschool. This was justified on the grounds that, having failed to get into grammar school, I would be educationally disadvantaged further by attending the local comprehensive. Her excuse for this piece of academic snobbery was that classes were held there in lecture theatres and that the first desk would be too far away from the chalkboard. There had been talk of sending me to a special school, but my family were not ready to accept such an open acknowledgment of my disability, and the excuse was again made about academic standards.

I was already aware at the age of eleven of my mother's political background: she had been an active Communist until 1965. I found it hard therefore to understand why she should act so far outside her own political ideology. I also found it hard to deal with the petty bourgeois outlook of all but a few of the girls at that private school. I was already identifying as a socialist and spent a lot of time arguing politics with the other girls. This made me even more of a social outcast since most of the other girls already regarded my disability, my lack of money, my accent and the council estate on which I lived as reasons to ignore me. I couldn't get rid of my disability, became more staunch in my socialist politics, got rid of my accent and was thankful when my parents put themselves into enormous debt and bought a tip of a house in Croydon.

I had begun to experience increasing difficulty with reading from about the age of thirteen. Knowing that to say anything about this would lead to further ridicule and isolation at school, and open disbelief from my family, I decided to ignore it. There were days when the world was shrouded in a mist and I would feign headaches and period pains to get me out of awkward situations such as reading in class. There came a day when the vision in my left eye suddenly almost disappeared.

Since I didn't use this eye I again ignored it. It was about three weeks later when I happened to notice that the pupil of this eye had dilated to such an extent that it was now noticeable to everyone. Suddenly I found myself in hospital clinics being peered at by hundreds of doctors, all making interested sounding noises and saying long biological words. I was now labelled. It was at last obvious that my learning and social problems were caused by my disability and not by my stupidity.

Now that I had this label – 'partially sighted' – and it was clear that my disability would become more acute, the teachers and girls at school found some semblance of the tolerance and understanding that they had previously lacked, and I slowly began to edge my way up the academic ladder. I was sixteen, the year of 'O' levels, and it was beginning to look as though I would gain a respectable number of passes which would send me on my way to art school and my chosen career as a painter.

During the summer of 1971, soon after the 'discovery', for the second time, of my disability, I spent some time in hospital. A second routine examination under anaesthetic in January 1972 resulted in the decision to operate. I was told that it was in order to save the rest of my sight: a new laser beam method was to be tried. I woke up in the afternoon of the ninth of February to tennis-ball-sized sore eyes and a dirty pink mist, and searingly painful lights. The sight-saving operation hadn't worked; the doctors hadn't reckoned on a rebellion in the form of a massive eye haemorrhage. As the pink mists began to clear, my world turned into an out-of-focus elongated distortion, seen through yellow cellophane. I had lost all my reading vision, and could now only read individual characters with a strong magnifier.

On Easter Monday 1972, I woke up to a new view of the world. A pale white opaque gungey mist had invaded. It took me all day to convince my mother that there had been a change, but by the next afternoon I found myself flat on my back in the hospital again with injunctions not to move. I stayed there for five weeks and after another operation was pronounced 'partially sighted' enough to be registered as blind. Every day I lay there and repeated an exercise of counting how many branches on the tree outside I could make out. Each day they became fewer until my image of the tree became a pink and brown blur, it being blossom time.

With my new label of 'blind' came the object which was to stigmatize me more, a shiny new, long white cane. The girls at school were horrified: all their collections for presents and prayers after announcements at morning assembly had been wasted. I had come back blind. It could almost be considered as an extreme act of defiance, and many of them showed their disapproval by refusing to have any more contact with me. My small circle of friends stuck with me, choosing to support me and risking their own popularity. Whilst I believed their feelings and actions were genuine, I was also aware that they were as steeped as I was in the romance of blindness: the helping hand, God's purpose for us all. But blind people were 'out there', begging on the streets, bumbling along with their tip-tap sticks, staring sightlessly and pathetically out at nothing behind dark glasses.

I survived in the school until after 'O' levels and into the sixth form, but only for one term. By this time I had begun to learn braille and a more constructive use of my white stick, other than tripping up people who got in my way.

Discussions about my future took place behind closed doors, and sometimes in my presence as though I wasn't there. It was decided I should go to special school and my mother's objections were mollified by the proof of the academic success that many girls achieved there.

In January 1973 I found myself, and the grey metal trunk my eldest brother had used to take to university in 1967, dumped in an austere fifth form dormitory in the main block of the school. Being forcibly confined with other blind girls in a school which thought it was a public school soon turned me into a staunchly outspoken socialist. I decided to be unconventional; dressing differently (stripey socks and outrageous make-up), wearing trousers at every opportunity and trying to organize the other girls into a socialist club. This was the era of the *Little Red Schoolbook* which I attempted to transcribe into braille with the assistance of a partially-sighted Young Socialist called Katey. My open support of the Irish struggle, reading pro-Sinn Fein poems at school assembly when it was my turn to choose a reading two weeks after the Birmingham pub bombing caused more than a little outrage and several stern pep talks, culminating in threatened expulsion from the headmistress.

The school ethos was mainly concerned with turning out well-educated, potential wives of professional able-bodied men. With the influence of my older brother and his wife (he was active in the International Socialists and she was a raving feminist) I continued to challenge these expectations of my future career. I identified closely with the other girls at school making strong relationships which, although they were not sexual, were emotionally very intense. I was also aware that some girls and even some teachers were involved in lesbian relationships. I knew that I wanted a free and independent life although I secretly subscribed to the idea of marrying a professional, sighted man. It was by chance and with the support of a visiting teacher of drawing who also happened to be a lecturer at Goldsmiths College that I succeeded in getting a place at art school, the first and last totally blind student to have ever done so in Britain.

Goldsmiths College was not just an art school. The various buildings on the New Cross site also held a part of the University of London, a teacher education college, and in the late seventies the Laban School of Dancing. The art students were mostly a bunch of individualistic, head-in-the-sand poseurs. It was not cool to be political. In any case if I had wanted to get involved in student politics I was effectively prevented by the piles of print material that littered the coffee bar and canteen. No one had heard of access to ink print information in those days and as I was the only blind student there I didn't feel I had any support to ask for it to be made available. Therefore I didn't know what was going on to the point where I carried on working in a prefabricated hut hard by the administration block during a very successful students' occupation in summer 1976. I hadn't even noticed the pickets and I can only presume that they had parted before me as I walked towards them as they still do today.

The social pressures of my peers precipitated me into a frenzied bout of heterosexuality, usually accompanied by drunkenness. It was only in 1977 that I became even vaguely aware of gay liberation. This was from the basis of a new found security in a relationship with a male student who managed to last out more than the usual six weeks of all my other relationships so far at college. For the first time since I had come to the college I had access to student political material because my boyfriend was reading the posters, leaflets and student newspapers to me.

I got myself elected onto the Students' Council where I muddled through, never having read the agenda papers and often not knowing what on earth everyone else was talking about. I also joined Gaysoc, partly out of respect for a close friend (and former boyfriend) who had come out as gay, partly because we had a gay president. Also, Tom Robinson was in the charts with 'Glad To Be Gay' and there was a general atmosphere of tolerance towards gays. From the safety of my heterosexual relationship I wore my Gaysoc badge out on the streets. I believe I didn't get gay-bashed partly because of the heterosexual relationship and partly because no one took my sexuality seriously because I was blind, and obviously didn't know what badge I was wearing. At the end of my final year I stood as a sabbatical officer for the Union. My platform as an Independent Socialist was 'put the U back into the Union' and I believe I mentioned my disability once, but only in passing. I lost, of course, hardly surprising since the elections were carved up by the various political groups, most of which I didn't even know existed.

Like every other aspiring young artist, I wanted to go to the Slade or the RCA (Royal College of Art) to do a post-graduate degree. The plan was to get through postgrad. school, get a part-time lecturer's job, a studio in Wapping and become a Real Artist. Very few women ever made it through, as evidenced by the handful of women art tutors at Goldsmiths. My failure to even get interviewed soon demonstrated to me that, even though Goldsmiths had accepted me despite my disability, I would have to fight very hard to get any further.

Being on the dole in 1979 was becoming a very common occupation. The woman at the employment exchange wouldn't even register me on the Professional Executive Register. She told me, 'Blind people don't need that register,' and that no one would ever employ me as anything other than an audio-typist. Realizing I couldn't hang around on the dole forever waiting for the Tate Gallery to offer me an exhibition, and also that my boyfriend, also on the dole, was not likely to be able to support me, I decided to go for further training. Since the postgraduate schools wouldn't have me, it had to be audio typing. Determined not to re-enter blind institution life, I headed for the nearby technical college who wouldn't have me either. After another series of battles with the employment exchange, the

Royal National Institute for the Blind and various principals of local technical colleges, I eventually got myself onto a TOPS typing course at a college in south-west London.

During the summer of 1979 I had moved into a collective house whose occupants were libertarian hippies, socialists, Christians and noisy heterosexual feminists. It was the latter who inspired me on my first day at the tech. to walk into the Students' Union office and demand to know where the Women's Group met. I was told there wasn't one but was invited onto the executive where I could form my own women's group. On my way out of the office that first day I fell over the only other disabled student in the college who was a wheelchair user. I had never spoken to anyone who used a wheelchair before, and we soon found ourselves immersed in a conversation about our mutual 'problems'.

I got hooked on student politics as there were many problems in the tech. Seventy per cent of the college students were Black, a significant number of the other 30 per cent were active in the National Front. There was rabid Thatcherism and an increase in popularity of the Fascist movements, both outside and inside the college. There was a feeling of hopelessness because of the prospect of unemployment facing most of the young people but also a great deal of anger and frenzied organizing arising from this.

I was sent as a delegate to National Conference in Blackpool. It was a wild four days, full of speeches, fringe meetings and late night boozy caucuses. But one evening sticks in my mind: an evening of hysterical debate including a heated row on the Irish struggle. There was a phrase screeched into the microphone by a hoarse-voiced member of Socialist Workers' Students' Organization: 'The government must be deaf, dumb and blind if they do not see the madness of this war.' I had never really noticed before this common use of the label that identified me as a means to imply wilful ignorance. As the debate continued I was to hear it again and again. It suddenly became clear to me that I was assumed to be equally as wilfully ignorant. It defiled my whole status as a person passionately concerned about politics and socialist ideologies in particular. These phrases

denied me my right to participate in the very same way that
the socialist movement refused to recognize my rights to
have access to information that would dispel my ignorance
on such subjects. I heard no more of the debate and to the
astonishment of my fellow delegates I stormed out of the
auditorium and locked myself away in the Ladies to howl
out my rage, alone.

As a result of a chance meeting in a Blackpool bar with a
student journalist, I was featured in *National Student* in an
article about disabled students. Suddenly out of the blue I
received a tape from one of the members of the self-
organizing group, the Liberation Network of People With
Disabilities. A few months later someone in my house told
me about an article in *Time Out* about the Liberation
Network. A woman's number was at the bottom of the *Time
Out* piece and it was with some feelings of fear that I decided
to ring it, not knowing who or what I would find.
Micheline sounded excited to hear from me and I was
invited to the group's meeting a few weeks later.

On a Saturday in November 1980, I entered Micheline's
cluttered flat. It was full of people with disabilities, deaf
people, people in wheelchairs and all manner of others.
There must have been about twelve of us. As we began to
talk I began to realize that these people were just like me. We
shared our battles and our triumphs through our life stories.
Everyone was given equal space and care was given to those
of us who found it more difficult because of being deaf or
having a speech difficulty. I spoke about my frustrations,
about not being able to read socialist and feminist books
and magazines. The groups discussed my problems and in
the empowering atmosphere it came as quite natural that
someone should suggest I start up my own campaign.

I wrote to Radio Four's 'In Touch' programme, venting
my frustrations and asking for like-minded people to
contact me. As the letter was in braille it was never
broadcast. Happily, however, Jenny, a braille transcriber at
the RNIB who herself was blind and had socialist
tendencies, intercepted it. Most unethically she discussed the
contents of my letter with other blind friends.

The result of this was a surprise telephone call from
Jenny herself suggesting that we should call a meeting. I

wrote off to *Time Out* and in early February 1981 found myself surrounded by eight or nine other blind socialists discussing the formation of the Alternative Talking Newspapers Collective.

I had left the technical college in February 1980 and within a few weeks had landed an audio typist's job with a trendy voluntary housing organization. Within hours of being in the office I was already hating the drudgery of being plugged into a machine. Words came into my ears and my fingers made the appropriate movements. I had no idea what I was typing and would leave the office each day disorientated and dizzy with the effort. Determined not spend my life in this manner, I continued to reapply to the postgraduate art courses. My persistence paid off when the RCA relented and grudgingly allowed me to take my place on a joint MA course in the departments of Environmental Media and Design Education.

The other students were horrified at my appearance in the college, unable to understand what on earth I could be doing there. I fled to the Students' Union where, within a very few days, I found myself co-opted onto the Students' Council. At this college there was a small but active women's group. Here I found an amazing group of women, full of caring and support for me. One woman in particular went out of her way to help me out. I felt ostracized by most of the other able-bodied students and so was more than just glad of her company.

Back in the Alternative Talking Newspapers Collective we'd started up our own taped socialist magazine, *Left Out*. A women's magazine, *Women's Tapeover*, was soon to follow, preceded by many pleasant evenings spent in the company of Jenny and her friend Sue. In September 1981 the magazine duly appeared, coinciding with the start of my office as the sabbatical Deputy President of the students' union at the RCA.

In recounting my coming out story in later years I have always sited this period of my life as extremely important to my subsequent emergence as a lesbian. I had not recognized my feelings for one of the women in the women's group as being of any significance. I had worried about this over-aged schoolgirl crush. Lesbianism wasn't in it. I couldn't be

a lesbian, they were butch pipe-smoking women in suits.
And in any case, I had a boyfriend. We reproduced articles
on *Women's Tapeover* which spoke about the lives of
lesbians. Their stories were like my own. Their feelings
were like mine and they weren't the stereotypical bulldykes I
had previously imagined them to be.

I became heavily involved in far left politics, becoming a
member of the Socialist Students' Alliance, the student
leftovers of the IMG's (Internation Marxist Group's) move
into the Labour Party. It was at one of their conferences that
I first came across organized lesbians and gays. They called a
caucus for lesbian and gay activists and I went along,
tentatively saying, 'I'm an, erm, bisexual, can I come in?' I
left that meeting with the phrase, 'I am a lesbian,' ready to
be spoken at any moment.

I was now faced with a real dilemma. I had just moved
into a flat with my boyfriend and I was beginning to feel
very guilty. Once having framed the thought in my mind
that I was a lesbian I found myself unable to keep silent
about it. I told my boyfriend who was horrorstruck and took
myself off to a lesbian students' conference.

The Labour Party had won the Greater London Council
(GLC) elections. Ken Livingstone was now in power, and
the Women's Committee had just been formed. In August
that year I found myself elected as co-optee for Women with
Disabilities, loudly proclaiming my lesbianism in my
hustings speech. I juggled my college work with
attendances at committee meetings which included the
Women with Disabilities Subgroup. Frustrated by the
bureaucracy of democratic representation in its convoluted
GLC version, I talked with other feminists with disabilities
about forming an organization for women with disabilities.

The same thoughts had been going through the minds of
two other women with disabilities. A friend of mine called
Sue from the Liberation Network had moved to London
and was now living next door to Patricia, another stroppy
feminist with a disability. Before I knew where I was we had
begun our organization, choosing Sisters Against Disable-
ment as its name.

We were fed up with the sexism in self-organized
disability movements and even more fed up with the

ableism of the women's movement. Our attempts to participate had been accidentally and sometimes deliberately obstructed. I was just beginning to get to grips with the Campaign for Ink Print Information, but *Women's Tapeover* could not keep up with the steady stream of new feminist writing that was emerging week by week. Patricia and Sue were more than fed up with being constantly left out in the cold, usually on the pavement outside women's events because of lack of physical access. We were very, very angry and more than ready for a fight.

We took direct action: battles such as the one over access to the Lesbian Sex and Sexual Practice Conference in 1983, the Feminist Bookfair in 1984, and the general battle to get the SAD access code used in public listings of events in feminist publications ... and much more.

Still active in the students' movement, I continued to struggle for recognition of our oppressions as women, lesbians and gays, and people with disabilities. I was elected for two years running onto the NUS Lesbian and Gay Committee and served for one year on the London Students' Organization executive committee. During this time we organized two national conferences for students with disabilities and more than a handful of steadily more accessible conferences for lesbians and gays. I found it hard to balance out these activities with my other commitments to the GLC Women's Committee. Then I was relieved from student and GLC battles and rewarded for all those years of unpaid activity by what some people considered possible selling out. I got a job after graduation in 1984 at the GLC in the Disability Resource Team.

It was a pleasure to be paid for what I had up until then been doing in my spare time. As more of us activists with disabilities benefited from the equal opportunities policies of the GLC and other local authorities by getting jobs with them, our activities in the Liberation Network and in SAD diminished. We were all burned out, exhausted by the battles and the fights within and outside our various movements. Some of us made a final effort and formed Feminist Audio Books – a library exclusively providing audiotapes of feminist writing for blind and partially-sighted women and women with reading difficulties. This was the first self-organized disability group to receive major funding from the GLC Women's Committee. Sadly, because of abolition, it was also the last. It is sadder still that the weight of being given funding may soon be lifted from FAB by the London Borough's Grants Unit proposal to cut FAB's grant.

Although many of us are now working around disability issues professionally, the lull in activity by self-organized disability groups such as SAD and the Liberation Network feels as though it might be coming to an end. Women with disabilities are beginning to meet regularly again and there is talk also of reactivating the Liberation Network. Most excitingly of all some lesbians and gays with disabilities are beginning to organize through groups such as Gemma (lesbians with and without disabilities), Gay Men's Disabled Group and the Brothers and Sisters Gay Deaf Group, to fight back from within the lesbian and gay movements. The first national conference for lesbians and gays with disabilities is currently being organized to take place early in 1988.

It feels like there are more of us coming together in all our groups to continue challenging our various communities on their continued exclusion of us. Towards the end of the GLC a conference was held for Black people with disabilities. The white-dominated self-organized disability movement shows some signs of beginning to think about racism from within. We know that we can't fight any more battles without involving all sections of the disability movement. We must now make anti-racist strategies a central part of the way in which we organize. Without this we will go nowhere.

12 'Irrespective of race, sex, sexuality . . .'

Gerry Ahrens, Ahmed Farooqui and Amitha Patel

Gerry, Ahmed and Amitha work for the co-ordinating body of a voluntary advice organization, where they have been centrally involved on the Equal Opportunities Policy Working Party.

Gerry: I'm a woman with a white father and a South-East Asian mother, brought up in the army as the daughter of an NCO. Because of my very varied upbringing I have found that I have never been able to analyse the political effects of any discrimination. My first political awareness of oppression was when I was discharged from the nursing corps of the army over lesbianism. Being eighteen and losing my job, my career, friends and being forced to come out to my parents in extremely unpleasant circumstances, profoundly influenced my life and identity. My first taste of oppression was not that of being a woman or Black but over homosexuality!

The gay scene was pubs and clubs full of role-playing lesbians into 'butch' or 'femme' and was just as alienating as the straight world. It was just by chance that I turned up at one of the early meetings of the first lesbian liberation groups in London and found myself involved in the early debates around socialist feminism, radical lesbianism, the Women's Movement and the sixth demand which named women's right to a self-defined sexuality. It was through this involvement and my direct experience of lesbian oppression that I found myself wanting to be a part of creating a new lesbian feminist identity along with other lesbian sisters. By the time I entered university two years later, my involvement in the student left politics and the local and national student, women, and gay campaigns was automatic. My lesbian socialist feminist identity was fully consolidated and formed the basis of my support network and closest friends. Any involvement in the race issue was around the anti-Fascist campaigns of that time. Not until the late seventies and the occupations around the overseas students, was I confronted with the issue of identifying as a Black person and the politics thereof. My personal experience of racism was common: that of ignorance and non-recognition. White feminist friends would not even accept the fact that I was Black!

After I left university, I worked for a Black community project and joined a Black socialist group. But even this didn't dispel some of the confusions that I was feeling. I found the sexism and heterosexism of the Black movement difficult to cope with and felt at that time that I wasn't considered Black enough either in my colour or my politics. At the same time the issues around heterosexual/lesbian women and socialist/separatist lesbians had created deep and painful divisions in the Women's Movement. In all the senses I felt that there was little support in helping me integrate my identity as a Black lesbian and ended up feeling totally alienated and with a complete loss of my self-confidence.

I could only resolve the confusion by refusing to be involved with any political activity. By the time that I began to work with Ahmed and Amitha, I had resolved within myself that I couldn't be anything other than a Black lesbian and that was in itself its own political identity, one that did not require validation from either the women's, gay or Black movements.

Ahmed: Ever since I was very young, I remember having very strong political views, mostly derived from my Father, but a weak sense of political direction. I had no sustained involvement in any kind of political activity – mainly, I think, because there weren't any models of political organization that I could identify with. I was involved at an abstract level with the struggles of the Vietnamese and the

Palestinians far away, or the miners (in 1974) nearer home. But there was nothing around that moved me enough to go out and change things.

I came out as a result of sexual frustration and a desire to be honest with myself. Surrounded as I was by supremely negative images of homosexuality such as 'the man in the dirty mac living out a lonely old age in a filthy garret', I still felt that there was for me a clear choice between expressing or repressing my homosexual desire. Expressing it would entail at least the possibility of a glimpse of happiness and fulfilment. Repressing it, on the other hand, would mean existing in a drab, twilight world of pretended affections out of which I could see no escape.

Even the awareness that I had a choice was of course a product of the way that I was brought up. My parents are broadminded, liberal and understanding to the extent that I probably could never match. It was because I was subconsciously sure of them that it never occurred to me that I could be rejected. So I made my entrance into a gay world which emphasized the politics of personal and sexual liberation to the exclusion of every other commitment and loyalty – familial or social. I became assimilated into the gay community and my identity as a Black person sloughed off me.

On reflection, those first few years on the gay scene hold a certain unreality for me. They seemed to have been lived by a different person. I have changed enough now to be shocked by the ease with which I let go of my Black identity, situated as it was in my real subordination on the basis of race and class, in exchange for an illusory equality with white men on the sexual plane.

Sexual stereotyping of Black people, conscious or unconscious, was, and is, prevalent on the gay scene. In the final analysis, it isn't much fun to have your personal and sexual identity derived from the fantasies of white men. Black 'macho' studs, or passive 'orientals', clones and leatherboys. . . . They all represent the obsessional, neurotic and fetishistic sexuality of a gay scene, created by and for white men.

In 1980, I and a number of other Black gay people came together to form the Gay Black Group. We wanted to situate

our experience of being gay in the Black community, and
being Black on the gay scene, into some political context.
We came together as a group almost by accident, but there
was a convergence of our experiences and a symmetry to our
ideas which made the first few months of our existence one of
the most stimulating and electrifying of my life.

Without knowing it we became a political organization
in that we shared an experience of oppression, a sense of
direction, and the will and the confidence to act. We took
issues of race and sexuality to the Black and gay
communities, again and again, occasionally with some
success.

It was at this point that I met Gerry. I had finished with
just being 'gay'. For me it wasn't just a question of being at
ease with my homosexuality: I was more concerned with the
way in which that sexuality expressed itself. I felt that I had
progressed from just wanting to 'be gay' to being 'Black and
gay'. The Gay Black Group also made me think much more
of the implications of being a man, of being an oppressor as
well as someone who is oppressed. It made me reappraise
my attitudes to oppression and the politics of domination
and subordination. So, when issues of equal opportunity
were raised in the organization where we also work together,
I was naturally interested in participating in the debates and
in the attempts to change the things around me. But the
actual impetus to 'act' only came when I met the right
people in the right context . . . that is, Gerry and Amitha and
the rest of the Working Party.

Amitha: I suppose, if asked, I would describe myself as a
Black Gujarati lesbian. Born in India, raised mostly in the
close-knit Gujarati community in England.

My first big act of rebellion against cultural expectations
of what an Indian woman should or shouldn't do was when
I left home in the face of family opposition to go into higher
education. For many years I was conscious that I was the
first woman in my very large extended family to do this.
Feeling like a pioneer I was also conscious of the
responsibility that I felt that I had. I thought that my
conduct, dress, attitude were used as a measure of what the
other young women of my family were or later would be

allowed to do. I was also very anxious not to become what my family said that I would become if I left home - you know, a westernised harlot with no respect for traditions.

In many ways that act gave a pattern to my life - the deep need to straddle the east-west in everything I do. Strangely, once done, this single act of rebellion elevated my position in the community. Many women admired my strength and the men, slightly awed, treated me as an honorary male. Eleven years on, this continues, though now there is perhaps more than a tinge of pity for my 'lonely' existence. I am what the English would call 'on the shelf': eccentric in their eyes. Yet in the eyes of the western world I am a young 'professional' queer. This does have a funny side to it.

I admire the strength of my kinswomen who stayed at home and who later on embraced arranged marriages. That's what they wanted to do. The story of those who didn't want this is often not a pleasant one and there the rigidity and the oppression of our traditions are exposed. I escaped with a few scars and I have no doubt that my greatest support was the knowledge that I wasn't economically dependent on my family.

In choosing my own path I recognized that I may indeed be isolated, lonely and rejected by my family in a racist, sexist, homophobic country. But at least in the midst of my misery I can own what I have instead of feeling I am a pawn in another's game with rules that I cannot stick to or change. Now I still have a large family composed of the family I was born into (some of it) and also of a family of friends, sisters, brothers, mothers and children that I have chosen.

In leaving home I became involved in student union politics, particularly round the issue of overseas students. I learnt how white activists can use other people's oppression to their own political ends by wresting the control and direction of sit-ins and occupations and so on, from the hands of those it clearly affects. I fell in love with a woman and went out with a man. It was a time of discovery and experiment.

In my spare time and during vacations, between 1976 and 1978, I set up what later came to be called the Standing Conference of Asian Youth Organizations. This group was set up to bring together young Asian people who could organize around issues affecting them – not least the worrying trend of the National Front gaining increasing numbers of votes, and in some cases Asian votes. In the by-elections, I rapidly became disillusioned by the men who not only ended up taking credit for the Group's existence but who also displayed a total lack of understanding about issues affecting Asian women in Britain. They could not grasp the value of setting up refuges for Asian women and to these men consulting with the community always meant consulting with other men.

From 1980 onwards I went on to become involved in the Black Workers' Group, unions – NALGO and ACTTS – and more recently, the Lesbian and Gay Workers' Group in our workplace. Over the years I have kept my distance from the white women's movement. I can't relate to their starting point and assumptions about my oppression. Things that they see as blanket oppression, I would see as possible sources of strength, such as arranged marriages. Having said that, I have never got involved in the Black Women's Movement. Perhaps because I was involved with other things, perhaps because at that time I was still trying to find my feet as a bisexual and felt isolated by straight sisters and excluded by some Black lesbians.

Today I would say that I am a Black Gujarati lesbian which sums up my politics and my identity. This feels wholesome and gives me the confidence to take up issues of racism and sexism in the Lesbian and Gay Workers' Group and issues of sexism and heterosexism in the Black Workers' Group, within the organization we work for.

Gerry: When I started with the organization in 1982 there were no Black or gay groups. You knew who was Black if they were a colleague, and who was gay if they had come out at work.

Amitha: I was appointed in September 1984 under the Race Relations Act and there was little or no idea why they wanted an 'Asian' worker. One of the first things that I noticed in my workplace was that there was an entrenched, hostile division between Black and white colleagues. What made things particularly difficult was that I felt I wasn't Black enough for my Black colleagues and that white workers picking up on the division used this to their advantage by divide-and-rule tactics. In the midst of the roaring debate about 'Black' as a political concept, and the work done towards eradicating racist practices in the organization, homosexuality did not get a look-in.

Ahmed: When I joined the organization in March 1983 I had the impression that though my colleagues could deal with my ethnicity as a factor in our relationship, they were rather baffled about how to incorporate my sexuality into our work relationship. My blackness was seen to be a public and political fact, whereas my gayness was seen as a purely personal matter. I became involved with the Union (ACTTS) when an Equal Opportunities Policy Working Party was set up by them in 1984. I joined in the debate because I felt that this was one issue to which I could meaningfully contribute. But the Working Party had a traditional management v. union approach, and there was very little opportunity to inject our personal experiences into it. Everything was argued round the premise that existing union members should not have to pay the price of an EOP, and we shouldn't be expected to do management's job for them.

Amitha: That's because the Union was too traditional and only involved in negotiations over pay and working conditions. There were very few Black or gay workers involved in it, and no attempt was made to recruit new members.

Gerry: I was a steward and felt isolated being the only gay/lesbian steward for two years, and for a lot of the time, the only Black person on a committee dominated by white male heterosexuals. My active involvement and participation was due to my previous political experience. I don't believe my being a Black lesbian was of any political significance until I was elected chairperson on an EOP platform. The Union reflected the workforce, as the whole organization is white female dominated and infused with a liberal social conscience. It had an EOP policy that it had not implemented and a proportionally higher percentage of men in 'leadership' positions.

Amitha: I don't think that the organization had thought very much about race and racism until it was forced to.

Gerry: Two reports on ethnic minorities had been produced and management had completed an extremely comprehensive draft EOP Employment Code of Practice. In the wake of a media flare-up over community advice agencies refusing to advise National Front activists, which affected both Union and the organization, a number of friends and colleagues, including us, took the issue to our National Conference and helped to get an anti-racism motion through. It felt as though anti-racism had become an important issue over a period of just one year.

Amitha: Then the Union Working Party on EOP in which the three of us were involved came up with a very well worked-out response to the EOP Code of Practice on Recruitment and Selection Procedures. Management amicably accepted our response. Looking back I suppose it was in their interest to have a happy, accountable workforce. In any case, codes and policies are only as good as people's commitment to implementing them. In the political climate we found ourselves in, EOPs made sense and were interpreted in their widest sense as applying to attitudes, behaviour, recruitment, training – through to the content and manner in which we delivered our service to the public.

Ahmed: I think that the GLC, as well as some of the radical London boroughs, did much to put EOP on the agenda of all voluntary organizations. They made it respectable to talk about it by linking grants with the proper adoption of equal opportunity policies. They gave power and legitimacy to those workers who, like us, were pushing our respective organizations to take issues of oppression and disadvantage seriously.

Amitha: As a result of all these events the Union also had to

take the issue of oppression seriously. There was a greater
flow of information, more exciting debates internally, and
with the formation of the Black Workers' Group and later
on the Lesbian and Gay Workers' Group, more politically
aware people began to organize around issues of their own
oppression.

Gerry: It's really strange how the special interest groups of
oppressed people came into existence. Management
organized a Black workers' meeting because they needed our
response to a report on ethnic minorities. What amazed me
was the number of Black workers who turned up. Though
small in comparison to the size of the total workforce, there
were 33 of us, but it felt like it was 66.

Amitha: There was a great feeling of solidarity between us
all and a common suspicion as to why management had
called the meeting.

Ahmed: At the meeting, what made the most impact was the
situation in which we found ourselves. Here we were 33
Black workers, called together by two white men, who were
to tell us how to go about discussing the issues of racism and
ethno-centricism. Our reaction wasn't surprising. We threw
the two white men out of the meeting.

Gerry: Even though we talked about the report on ethnic
minorities for a bit, more importantly we discussed setting
up an independent Black group with our own structures
and demands. Having been given the opportunity to come
together, we didn't intend to let it go. That decision to
organize ourselves as a group was a really important step
forward for us as workers and for the organization.

 Setting up the Lesbian and Gay Workers' Group was very
different. Partly it was in response to the Black Workers'
Group and because Ahmed and I were both Black and
lesbian/gay. It had its first official meeting after a Union
talk on heterosexism. There were not many of us in the
group to begin with, and so the issue of having two separate
groups for lesbians and gay men wasn't considered to be
organizationally viable.

Ahmed: I must say that I didn't think much of the group when it was first set up because I felt that it wasted a lot of time whinging about all the things that were 'being handed to the Black workers on a plate because anti-racism was currently fashionable'. There was a considerable under-current of racism in our early discussions. I felt that no attempt was being made to arrive at an analysis of our situation based on the specificity of our experience as lesbians and gays.

Gerry: Politically speaking, though, there wasn't the same organized pressure over the heterosexism issue, and management couldn't initially see any reasons for our existence. The disparity in numbers between the BWG and the LGWG meant different tactics. Both needed time to develop their separate objectives and political identities – which, by the nature of their oppressions, were different, even though they both were under the umbrella of EOP.

Amitha: I wasn't involved in setting up the Group, having then not accepted my lesbian identity, but from what I could see there was a lot of resentful and suspicious comparison between the BWG and the LGWG. I saw the formation of the Black Workers' Group and the concessions that we had won as a lever or a rolling stone which would have a knock-on effect. In setting a precedent, the BWG created the opportunity for others to make their demands and needs widely known from an organized base. Since the formation of the BWG and the LGWG, the administrative workers and the volunteers have set up their own autonomous groups, and Disabled Action has just taken off. Correspondingly, there is now less suspicion between the LGWG and the BWG. I think this is because we have our own distinct identity and proper base. There is far more talk of building bridges.

Gerry: Friends have said that many members were suspicious of my political motives, and perhaps Ahmed's as well.

Amitha: Yes, and later when I came out as lesbian,

suspicious of me too. But I found it really helpful to have known you both because you were in both groups and involved in the Union and the EOP Working Party. Apart from some of our managers, the Union was noticeably fearful of the new autonomous groups, probably because some members were afraid of losing the Union's power base through divide-and-rule tactics. I guess we dealt with it by changing the traditional union structures. All oppressed groups were able, if they wished, to elect their own shop steward to represent their interests in the Union. This didn't endanger either the Union's negotiation rights or the groups' autonomy. There was nothing novel about the idea, but that alongside with liaison meetings of all the groups and the Union around specific issues, helped to strengthen links between us all.

Gerry: Having a Black lesbian worker as chairperson and more Black/gay stewards played an important role in changing the Union. The potential for other oppressed groups to be autonomously organized also put pressure on the Union to question its structures and attitudes.

Ahmed: I don't think that the Union actually changed in any fundamental way. I think that what happened was that a lot of traditional union members, that is, the white, heterosexual male stewards who normally formed its backbone, for once took a back-seat, and allowed us to get on with it – to organize in our own way which we did. Now, this may be a very pessimistic analysis, but there it is.

Amitha: In a way that's right. There was and there still remains a feeling that some Union members feel as though they have 'allowed' us to exist autonomously and have special union representation.

Gerry: But the Union cannot now afford to go back on its decisions. I do believe that the debate round grievance/disciplinary issues and discrimination by members will really test both the Union's commitment to EOP and to fighting oppression, as well as how different oppressed groups tackle their own attitudes towards other oppressions.

Gerry: Unions could have a role in organizing workers with specific oppressions by acting as a buffer between groups and management; providing a wider political context for organizing in; and for providing liaison, information and support. But the Union must be clear about the demarcation between their role and the self-determination of oppressed and disadvantaged groups, otherwise autonomous groups will be sucked in and dissipated. This would weaken the fight against oppression and allow a continuation of oppressive practices.

Ahmed: I think that the Union should support developments towards workers organizing around issues of oppression as long as it is within a progressive ideology. It should be receptive to pressures for changes in its structure to take account of what oppressed groups say – for instance, it should move away from the very formalized committee structure towards a participative workshop-type framework. The Union should also be aware that EOP has a price tag for its existing members and that you cannot achieve equal opportunities on a no-cost basis. As far as other union members' attitude towards us, I think that we did get an enormous amount of support from like-minded colleagues in organizing around issues of race and sexuality. Without their support we could not have gone very far. But it is important to remember that there were those colleagues who expressed their hostility not through obstruction or outright opposition, but through silence.

Amitha: It wasn't just through silence. Their hostility and antagonism was shown through non-attendance at meetings and by their obstructive behaviour when they did turn up.

Ahmed: Being in at least two oppressed 'specific interest' groups we were able to mediate differences and act as a bridge between the two when necessary. Let's face it, both groups had, and still have, people who have no understanding of the other's oppression, or in many cases, no sympathy either. But the fact that each group came into existence in its own time and for its own reasons, and found its own identity and direction, means that we need have no fear about it losing its autonomy *vis-à-vis* the other groups. What would be more difficult would be for each group to resist both poles of power (management and union) and not become a caucus or adjunct of either.

Gerry: Autonomy is fundamental but so is unity. Without both, divide-and-rule tactics will open the way to ranking oppressions and putting the groups against each other.

Ahmed: When you are Black and gay and you open yourself up to the realities and contradictions inherent in this combined identity, it provides a better basis for understanding other people's experience, both intellectually and intuitively. I think you can be oppressed through being exploited, harassed, discriminated against; or through being ignored and looked straight through. The important thing is to be open about yourself – both in terms of where you are oppressed and where you oppress others. It makes you aware of how much power there exists within yourself, not only to resist oppression, but also to oppress others. We all have capacities to do both – sometimes we forget one in our concentration on the other.

Gerry: In my case, it means that I am always aware of the political and personal contradictions in being a Black lesbian. Wearing so many 'hats' can be very manipulative because of being involved in everything but it also opens one up to being oppressed within the different groups. Gays can be racist, Blacks can be heterosexist and sexism is rampant in both. The pressures to be either Black or lesbian make it very difficult and confusing to develop being Black and lesbian.

Amitha: It was the Equal Opportunities Policy which cut through all the contradictions. The comradeship, energy and commitment of the core of the Working Party, comprising as it did a lot of very different people, was an example of the possibilities of uniting diverse interests and oppressions to the mutual advantage of all concerned, including management. It was in their interest to have an efficient, mutually agreed Code of Practice. Instead of wasting energy arguing over contentious issues and different oppressions, we used the issue to clarify and increase our understanding and feelings about our oppressions and those of others. The Working Party helped me to express my lesbianism in a positive way in that I could come out, and it helped me to deal with the suspicion and fears of colleagues Black and white, gay or straight, male or female. It has confirmed my belief in the snowball effect around EOP issues, but also made me aware of, and have strength to cope with, backlashes – such as the question 'which group or interest are you representing?'

Gerry: The EOP Working Party was also an amazing learning experience. Working so positively and with such support with different people confirmed my belief that oppressions shouldn't be ranked against each other; and that an EOP debate could act as a central focus around which a unity between different oppressions could be achieved while recognizing and accepting our differences. Having to tackle procedures restricted by legislation also forced us to apply political theories to practical realities without too much compromise. It was rare to have six Black gays working politically and personally together in the same workplace and that helped me integrate my identity as a Black lesbian.

Ahmed: What I found really exciting and stimulating about our Working Party was that there was a great deal of openness, a willingness to listen and learn on the part of all the people. People didn't try and score points off each other – contributions were acknowledged and applauded, rather than criticized or tested to destruction. The warmth and affection that we felt for each other will always be with me.

13 Voices in my ear

Lisa Power

I was standing in the Hemingford Arms one Friday evening, minding my own business, having a drink with a few friends, when Simon introduced me to someone he knew called Keith.

'Keith's a volunteer for Gay Switchboard,' he told me.

'That's interesting. I've been thinking about doing something like that,' I said, more out of politeness than accuracy. Seven years later, I'm still a volunteer.

I don't exactly have a clear sense of perspective on the subject myself. Paradoxically, it's very easy to talk to other volunteers about the calls, the personalities, or the organizational dramas; it's a standing joke amongst Switchboard volunteers that whenever two or more of us get together, that's all that we can talk about. Friends of volunteers have been known to refuse dinner invitations unless Switchboard as a topic is banned, and lovers often jokingly refer to themselves as 'Switchboard widows'.

The organization is infectious; many people have joined intending to make a small, easily-managed commitment and ended up doing three or four shifts a week and taking on extra work until sometimes their whole life becomes bound up in the organization. That can bring its own dangers. It's a problem common to lesbian and gay organizations that there is often a handful of stalwarts without whom things seemingly would not survive, and yet reliance on such martyrdom leads to over-involvement, resentment and burnout for the martyrs and under-involvement, resentment and alienation for others. If organizations don't manage to balance the two, they can topple.

Keeping some sort of balance is something I suspect to be close to the corporate heart of Switchboard, though usually unspoken. Though at any given amount it looks as if it isn't going anywhere, it's always on the move, lumbering from crisis to crisis. Volunteers constantly tug in all directions while others bewail the imminent end of the organization – just as they did last week, last year and (in a few cases) last decade. Change is slow and unspectacular but nevertheless constantly occurring, allowing the organization to keep its balance where most of its contemporaries - Icebreakers, *Gay News*, GLF and many others - have slipped and lost their footing.

Despite the hype, Switchboard is very special; not because of its size, or its range, or its particular achievements but because of the way in which it has endured and grown and responded to a perceived constituency. Of course, in reality there is no united lesbian and gay community with a common set of needs and yet Switchboard attempts a near-unique balancing act of serving some of the needs of all of the people as much of the time as possible. The changing history of Switchboard is in many ways the history of changing needs of lesbians and gay men and a reflection of a growing understanding of our diversity.

I really only went along to the interviews for a lark, as company for a friend. I found I was the only woman in the upstairs room of the Albert in Kings Cross, listening to a man in a leather jacket giving an introductory talk which seemed to assume that we were all men. Later, two men took me into a corner and fired questions at me for what seemed like ages, but can only have been about half an hour. They seemed embarrassed at having to ask a woman questions about sexism and feminism. It wasn't till years later that I realised they hadn't even remembered to ask if I was a lesbian. I remember a lot of questions about gay men, Heaven, leather bars and the geography of London. Since I was living with the most out gay man I know, I wasn't short of an opinion on anything to do with anything in faggotdom, or at least the social side of it. Getting onto Switchboard was the easy part.

In December 1979 I became one of two lesbians and sixty-five gay men providing a twenty-four-hours-a-day information service and helpline for the gay community. You didn't say lesbian and gay then. Although we were officially the London helpline, we got calls from all over Britain and from all over the world. We still do, because of the amount of information we carry on just about anything gay (and lesbian too now) anywhere. In fact, we probably carried more information then about social and campaigning organizations – a myriad world of Chipping Norton GLFs and Llandridnod Wells CHEs that no longer exists, replaced with a few regional commercial meccas and a London explosion of hotels, plumbers, shops and other services. In many ways, that's what's happened to the lesbian and gay helplines too. Then there were new Switchboards springing up all over the place, sometimes with more enthusiasm than resources and occasionally with decidedly dubious intent or policy. Now there are fewer each year as they suffer from dwindling finances and members. The National Association of Gay Switchboards has fallen into disuse. Only London Lesbian and Gay Switchboard seems to grow, still balancing on a tightrope – a difficult and dangerous trick.

Partly, it's survived because of its very size and range; with hundreds of thousands of people calling us every year, there's a clear demonstration of need for the service. It's always there to answer the phone and the number is easy to find – these days it's even in Thomson's Local Directories. But also it's survived, I think, because of the motivation that the constant flood of callers provides the volunteers with – everyone in the organization. No matter what else they do within the group, every volunteer must do at least one shift on the phones every fortnight. All of them have to hear people's needs regularly and at first hand, and judge for themselves how well they (and other lesbian and gay services) are meeting them. So far, that's prevented the organization from losing itself too much in theoretical debate or argument. It's prevented the volunteers from losing sight of the multiple realities for lesbians and gay men in this society, until they lock ideological horns or lose organizational drive – the twin causes of many groups collapsing.

I was sitting in the office recently, finishing a shift. The night shift volunteer was standing next to me getting ready to come on to the phones and as I came off a call he started to chat to me. I explained that I hadn't been around as much as usual lately because I was pissed off with the way some people were behaving. 'Oh, take no notice,' he said, 'That sort of thing isn't really important. I just consider it a privilege to be answering the phones and sometimes to help people. That would keep me here whatever the problems.'

Another of the major difficulties which beset lesbian and gay organizations increasingly, apart from the motivation of current volunteers and members, is the getting of new ones. Even when there is clearly a need for the service provided, there are often far too few people willing to involve themselves in providing it, so that when the originators leave, the service dies. Throughout its existence, London Switchboard has always had more would-be volunteers than it could take on. (One of the originators once told me that his memory of the first few weeks of the organization was of people literally waiting in turn to answer the phone every time it rang.) This luxury has meant that the group has been able to evolve a fairly sophisticated selection and training procedure. Though this comes in for constant robust internal criticism and revision, it is more thorough than that of many professional advice and counselling organizations and is increasingly used as a model by other organizations. It's certainly come a long way from the upstairs room at the Albert. The numbers may partly be due to the reputation Switchboard enjoys as a good training ground for employment, mainly in the voluntary social services (every time the organization manages to build up a core of daytime volunteers, half of them find jobs) but the largest group of prospective volunteers are past callers, people who, having found the service useful, want to contribute to its continued existence.

I can't tell you more than the bare bones of what happened before I arrived, though the polite version is available in old back copies of *Gay News* and Annual Reports. Switchboard was formed in 1974 out of an alliance between the old Gay Liberation Front office collective, who donated the office, and *Gay News*, who donated the publicity and energy to get it off the ground. The story runs that *Gay News* were having trouble getting any work done because of the number of people who used their phone line as a combination information service and helpline. Having some information on helplines in other areas and countries, they realized that such a service in London would both take the pressure off them and be an asset to the community. The idea, once publicized, took off like a rocket and from the start the service ran seven days a week. Just over a year later, it went to a round-the-clock service. The real explosion in calls, particularly from isolated people, happened in 1977–8 when Switchboard began to advertise in local papers and Tom Robinson put the phone number on the single sleeve of 'Glad To Be Gay'. At around the same time, after a number of bitter arguments, all the remaining women in the group left to join with women from Icebreakers to form Lesbian Line.

It was at a time when many lesbians, angry at the lack of weight given to women's issues within the mixed movement and at the continuing sexism of many gay men, chose to prioritize work with the women's movement. The decision of most lesbians with any political sensibility at that time to do this left many mixed gay organizations in a quandary. Should they accept the verdict of their women ex-members and work as single-sex organizations? Or should they take a hard look at themselves, try to learn something from what had happened, make the necessary changes and hope to attract more lesbians? Those with a clear commitment to serve the whole community opted, at least theoretically, for the latter and in the early eighties a token lesbian was worth her weight in gold as a range of groups struggled to maintain a semblance of political balance.

It wasn't just a matter of image for Switchboard though, or a way to make a few right-on gay men sleep easier in their beds. Even with no lesbian volunteers, some women continued to call; women who'd never heard of Lesbian Line, women who couldn't call during the hours they were open, women who'd swallowed media distortions of separatist groups, women who preferred the service or needed information Switchboard had. With the wide and growing publicity for the service, more and more women called. Their needs alone would have been enough reason – were enough – for a number of us over the next three to four years to stay in a male organization, with largely male resources for mainly male callers and to join with some of those men to change it. In my first few years in the London activist network I was several times courted (it seems the only appropriate word) to join currently all-male organizations as a token lesbian but none of them offered, alongside the assumption that this would be a privileged or welcome position, the incentive that Switchboard did: the callers.

At one point I left Switchboard for a few months. The break was intended to be a long one, possibly a year or two. I felt disillusioned, stale and cynical and I wanted to take a break before I started taking it out on the callers. Too often over-involved people burn out without realizing it and end up damaging their cause and themselves. I thought that if I didn't get out I might end up being thrown out. I went along to other organizations, joined one or two things, went out a lot. For some reason (and I really can't remember what I was doing there) one day I found myself rather out of order at the opening of a new leather shop in Hoxton. I'd been muttering unhappily to a couple of friends about how hopelessly disorganized a particular campaign I'd got involved with seemed to be when a strange man next to us started a similar but louder tirade about how useless Switchboard was, how everyone knew they were ripping off money from their fund raising and what a lousy job they did in his (extremely small and third-hand) experience. A couple of volunteers started to argue with him and I joined in with anger. When I calmed down I realized I was defending an organization I refused to be in, though I had nothing good to say for the one I'd left it for. I reapplied to Switchboard the next day.

It took a long time for the penny to drop with me about why I was so apparently popular in men's organizations in the aftermath of so many women deciding to work separately. I'd not been in London long and those lesbian and gay friends I had were involved in squatting more than gay liberation. In Lancaster, where I'd come out, there had always been a mixed scene; in many places outside the big towns, most of the lesbians and gay men continued to hang

together for at least part of the time because there didn't
seem enough of us to consider doing much else. I'd helped
to start up a mixed-sex Lancaster Gay Switchboard and
learned a lot from radical faggots. They taught me bravery
in the face of bigotry, the way that anger intelligently
channelled can move mountains, the use of laughter as a
weapon and a source of strength. They taught me what I
still believe (and no amount of misogyny or gynophobia or
general bad behaviour on either side can shift me) that
though there is much that is different for lesbians and gay
men, there is also much that is common. As far as much of
the rest of the world is concerned, we're all just a bunch of
queers. It seems to me that we're stronger fighting that
together than apart and in the last few years a growing
number of successful campaigns have strengthened this
belief.

I remember my early shifts as tremendous fun. I realized
early on how much I was getting out of the callers and the
fact that some of them seemed to get something out of me
too increased my confidence in other areas of my life. I
wasn't a particularly happy person at the time; lonely, in a
rather dead-end job and with few personal relationships. In a
funny way, it helped me a lot to find that there were people
worse off than me and to learn through the callers that there
were a lot of different ways of being strong. Many of the
calls were for information, but many of them were from
people who were confused or desperate. Despite the current
fear of AIDS and the moral blacklash increasingly in
evidence in the late eighties, most callers now take far less
persuading that homosexuality can be part of a valid
lifestyle. They may be worried about how to be gay, but far
fewer of them are as desperate not to be and though they
may be afraid of reaching out to the gay world, mostly they
know it exists. As near ago as 1980–1, many didn't.

I remember sending far more callers on then to general
befriending and support organizations (of which far more
existed) and fewer to specialist social groups and youth
groups (which have blossomed since). Violent abuse, death
threats, bomb warnings and evangelical types were also far
more common on the phones then, though received
Switchboard wisdom says that's because they have more

trouble getting through now and tend to get discouraged and give up quicker than genuine callers. I soaked it all up, even the abuse. I know it's something a Samaritan would consider unprofessional, but I enjoyed getting verbal queerbashers to hang up on me because *they* couldn't handle what I was telling them. But the genuine callers were always far more interesting and more testing.

'I don't know how to put this – you won't be embarrassed about this will you? ... I'm sorry to waste your time ... It's difficult to say the words ... I don't know why I can't just pull myself together ... I've thought about this for years and never told anybody ... I suppose I've always known that I was a bit different ... do you understand what I mean?'

'Oh, my dear, don't tell me to go to one of those dreary little do-gooding tea party groups. I don't want to learn macramé or flower arranging, either. All I want out of this life is to meet a few men with something more between their ears than the latest Donna Summers hit. Is that too much to ask?'

'I'm sorry, I can't speak louder. My husband's asleep upstairs and so are the kids. You don't mind, do you? I often ring at this time of night for a chat, it helps to stop me from going spare. I knew I made a mistake, marrying young, but it took me a while to work out what was wrong. I want to do right by the kids, give them a good home. In a few years ... I'll have my own life then. It's kind of you all to spare me the time.'

'Hello darling, what's on tonight then? Nice to hear another girl's voice. The fellers down there are always good for a laugh but they don't know what any of the places are like. Have you been there? Got a girlfriend?'

'The others at school keep making fun of me and saying things. I don't know how they found out. They keep picking on me, but I can't ask a teacher for help. They'd want to know why and then they'd tell my parents. My dad says that queers are all sick in the head and he'd kill one if they ever touched me. What will he do to me?'

Working on a Switchboard – particularly London, where the phone rings as soon as you put it down even now they have five lines – is a continuous education and a continual reminder of your own privileged position and relative security in the gay ghetto. Trying to dissuade a father from sending his gay teenager to a psychiatrist; calming someone who's just been beaten up in a police cell; sharing someone's joy at discovering that there's another lesbian in the next village, all serve to remove some of the complacency which can so easily set in. Despite its short-comings and my own, working on Switchboard gave me the tools to work out some sort of political consciousness, the level of articulacy required to stand up for what I started to believe in and the confidence to take the sort of shit that comes to any woman who does that, anywhere.

One of the most positive aspects of Switchboard that I've seen over the past seven years, apart from the callers, has been the way that many of its members have continuously struggled to put their politics and convictions about gay and other rights into practice (though some of them might not care to put it that way) and the strength that working on it has given some people to do so elsewhere. Ex-Switchboard volunteers didn't just help to found Lesbian Line. Others left for a wide range of other organizations throughout the world. In particular, the Terrence Higgins Trust – employees, hierarchy and all its different work groups – has a strong flavour of Switchboard past and present.

But there's a depressing flipside, too, in the way that in some areas the organization has continually fallen short of its own ideals through an inability to admit that such shortcomings could and do exist. Switchboard is still almost as white dominated as it was male dominated when I joined. The inability, so far, to properly confront issues of race is largely due to the huge number of white volunteers who simply find it too painful to accept that, because of their culture and upbringing, they tend to behave in a racist manner. It's interesting that gay men on Switchboard found it much easier to accept that they didn't automatically know best for lesbians than white people on Switchboard find it to accept that they might not know best for Black people. I suspect it's an assumption Switchboard shares with the wider white-dominated gay community – a reflection that, for once, the organization ought to be ashamed of.

Perhaps the major requirement for change on Switchboard is a combination of the overt needs of the callers, and the needs of a group of self-interested and highly-motivated volunteers who find a reason to stay in the organization. Lesbian issues came to be taken seriously only when there were a number of lesbian volunteers (and quite a few men supporting them too) who were prepared to be loud-mouthed, difficult, overworked and sometimes thoroughly disliked within the organization. Without that we wouldn't have a selection and training procedure which demands that all new volunteers give equal weight to understanding of lesbian concerns and knowledge of lesbian information as well of that of gay men. Nor would we have a public image that clearly conveys the mixed nature of the organization: in early 1986 the name changed to Lesbian and Gay Switchboard which confirmed our status. Nor would we have an information system which carries every piece of lesbian information any of us can find, lesbian benefits to balance up the years of drag show fund raising, and a closed Women's Caucus which supports whatever work we do in the organization. Previous attempts to open a dialogue on race issues (let alone institute anti-racist practices) have ended with anger and hostility on all sides and, unsurprisingly, there are few current Black volunteers ... but the calls are still coming in. Policies won't be enough – practical action needs to be taken.

Since Switchboard policy and response is shaped by the callers as well as the volunteers, there is bound to be an emphasis at any given time on whatever issue looms largest amongst the calls. In 1983–4 there was a sudden upsurge in legal calls, mainly centring around 'pretty police' activity in the London area and a spate of cottaging entrapments. Switchboard became a vocal opponent of the tactics, providing material for parliamentary and media attacks upon the practices. The death of *Gay News* provoked a considerable growth in out-of-London calls for information no longer available in that magazine's supplement, while at the same time making it far more difficult for us to obtain the information the callers needed and throwing an internal emphasis on that side of our work. Simple pressure of calls has taken us from one to five lines over the years and the only reason we have stuck at five is because the office is simply too small to take any more. Now that the calls are almost constant, allowing little time for relaxation and getting to know other volunteers, the group is having to explore the possibilities of support groups and regular discussion weekends.

The best example of this and of the way in which Switchboard tends to mirror the mainstream gay (and still mainly male) community lies in the organization's response to AIDS. From what seems now like an almost total lack of concern when the news of the virus first reached the organization, there is currently a major emphasis within the organization and a constant campaign of re-education of both callers and volunteers. Everyone is required to attend inservice training providing factual updates, bereavement-counselling techniques, safer sex discussions; all AIDS and HIV related calls are monitored and there is constant discussion on shift about how we handle the calls.

I remember the first inservice training on AIDS that Switchboard held. The discussion went round and round in circles as many of the men present refused to face the reality of the issue. Two men held a long argument about whether the whole thing was an establishment plot to repress gay men's right to a freely expressed sexuality. Another said, 'Well, if I cross the road I might get run over, and if I have sex I might get AIDS. It's just one of life's risks.' Fury was expressed at the idea that some gay men might have to change their sexual habits and scorn poured on the idea of trying to tell that to the callers. One man who spoke about already having made the decision to only have safer sex was ridiculed by some of the others. I myself was grimly unsympathetic, pointing out the years of government and social inaction on cervical cancer, a sexually-related disease from which only women suffer and which could be drastically reduced by simple health education and changes in heterosexual male habits. I don't think I'm the only volunteer who's ashamed of their early attitude to AIDS and I'm only glad that we had the sense, collectively, to listen to reason before the calls began. It was Switchboard volunteers who eventually organized the first London public conference on AIDS.

AIDS has changed the whole face of Switchboard. It's no exaggeration to say that almost half of our callers now either raise the issue or need to have it raised with them. It increases the pressure on volunteers and on the phone lines dramatically, because whereas any other sort of information call may take a minute or two, an AIDS call can take half an hour or more because the information may lead into a discussion of the caller's lifestyle, moral attitudes and emotional needs. The general level of pain and fear for all gay men who call is now higher and just below the surface, as many of them seek to come to terms with the virus and its effect on their lives. For those just coming out onto the scene, it's an established fact that many can come to terms with, but for those who have set patterns of sexual behaviour or who've put themselves at risk in the past, it's a great problem. Many people who have been out for a number of years have friends and lovers who have died or may die. Volunteers need greater counselling skills and better personal emotional support than ever before. Every shift, they face people who have lost lovers, lost jobs or lost families through AIDS or (more often) the fear of AIDS; every shift they have to help people think through the new consequences of future sex or face the possible results of past ignorance. It brings a new light to conversations about matters such as sexual dishonesty in relationships. I personally find it hardest to deal with married men, still sexually active with their wives while seeking casual unsafe sex with gay men and refusing either to change their sexual style or to consider the possible results. Early on, someone said to me that nobody really took AIDS seriously until someone they knew died through it and when the first ex-volunteer died, many of us felt the shock waves. With AIDS and HIV, the balance on Switchboard has shifted from Cloud-cuckoo-land to grim reality.

There's so much more that I could say about the development of Switchboard. I've avoided the stuff that's on public record – the big fund raising events, the grandiose announcements of plans, the celebrations of our survival. What still seems most important to me, after seven years, is still the callers and the way that we do or don't service their needs. Whatever we need to go through to continue to do that – raising money, training new volunteers, finding more efficient ways of managing our information and our office, contributing to public debate on the state of lesbian and gay rights – I hope we have the sense and the energy to endure. Switchboard as an organization has probably had some effect on more of us, as callers and as volunteers, than any other single campaign or group has done in the recent history of lesbian and gay rights in this country. I hope that we are never foolish enough to take what it does for granted – because that is when it will begin to crumble and fail like so many others have done.

In joining London Gay Switchboard, I'm not sure quite what I expected. What I got was a group of men who ranged from those with a more developed line on women's issues than mine to those who were frankly misogynistic, and a woman who went on record as saying that, in her opinion, feminism put women off being lesbians. And all this within an organization which within a year changed my life, my career and my character. It sounds rather extravagant, but then my whole relationship with the organization could be called that. We may not be lovers any more, but we're still very good friends despite a few attempts to pull us apart. Don't ask me to be objective.

14 The liberation of affection

Bill Thorneycroft, Jeffrey Weeks and Mark Sreeves

Bill Thorneycroft (born 1926), Jeffrey Weeks (born 1945) and Mark Sreeves (born 1958) talk about becoming gay, about gay male identity, about gay male relationships and about the gay male community.

Bill: I had been having sex, occasionally, with men since I was about fourteen but I had no gay social life at all. I just used to do a bit of cottaging, picking people up, particularly during the war; that was the heyday in picking people up so easily – in crowded trains, in the blackout – but it was always just the one-off. People I met never became friends, people never spoke in those days at all, in fact, I found that if you did try to speak they always ran away.

In the fifties I got into a set of about a dozen or so gay men in South London. I had been travelling the country flogging Soviet magazines – I was working for Collet's bookshops – and I stayed with a comrade in Edinburgh who kept a boarding house. It was a terribly cold winter and she said, 'You won't mind sharing a room with my son, will you?' So we got into bed together. He was very much more out than I was and he knew where the gay scene was, not only in Edinburgh but also in London. He introduced me to this world that I had never really come across before. Most people met through casual pick-ups, going through to the Black Prince, which was the equivalent of the Vauxhall today.

The sort of things we did was go to private parties, go to gay clubs, troll around pubs in South London where they had drag shows. I never did like drag shows and I didn't want to spend the evening in the pub but I did it just to be with gay people. We were all pretty open with each other but very discreet outside. Most of them were pretty determined to have a totally straight image outside the ghetto. It was very much a sort of double life. We camped about and we had our little parties, but we never really discussed it; just accepted it as a fact of life. I used to talk about being gay to my straight, but enlightened, friends – mostly women; it was a relief to me and they were perfectly happy to talk about it. But once I got into this set of gay men, it took over my social life almost completely. I more or less gave up cottaging for a while. However none of them actually shared my interest in politics. . . . Most of them were clerks or shop assistants, although there were one or two manual workers, a couple worked on the railways; nobody was upper class. I was an electrician, doing house wiring and things like that in the fifties, and then my lover and I had a greengrocer's shop with another gay man. My lover and I lived together for eight years and then when we got rid of the greengrocer's shop, he 'went back to mother'. I still see him but we don't have sex any more.

Jeffrey: My first sexual encounters were in South Wales, where I grew up. My very first was with someone I was at school with, but he subsequently got married and vehemently denied he was gay. The first sexual casual pick-up I had was also in South Wales; this must have been about 1965–6 when I was nineteen or twenty. I was a student in London but I was at home on this occasion when I met someone in the park. We had sex in the park and I felt a tremendous nausea for what I had done. I can remember walking away, swearing that I would never do this again, feeling physically sick. Of course, by that evening I couldn't think of anything else and it set up a pattern of repetition which I followed once I went back to London. It wasn't difficult to pick up people for casual sex but it was difficult to transfer that casual sex contact into any sort of relationship.

Building up relationships was very much like collecting little islands – you jumped from one to another to another to another – and if you were lucky you eventually had a network. By the time the gay movement started in 1970 the gay friends I had were people I had picked up or met through a pick-up; I probably knew about half a dozen gay people intimately. Some of my friendships from then I have retained and someone I met twenty years ago I still live with. It is not as if that period was a failure in terms of personal relationships but it was very hard work to build up those relationships. It was that I think which was fundamentally transformed by my involvement with the gay movement.

'Swinging London' of the mid-sixties was not a particularly exciting place for 'queer people' as we called ourselves. There was a generally growing permissive attitude, although I don't think that the attitude towards homosexuality was particularly permissive. But I didn't find it at all difficult to come out to my student friends. I graduated in 1967 and then I did postgraduate work till 1969 and so I was in a student milieu until a year before the gay movement started. The straight people I was friendly with were quite realistic about my gayness, even intrigued by it and grew to know what I did and who I met. I managed to introduce some of my gay friends to some of my college friends – some of my college friends also turned out to be gay. The first person I ever came out to as a student was a person I suspected of being gay and everyone else thought he was gay; in fact, he vehemently denied it after I came out. Ten years later, of course, he did come out after a rather agonizing process and he is now a gay activist himself in South London and the Labour Party.

I think I was mentally prepared for gay liberation in 1970 when it came along and when I did encounter it it swept me along quite easily. I was emotionally prepared because I had just had what seemed to me then an incredibly traumatic experience. A close friend who was gay – we were never quite lovers but we were inseparable for a while – went off with a woman and I was incredibly devastated by this. It was not just that he had gone off with someone else but he had actually gone off with a woman and it seemed to me like a betrayal of my identity. This happened just before I went to the first gay liberation meeting in London. The second element was that I had just started working at the London

School of Economics in October 1970, which was exactly the same time as GLF started meeting there and LSE was in one of its periods of turmoil which involved me as someone working on the staff and excited me politically. Going to the first GLF meeting brought together these two aspects of myself as I saw for the first time the emotional need to have a context where I could be open and proud of my gayness, as well as the political context where my sexuality would seem relevant to all the other things that were going on around me at work and in the country at large. It was an immediate transformation of my personal and social outlook and it started in me a new sort of excitement – it was as though you'd been shot full of adrenalin. For three of four months I couldn't think or do anything else. Within the first month of my being involved with the gay movement I met Angus, who became my lover then and remained my lover for ten years. We still live together. Immediately, therefore, I was involved in the gay movement and for the first time in my life in a couple relationship. Everything I did personally and everything I explored in my own life seemed part of this much wider political and social movement. There was a period of incredibly intense excitement which, I think, probably sustained me for the next five or ten years.

Bill: The gay movement for me really started with the South London GLF in 1972. The impact it had on me was that here were a lot of gay people who were interested in politics; for whom it wasn't just a social thing to do after work. They were a totally different set of people from the ones I knew before. They weren't very conventional, they were mostly younger and were into being public and talking about it. Also I remember a very, very early meeting when somebody said, 'Let's think of the reasons why we are glad to be gay,' and I thought, 'Rubbish, there aren't any, what nonsense.' When I actually began to realize that there were advantages to being gay, that changed my whole attitude – up till then I had always thought of it as something to be sorry for, to apologize for. That was the turning-point in my whole attitude to myself.

Mark: I suppose the point at which my public coming out

started was 1976-7, though I'd known that I was gay from a much earlier age. I was aware that I was attracted to boys and men from about the age of twelve or fourteen, but although I was brought up in London I still didn't find it very easy to have any sort of contact with other gay men. I was extremely scared of actually meeting people and, having read *Homosexuality* by D.J. West, it really terrified me, the prospect of meeting these strange people. It didn't give me a very positive image to actually find other people, but I used to go to South London drag pubs, such as the Vauxhall, with schoolfriends when we were in sixth form. I wasn't acknowledged as being gay. I went with a lesbian and some other friends. At the end of 1976 I actually met several people, whom I could talk to, who acknowledged that they were gay and, as a consequence, I then subsequently admitted - and that's the word I still use - that I was gay. It was like a little explosion because it wasn't just a question of telling one other person; I had to tell my parents and I had to tell all my schoolfriends and make sure that my world existed and to a great extent it did. I'd left school in 1976, I was unemployed and it all happened through a drama group at the Royal Court Theatre where I met people who were out. There was a youth group being set up to perform a play which was about teenage gay men and lesbians and their experiences. I got involved in that so that by mid-1977 I was performing in a play which was actually saying that I was gay.

I had initally met a lot of people who were gay but I didn't really identify with them and sort of felt, 'Yes, but is this it?' I really wanted to meet people I felt far more at ease with and at that time it was the still the punk era and I met a lot of other people who were into that. I knew a lot of other people who were both gay and punks; there was no question of having to esablish yourself. But there was a great thing about the Prince Albert - whether or not the Prince Albert would let people in who were punks. Being gay for me meant identifying with people who were of a similar age to myself and with a particular way of dressing. At the same time I can remember going along to clubs, like the Vortex, and being slightly hassled because I was kissing my boyfriend. He was a follower of Sham 69 and I remember going to a concert of theirs at the LSE and almost getting beaten up by skinheads.

I had an image of GLF existing through meeting people and talking to them, but the only physical evidence I saw at that time was badges saying GLF. I wasn't quite sure whether GLF was an actual entity or an attitude of mind.

Jeffrey: I like the idea of seeing the gay movement as an attitude of mind. For me it was fundamentally feeling part of a community, a word we didn't use in those days. From the mid-sixties I had had a homosexual identity and I did say to people that I was homosexual; but in the early seventies that had a completely different meaning. It was in the context not of an isolated individual saying it to another isolated individual, but actually feeling that this identity had a social location, a political and moral location, because it involved a whole series of things which meant you weren't just a voice crying in the wilderness. So what fundamentally came out of those early years was this sense of community. There were differences between lesbians and gay men in those days as there continue to be; there were differences of race; there were differences of class; differences of interest; so the community isn't a particular thing – it's a whole series of different things. But the fundamental point for me was that it involved a positive recognition of *my* identity and mutual recognition of *our* identities and that made it much easier to form more personal sorts of relationships on various social levels with other people you met naturally through the things you were doing, whether it was political or social or whatever.

Mark: I certainly found quite a distinct difference between actually going out looking for sex, which I often associated with going to discos and, on the other hand, just making friendships which happened in a much more natural and less forced way. Actually, it just happened because I found I was engaging with people who had similar interests to myself.

One early significant occasion for me was actually meeting someone in a bookshop in the Finchley Road when I was about sixteen. There was obviously some sort of sexual element to it but I just didn't know what to do next and expected this man, who was about two or three years older than me, to, in some way, tell me or indicate to me and so I followed him without talking to him. There was all this unstated sexual intention and we went to the toilets at Finchley Road tube station and I didn't know what was going to happen. He went into a cubicle and I thought I should follow him but he pushed me away, locked the door and left me standing outside. It was totally outside my experience and so I just stood there and walked out. I just didn't know what to do – that was it. It was very disappointing really.

Jeffrey: When I first recognized that I was homosexual, I could recognize my feelings but I didn't know actually what you were supposed to do – not just to meet people, that was difficult enough, but I didn't know what to do physically. My fantasies were never about specific sexual activities, they were always on the level of some emotional transcendence – someone would come along and embrace me and that would be it; I couldn't really envisage what the nitty gritty practical things were.

Mark: I never fantasized about particular sexual activities until after I had had sexual activities.

Bill: I was the same but I still find that I'm totally different from people who think of sex as just screwing. When I first thought about fancying men, it was about kissing and cuddling. It was just a great romantic thing, when one somehow fell into this man's arms – like Hollywood films. I think it's straight from Hollywood really; but instead of falling into the arms of Barbara Stanwyck, it would be Tyrone Power. My sexual encounters seldom included fucking. After my first I felt totally guilt-ridden and swore never to do it again.

Mark: The feeling of guilt is quite predictable, or certainly one of nausea or revulsion or fear. Presumably it's also a lot to do with isolation, a lot to do with the fact that there was no one to talk to about the sexual experiences you were having and the only surrounding attitude was one of, 'This is something which shouldn't happen', whereas the situation when I had my first sexual experience was one where I knew other people who were gay whom I could talk to. It was a question of a different sort of climate, different surrounding circumstances. I was not going back into a situation where I only had myself to talk to.

Jeffrey: There was something very odd about attitudes in Britain in the seventies towards sex. I found when I got involved in my relationship with Angus in 1970 there was a real sort of tension. On the one hand what the gay movement had done was to involve me in a very intense one-to-one relationship, a couple relationship, and at the same time the ideology that the movement was instilling in me was away from the idea of couple relationships and away from the idea that sex should be conventionally tied to relationships or a single relationship. I think that this was a tension, a sort of contradiction which went through all the seventies, a real problem about sex which was never really confronted.

I wrote a lot about gay politics during the seventies, including a book on it, but when I look back on it, I don't actually talk about sex at all. What I am talking about are the contexts in which people have sexual relationships. My work has been mainly about the development of a sense of identity and of a sense of community, the development of relationships but not actually about sex. Yet in the States at this time there was a real explosion of sexual activity, of public sexual activity, the development of gay saunas, the development of sexually explicit magazines; there was a huge migration, really, to New York, San Francisco, Los Angeles by gay people, a whole burgeoning of a literature and expression of new sexual activities which I don't think was really echoed to the same extent until quite late in the seventies in this country. Gay politics here was much more about what we conventionally regard as political activity. Actually for radical gays it was much more about the relationship with the Labour movement; much more about building social identities; about relating to the need for social change. Lots of the most active gay activists in this country had pretty poor sexual lives in the seventies, I think. They spent so much time talking about gay things that they didn't actually have much time to do many gay things – which is why I think the really crucial thing that happened in the seventies was not the liberation of a particular sexuality but actually the liberation of a particular set of relationships through which people could enjoy sex, or not have sex, as the case may be.

Mark: I certainly identify with the attitude of a contradiction between my one-to-one relationships and the image of what should happen to try to get away from the heterosexual attitude to relationships. It's only now that I feel that I could actually decide to have a relationship which is specifically going to be monogamous, which is a really big change for me . . . that makes me think immediately of AIDS but I'm not sure. Previously, my close relationships would have been with people where we would perhaps be living together or just lovers, but they would have been quite explicit that they would have been non-monogamous. If either one of us wanted to sleep with other people then that should be OK and it was a question of something we could work out and that would not necessarily break the relationship even if in fact it actually did. It was as though there was a sort of non-resolved question of wanting to commit myself to a particular idea of having non-monogamous relationships and not buying into the feelings of jealousy. And, personally, I don't see the difference between emotional jealousy and sexual jealousy. If my lover was having sex with someone else and it was just a one night stand or something insignificant, it would be far less important to me than some sort of emotional thing that he might be having with someone else. But this jealousy actually happened because it was a question of making a decision wthout actually thinking through the consequences of it. It was something which I don't feel I have totally resolved in myself now.

Bill: I don't know if anybody feels they have, but this is a thing which I felt was central to the gay movement of the seventies and I think I would go so far as to say that I assume that most of my close friends feel, like Mark, that it's fine to have special relationships but it isn't fine to have ones where you aren't allowed to have anything else and also that there's nothing more deadly to a relationship when you are trying desperately not to have it off with anybody else because you feel guilty about it.

Jeffrey: You feel guilty if you do and guilty if you don't, that's the problem.

Bill: I know that it isn't always possible but the idea is not only not to feel guilty if you do, but to feel quite happy about it and about your lover/lovers doing it too. I think this is quite realistic except during that period when you are 'in love', which I think is a hysterical state where you can't even bear for your lover to go to the loo without you going too. But when that's passed I think that being able to have sex with other people is an essential part of your relationships; otherwise, one does, or I do, feel very trapped, feel the sort of heaviness of a conventional marriage.

Jeffrey: I think that lesbians and gay men have been very creative in the sort of relationships they have tried to develop over the last fifteen years – because it's very easy simply to copy the models which we are presented with. The problem is that try as you might to obliterate jealousy, jealousy keeps cropping up – that's certainly my experience. I don't think it's reasonable to expect that you will ever get rid of jealousy or fear or anxiety. What is realistic is that you should not allow these feelings to hamper either your own or your partner's development. I'm beginning to wonder whether a certain amount of agony isn't inseparable from having relationships anyway; that's what relationships are, in fact, and that's the pleasure of them. I think relationships, in the end, are involvement with other people and that does lead to all sorts of tensions and conflict. The illusion that I had and perhaps many others had in the early seventies was that somehow we could reach a blissful state where all tensions and anxieties would not be there and we would be sexually, as well as emotionally, free. That's one of the utopian hopes of the early seventies which it's right to abandon – we should be more realistic, but that does not mean trapping people in relationships which are sterile or unsatisfying.

Bill: There's something I'd like to mention before we go too far away from the halcyon days of the gay movement. I don't know whether it affects anyone else but what happened to me was that for the first time in my adult life I began to feel part of a community. It was the actual feeling that you could walk down Railton Road and go to Brixton and you would meet several gay people in the street who would recognize you and probably kiss you. It's all out there on the street and it's the closest I've ever been and probably the nearest I will ever be to actually feeling part of the world. Like a lot of people in the sort of society we live in, you feel very isolated from everything around you and you don't know the neighbours and you are only barely on speaking terms with the shopkeeper. But what happened to Brixton and it still, to some extent, exists there is a feeling that there are gay people in all these houses and you're probably going to meet them when you go into Woolworths. That was an enormous transformation from the world where you only met gay people at specific times of day in specific places under specific circumstances.

Mark: I can't say that to the same extent, but where I live at the moment I know a lot of people within five minutes' walk and there are ten or fifteen gay people I know who live locally; there are people I can visit without any great effort whatsoever, whom I'm likely to meet in the shops.

Jeffrey: It's also a sort of invisible network. I don't think that it actually needs to be geographically located. I feel part of a London-wide network of lesbian and gay friends. Just by knowing that they exist and knowing that if I went to places whether it's a bookshop or a coffee shop or a pub or the streets of Brixton or Tescos or Budgens in Crouch End you bump into people you know or might know. The interesting thing about it is when Bill's talking he's describing a sort of village atmosphere and, of course, it's a re-creation of a village sort of atmosphere, but it's a village of choice, a community of the mind rather than one you were born into.

There's an interesting historical paradox in the impact of AIDS on the gay community because without the existence of an international gay community I don't think AIDS as a disease could have had the rapid impact it's had on gay men. On the other hand, without the gay community there would not have been the collective response of support which has made it possible for many gay men to live with AIDS or the fear of AIDS. I think the real historical tragedy is that AIDS has emerged just at the moment that the gay community was reaching a sort of maturity and openness. It's a tragedy which will probably set us back a generation. People are already beginning to think of pre- and post-AIDS periods just as we in the seventies grew accustomed to thinking of pre- and post-gay liberation periods. There are two really significant dates in recent lesbian and gay history – 1969–70 with the emergence of the gay movement in America and Europe, and 1980–1 with the emergence of AIDS as a major threat to the health of gay men. What's really moved me over the last three or four years, as AIDS has become a major threat in this country, and especially since spring 1985 with the rising public hysteria about it, is that it's brought out tremendous reserves of strength in lesbians and gay men which show the importance of the achievements of the previous fifteen years.

Mark: I was in a relationship from about 1981 to 1984 and, in a sense, I did not think AIDS affected me very greatly and it was not very high in my consciousness. It was there certainly but, at the same time, I was not willing to think about it and what impact it could have on me. But since the end of that relationship, I have just been very clear – or attempted to be – about what I am going to do sexually and what I am not. In terms of actual support, I think for me personally it's been within a gay men's group. AIDS is an issue which has enabled people to talk to one another and also think about issues which they might otherwise not have thought about – specifically about death at an early age. When I meet people who are HIV positive or who have got AIDS, I am always surprised at how positive they are; it's personally inspiring for me to meet people who have thought out what they are doing about their lives and the changes they have made.

Bill: I was wondering recently what effect the AIDS hysteria has had outside the gay movement and I was talking about it a bit in a pub I use down in Sussex. Obviously, the real nasties, *Sun* readers, are just as they have always been, vile and pretty anti-gay. But other people have voluntarily talked to me about being gay in the context of AIDS. They never would have initiated it before, although they knew I was gay. One of them, the landlord of the pub, got pissed and kissed me on the mouth and talked about the problems of these demarcations – and this is in spite of all the AIDS hysteria. I think there's a possibility of overestimating the negative effect, because one sees newspapers and thinks, 'Oh, my God, they're going to start shooting us at any minute.' It doesn't seem to have had as bad an effect on a lot of people as it might appear – they haven't immediately turned round and gone back to the very worst anti-gay feeling.

Jeffrey: I don't think that it will halt the development of a sense of gay community and, in a way, it makes it more essential that there is a gay community. There's an important element in this crisis and, in a sense, the government's reaction, belated as it is, shows a recognition that the crisis, as it affects gay people, can only be stopped or delayed, deferred or whatever through involvement with the gay community – and that's an odd recognition in this climate.

Bill: It's certainly very odd to see government posters use the words, 'gay or straight'.

Jeffrey: For many people involvement in campaigns around AIDS is having a similar effect to involvement in gay liberation campaigns, in that you get a tremendous sense of common feeling, almost a sort of euphoric sense of working together. I have heard people describe their involvement in AIDS support groups in the same terms as

people used to describe their involvement in the Gay
Liberation Movement.

Mark: In order to combat the spread of AIDS among gay
men specifically there's a need for more communication,
and a greater amount of closeness and explicitness about
issues between us. But at the same time it's wonderful that
the government is recognizing the kind of work that gay
organizations have put into this issue.

Bill: But they are trying to keep it as quiet as possible. Did
you see the poll published in the Sunday newspapers about
public attitudes to AIDS which avoided any reference to the
Terence Higgins Trust or any of the other gay support
groups?

Jeffrey: I think what our discussion shows is the
importance over the last fifteen years, and particularly in the
age of AIDS, of the friendship and support networks which
we have developed. It seems to me that the really critical
thing that has happened since the emergence of the gay
movement is the affirmation of our identity through a sense
of community, through an involvement with each other.
The message I draw from this is that the gay movement is
not ultimately about the liberation of any particular
sexuality but actually about the liberation of a whole set of
relationships; an affirmation of relationships which are
sexual or non-sexual, relationships through which sexuality can be realized or transformed or denied or changed or
just lived. The really important thing is that a public
context for this has now developed and I don't think that
this can be fundamentally changed despite the impact of
AIDS and the revival of the moral right. It's now a
sociological and historical fact that gay men and lesbians
have constructed this dense network of relationships and
communities. We are on the map for keeps.

15 Amnesia and antagonism: anti-lesbianism in the youth service

Val Carpenter

My boss knew he had taken on a lesbian when I was appointed. A straight feminist had brought me out by telling him she 'thought' I was a lesbian. I'd only met her once, so perhaps it was her way of telling me or him or someone else that she was 'in the know'. Whatever her intentions, he turned out to be a good old-fashioned liberal. He called me into his office and proceeded to deliver a very embarrassed speech about how he would support me and anything I might do. I think he expected that to be the end of it, since he continued to be surprised and concerned every time lesbianism came up, in whatever form, over the following seven years.

Sometimes he would interpret my involvement in discussions or groups as me being 'got at' by outside influences. At others, he would simply imply that I was going overboard – not quite being myself. Had he lost his memory? I asked myself that question on many occasions and wondered how I was supposed to refresh his and other people's memories without risking the accusation of going on about it all the time.

I work for a national voluntary youth work agency. My job is to help youth workers develop their work in ways which are relevant and accessible to girls and young women. We – me and the five other women with whom I work – develop resources and printed materials, and get involved in training youth workers. It is a fast-growing area of work. Unfortunately there are still many people who think it is nothing but a fringe event, an extra little treat grafted onto their work without need for fundamental or organizational change. And the organization I work for is a little like that too.

I wasn't there long before things started to happen. My first little skirmish took place over a film, one about rape. It had been purchased by my immediate boss just before she had left to work somewhere else. I therefore inherited the dubious honour of making it available on loan to youth workers.

The film was dreadful. A white middle-class man gave a lecture to American High School students about how to avoid rape, giving demonstrations to some of the young women of how to avoid him raping them. No relevant issues were raised, no acknowledgment that rape is about male power, or even that it is wrong. The message seemed to be that women who are raped are at fault for not having successfully avoided it. Nor was it of much use to youth workers, as what it boiled down to was a couple of blocking techniques, a punch and a bite: a self-appointed, self-defence expert showing off.

I'd seen the film myself in a mixed audience of youth workers, and it had left many of us women upset and shaken. We were critical, and also complained about the audience being mixed. We were slated for our views, and spent the rest of the weekend being ignored or branded as extremists. Most of us who'd complained were lesbians.

I wasn't therefore able to recommend this film when a few months later a woman from Nottingham requested a loan. I explained why. The same afternoon, my departed hetero-sexual colleague, who had bought it, and who had shown it at the conference, was on the phone: would I change my mind? My answer was no, and about an hour later my boss called me into his office to put the pressure on. I never gave in, but within weeks the networks were buzzing with the news that I was into censorship and as bad as Mary Whitehouse.

Sometimes heterosexism is crude. But just as often it's too subtle for you to pinpoint, especially if you're working in liberal organizations with well-intentioned colleagues. Nobody openly pointed to my lesbianism, over the film or subsequently, as the feature causing them problems. It has always been my 'extremism' or my 'unpreparedness to compromise', even though of course I have to compromise all the time.

The irony is that what gave me and other lesbians the ability to develop a fuller understanding of rape at that time (1978) was the very fact that we are lesbians. While heterosexual feminists recognized rape as an important issue, they still had an investment in men, which to some extent meant not upsetting those men too much. It was as difficult for them to develop a public analysis of rape eight years ago as it is for them today publicly to acknowledge the extent of sexual abuse of girls and young women inside and outside the home.

I'm not writing-off all heterosexual feminists. Their position is complex, sometimes contradictory and occasionally uncomfortable. Nor would I dismiss their contributions to the analysis of sexism, or deny the contribution, in my own profession, they have made to the re-emergence of work with young women. But while they gave support and commitment, it was lesbians who were at the forefront of change when the Girls' Work Movement came to life in the late seventies and early eighties. And it was lesbians who, without heterosexual credentials or cover, took the heavy risks and, consequently, the heavy blows. It was our unclouded commitment to women, and greater insistence that the fundamentals of sexism should be tackled without compromise, that brought youth service attention back to the young women who for decades had been excluded by boys and men. Without lesbians there would be no Girls' Work Movement today.

There would also have been no organization to employ me had it not been for our foresisters at the turn of the century. At that time (1911–39) there were girls' clubs all over the country. Many of the organization's leading figures were, and still are, 'spinsters' who 'teamed up with each other' or with women outside the youth work world. These unmarried women were thought to be a good influence on the girls and good role models. There was little room for lesbians to be out in the first half of this century, unless of course they moved in the right literary or aristocratic circles. As a result there was no public discussion of lesbianism and rarely any acknowledgment that these 'splendid', 'dedicated' and strong examples of 'magnificent womanhood' were in fact lesbians.

It was because of this denial of the importance of lesbians and lesbian strength within the organization (by lesbians as much as heterosexual women) that heterosexual women were encouraged to take over key positions. Before too long heterosexual women had in fact taken over and they began to encourage men into the organization and to instigate the mixing of boys and girls into provision previously available to to young women on their own (but preserving the boys' clubs). Men soon outnumbered the heterosexual women in the key positions, and by the sixties the organization had changed in perspective and in name. Single-sex work with girls had not only disappeared. It had become taboo. The single women who hitherto had been considered a good influence on the girls were relegated to obscurity whilst the married heterosexual women were left to emerge as the (acceptable and healthy) role models. Women youth workers, both lesbian and heterosexual, had almost disappeared, and this all in the name of 'fair play for men' which heterosexual women claim, whilst simultaneously denying lesbian energy, strength and commitment.

The emergence of informed lesbian feminist workers in the seventies brought a wave of energy and projects; setting up girls' nights, girls' work conferences, women workers' groups and training events. Our national women youth workers' conferences were widely successful with heterosexual women. They liked the good organization, the atmosphere of safety and support and the well-run crèches we'd organized mainly for their benefit. (At that time the lesbians involved in the organizations of the conferences had all long since made positive decisions to be child-free.) They joined in our events for young women, and devoured our publications, because it gave them the springboard for taking action themselves. Most of all they enjoyed the space we created for them to get on and do their work in relative peace.

However, heterosexual women still complain that lesbian workers are 'too threatening', we're 'too exclusive' and we're always 'pushing lesbianism down their throats'. Perhaps the biggest insult of all is when they claim that we've taken over girls' work!

Meanwhile it is male colleagues who have largely benefited from this anti-lesbianism. Not always content to watch from the sidelines, some of them have joined in with their more confident brand of anti-lesbianism. The result has been a consolidation of their power as men, over heterosexual women and lesbians, within the work, and the organization.

Work with girls continues to be undermined and marginalized because ultimately it is the boys – well, the heterosexual ones – who count. Single sex work with girls and young women ruffles the feathers and produces a frantic and strident response, a response that can also be physically aggressive and violent. The platform of this abuse is inevitably anti-lesbianism.

All young women who attend girls' nights at their youth centre, or who go to girls' days and weekends, and every woman youthworker involved (whether in single-sex or mixed settings) is likely to get labelled a lesbian. This is enough, it would seem, to precipitate the verbal and physical abuse which follows. Heterosexism ensures that the gut reaction of every heterosexual woman and young woman, as well as many lesbian workers and young lesbians, is to deny the 'accusation' – for that is certainly what it is meant to be. We've all got a lot to lose: our jobs, friends, respect and our safety. In the end it's our integrity and knowledge that the pay-off isn't big enough which stops many lesbians from colluding. A few heterosexuals struggle, mainly unsuccessfully, not to be anti-lesbian themselves and against the desire to render their own position safe.

In any case, virtually no heterosexual feminists have an analysis of heterosexism, which would enable them to deny they are lesbians without making it seem as if they are happy not to be. So, in making their denials, they often make unseemly proclamations about their own hetero-sexuality, in the worst cases (only too common) dis-associating themselves from 'radical feminists' (read lesbians) and presenting themselves as the ones who are the reasonable moderates. And there are many others who simply remain silent in the face of overt anti-lesbian comments.

Male power, both in male colleagues and in the boys using the clubs, is increased by the lack of a concerted resistance to this anti-lesbianism. As soon as any woman gets a bit uppity, or any two or more women or young women want to spend time together, or even if we just plain disagree with the men or boys, the ultimate sanction can be applied: call her a lesbian – that will soon bring her back into line. And it all too often does.

While nothing is challenged, nothing is changed. Anti-lesbianism controls all women's lives and the result in youth work with young women is that lesbians and young lesbians are presented as the unreasonable and unacceptable face of the work. Meanwhile, with our ideas and work dismissed, heterosexual women colleagues are welcomed as the ones who can provide the model of acceptable girls' work.

While this struggle has been in the making, gay men in youth work have remained silent. Perhaps they have been fearful that supporting lesbian colleagues would mean they too would have to come out. They may have been reluctant to lose the tenuous support and camaraderie of heterosexual men and women who think of them as safe. Or they could be afraid of the implications girls' work might have for their own work. Whatever the reason, gay men have never united to take action or develop work with young people which challenges heterosexism – or sexism for that matter. They probably fear that coming out and working around issues of sexuality would leave them vulnerable to accusations of paedophilia (child sexual abuse by any other name). It's something both they and lesbians have always been blamed for, despite the now well-publicized fact that it is heterosexual men who commit by far the most assaults on boys, as well as girls. In addition, it is an unfortunate fact that some gay men *are* paedophiles, however few in comparison with heterosexual men. For all these reasons, their fears in this respect as youth workers are based on the realities of heterosexism.

Some gay men are out to their colleagues, especially perhaps to heterosexual women, while remaining in the closet with the young people with whom they work. But the absence of an analysis; of sexism and heterosexism has rendered them unable to develop any anti-heterosexist perspectives within their work. Such inaction provides an ideal foil which leaves their assumed image of heterosexuality intact. Such pacts of silence with heterosexuals inevitably work against the challenges to heterosexism being made by lesbians. Thus lesbians are left to challenge the oppression alone. In doing so, we have to come out every day and, once we're out, it's on our record for life. In the absence of an analysis of heterosexism, heterosexuals can (and do) reduce our gayness or lesbianism to just living with someone of the same sex, thus enabling them to remove the possibility of challenge from our relationships with them. It's our work around heterosexism which makes a direct and daily challenge to them, and in a sense this work is a pure act of coming out in that it no longer allows them to treat us as one of the girls (or boys) who is really just like them.

We make daily decisions about whether or not to say, whether or not to interrupt the assumptions being made about our presumed heterosexuality. We weigh up the risks and possible repercussions of each and every situation. We come out to colleagues who, like my boss, know but seem to lose their memory with annoying regularity. We constantly come across situations where colleagues treat us as if we were just raising points of sexuality to be difficult, or as a piece of axe-grinding. We know, and they know, that if we were not on the project, in the meeting, or in any way involved, the issue of sexuality would simply be entirely glossed over. In short lesbians and gay men are assumed to influence young people over their sexuality, whilst heterosexuals assume themselves to be neutral.

In many ways we've come full circle: in the early days of lesbian feminism, lesbian theorists demonstrated that anti-lesbianism is the most intense form of woman-hating. After several years of thinking of sexism and heterosexism as different forms of oppression, we've come back to seeing them as inextricably linked. In fact it has been mainly the lesbians in the girls' work movement who have been developing a determination to make the links between all oppressions, and who have become very clear about the need for that work to be accessible to *all* young women.

When we were first creating the model for girls' work, those of us who are white, both lesbian and heterosexual, developed work that was racist, that is, based on our ideas about how sexism affected white girls, and what kind of provision white girls might need. During our efforts to spread our ideas about girls' work we encountered much anti-lesbianism, while at the same time we began to be challenged about our racism by Black women, among whom were some out Black lesbians. It was during this period of considerable stress and pressure that we began to move towards a multi-oppression analysis as a basis for training and for the work.

But of course, it wasn't quite as simple as that. Much of the confrontation around oppressions arose through the national women youth worker conferences, which, as I have already mentioned, were predominantly organized by lesbians. However, getting agreement at the planning meetings that we could have lesbian-only workshop space was hard work. So was dealing with the repercussions when we distributed the finally agreed programme. On two consecutive years the venue, one used for many conferences, tried to cancel our booking. Meanwhile individuals and organizations also wrote to my boss complaining. Some employers tried to make potential participants swear allegiance to heterosexuality before they would pay their conference fee. Many heterosexual women stayed away specifically because there would be out lesbians there.

Most of the problems found their way to me. My boss again felt I was being influenced by outside 'extremists'. He wanted to withdraw our organization's financial support for the conference, and tried to discourage me from remaining involved. I thought it unlikely that it would come to a showdown about me being a lesbian, but felt clear that the chances of being disciplined were high. The pressure was on.

There seemed nowhere to take discussions of these dilemmas except to the conferences' lesbian workshops, where they took up almost all the time. Any time left over was spent on the heterosexism we were experiencing from heterosexual women at the conferences. However, we never put heterosexism itself on the conference agenda, nor did we ask heterosexual participants to discuss it.

But after two years of such conferences, things began to change. All the women in the conference planning group had so far been white, and we were only just beginning to respond to Black women's demands that we examine our racism, and tackle it. The following conferences did place racism on the agenda, and all white participants were expected to take it seriously. Our fear was that not to focus solely on racism would mean it slipping onto the edges of our concerns once again. In our attempts to take racism seriously we denied the importance of heterosexism by allowing it to remain excluded from the agenda. It was then very hard to come back to it. We didn't yet know how to challenge the anti-lesbianism from the very heterosexual colleagues we depended on, or indeed how to challenge heterosexual Black women's anti-lesbianism whilst maintaining a challenge to racism. Meanwhile the anti-lesbianism from our organizations and from heterosexual workers did not abate. As white lesbians, because of our racism, we had not been able to work out a joint analysis of heterosexism with Black lesbian workers, because we had no knowledge of the implications and ramifications of heterosexism in their lives. In short, our singular approach and our racism, along with heterosexuals' inability to take heterosexism seriously, combined to close down the possibility to focus on heterosexism at these conferences in a generalized way.

There followed a period of reassessment – one that was widespread among feminists in general – through which we examined oppressions and questions of priorities and hierarchies, something we are still centrally concerned with. In girls' work, for example, we began to learn from our experiences and commit ourselves to ensuring that facilities were genuinely available also to Jewish young women – that we tackled anti-Semitism; that young women with disabilities were not excluded, and that we looked at our oppressive attitudes to disability and the institutions in which these were enshrined. Our increasing understanding of heterosexism brought many of us to realize the importance of diversity in our training work – taking a multi-oppression approach.

It was by placing racism and heterosexism, along with sexism, at the centre of my training work that helped me stop being nervous about challenging heterosexism. Whilst I worked only daring to place sexism at centre stage, it was difficult to give racism its rightful place in our considerations. In fact it would keep slipping off the agenda. But if it was difficult to keep racism on it, it was impossible to even breathe the word heterosexism. We'd been playing safe for our own survival, and scores of heterosexuals went unchallenged in their continued acts of heterosexism. But everyone was left feeling dissatisfied, because everyone knew, or feared, there was more to this than they were letting on. People were left feeling disconnected from sexism until we made all oppressions centre-stage. It was only then that people were able to make the connections to their own lives and their other experiences of oppression, and how different oppressions overlap and intervene.

It has made it easier for participants in training courses to understand the concept of oppression, to recognize oppressive attitudes and behaviour, and to identify oppressions which may be new to them: heterosexism is often a new concept to heterosexuals. It's touching at their core because it helps them to recognize and understand their own experience of oppression, or what life must be like for their own sister, brother, mother or a member of the youth club. It creates the possibility for them to meet the lesbian or gay man inside who may be trying to get out. It's helping them to understand the immense pressures on them to stay forever in the closet. Just as important, gay men are beginning to recognize other connections as they come to understand male sexual abuse and male violence, whilst white lesbians are making the connections with their racism.

So our gains in youth work have been marked by surges of confidence based on a developing analysis. We have been able to take on increasingly risky campaigns and projects. At first it was difficult enough to claim single-sex space for girls (and maintaining it still isn't easy), and to challenge the male resistance and violence that often ensued. More recently it has meant developing a sex education practice for all youth workers which means avoiding heterosexual assumptions and presenting lesbianism as a positive option, something which sticks in the throat of many workers. It has led to the establishment of a network of groups for young gays and lesbians. And we are developing our work so that it meets the needs of incest survivors.

Despite the growth of our work and our self-esteem, we still remain marginalized and at risk. We've created so much space for heterosexual women workers to carry out projects, and yet up till now they have not returned the compliment. It's not unusual on girls' weekends or at women workers' conferences for them to be demonstrative with each other, or with the young women, while we remain caught in the straight-jacket of frigidity while we are in the public eye. It remains perfectly acceptable for heterosexual women to enjoy the benefits of relaxing in an all-women atmosphere, even kissing and hugging with other women, while dropping Tom, Dick or Harry into conversation as convenient. But as soon as any lesbians stand 'too close' to each other, or to them, they get jumpy. All lesbians are familiar with this response. We recognize their resistance to having our lesbianism made as public as they make their heterosexuality. It is difficult to relax with them, and even with each other, under such circumstances, perhaps especially in those 'social' events where we have a perfect right to do so, events which we ourselves have organized.

This catalogue of pressures and constraints is not the entire story of my life as a lesbian involved in work with girls and young women. It's the part that can be told in an article which is tracing some of the effects of heterosexism. Just to give a flavour of the more joyful side: as a result of so many of us being out and being there, many other women workers, and many young women have come to feel that the time was right for them too, that they too have lesbian potential.

Some have come out there and then, while others have waited until later, like Ruth at a club I once worked in. She and her best friend cried when they heard I was leaving for another job. I'd had them sussed for ages and had been encouraging them to articulate their growing awareness of their lesbianism. I told them not to worry, that I was sure I'd

see them again – on the scene. They seemed delighted that
I'd said it, and to know just what I meant. Four years later I
saw Ruth – on the scene.

I know some young women rightly feel that they came
out as a result of their own strength – and of course many of
them do come out without any youth work involvement.
But ideas and structures don't come from nowhere, and nor
does strength. What we've helped to provide is the backdrop
that makes it possible for today's girls to grow into young
women, and into women, confident in their lesbianism.

Epilogue

Throughout its life of eight years, myth building
encouraged people to think of the unit as being on the
margins of the organization.

The organization fostered and developed such myths
because they were then freed from having to take on board
the understandings and implications of carrying out the
work. However, a multi-oppression approach demonstrated
to youth workers once and for all the importance of making
the connections, and that Girls' Work *is* Youth Work. This
was too much of a threat to the rest of the work of the
organization which is rooted in competition and activities.

Four months after this article was written the unit
focusing on girls and young women was closed down by the
management of the national organization, and we all lost
our jobs.

16 Lesbian mothers – the fight for child custody

Sue Allen and Lynne Harne

This piece has been written by two white lesbian mothers, and records some of the history of our struggles in the seventies and first half of the eighties, both struggling for political recognition within the feminist movement, and in surviving under male supremacy.

It reflects two particular experiences, both of which have common threads, but which are also different. We do not claim to recount the many different experiences that other lesbian mothers may have had, coming from different places, or also having to deal with racism and able-bodied-ism.

However, amongst the most crucial issues for all lesbian mothers is the fact that male supremacy states that lesbians should not be permitted to bring up children, or, where this is permitted under limited circumstances, that it should only be in a manner that allows for male control to continue. For both of us, at the crux of the matter has been our experience as lesbian feminists and separatists (as far as one can be a separatist and a mother, and still survive in this world – which isn't very far) struggling to bring up our daughters in a world which is totally hostile to us.

We are perceived to be directly challenging the authority of the father and the system of male control, by wanting to bring up our children without men. It must, therefore, seem contradictory that we are writing for a 'mixed' gay book, when we feel we have little in common with gay men, or with the sexual politic which is centred around the freedom of sexual practice – of whatever variety – and which is often fundamentally anti-feminist. Further, gay men have shown little interest and given little support over the issue of the oppression of lesbian mothers.

However, as lesbian feminists we have few opportunities to express our views or record our struggles. We do not have access to the relative wealth of the male gay community, and we have largely remained invisible. We are becoming increasingly marginalized as extreme even within the confines of the 'lesbian and gay alliance' which has grown up over the past few years. We therefore feel it is important to write down some of our herstory and particularly to demonstrate why our struggles, from fairly early on, have been located within the Women's Liberation Movement rather than within Gay Liberation. It is important that it is recorded, before it can be said that it never happened, or before it is forgotten. Furthermore, any collection of contributions about lesbian and gay concerns would be seriously lacking without information about this crucial part of lesbians' struggle.

We also hope this piece may contribute to the understanding and struggles of other lesbian mothers, so that the wheel does not have to be constantly reinvented.

Of course, there have always been lesbians bringing up children, but because being a lesbian has so frequently been hidden, this has contributed to the notion of rarity.

In 1976, in one of the few lesbian custody cases which have been reported in a law journal, a judge commented on how 'rare' it was for a child to be growing up in a lesbian household, and how he was treading in 'uncharted waters'. Needless to say, he gave custody to the father. Growing up in the fifties and sixties, however, some of us can remember children being brought up by two 'aunties', women who we realized later to be lesbians. Whatever the herstory of those generations of lesbian mothers who preceded us, it is clear that there was little opportunity to speak or write about it – or, if there was, such writing has been suppressed and we have no access to it.

In the late sixties and early seventies, with the newly-emerging second wave of twentieth-century feminism, being a lesbian mother was still a difficult and isolating experience, even where custody was not a problem. We know from what we are learning from older lesbians that many of them 'waited out' marriages, which they felt as young women they had no real option to avoid, until the children were adolescent, and then began their lives as lesbians. Others kept up the appearance of heterosexual family life, while secretly relating to women all the while, so great was the pressure to appear heterosexual – and married.

Although the lesbian custody issue began to highlight the existence of lesbian mothers in the mid-seventies, the difficulties that all our predecessors experienced, and also the difficulties of our own generation who are lesbian mothers but have not had to fight specifically for custody, have remained largely hidden.

Even where a lesbian mother does have custody of her children – either because the father does not want them living with him, or because he does not know about the mother being a lesbian – there is the constant fear that until the child is sixteen the father may turn round one day and go for custody. For those of us who had no immediate custody problems, but where the father had access, there has always been the painful undermining of our lesbianism and feminism that the father perpetrates on the child, turning them against us at the most opportune moments. There have also been the threats of violence and constant verbal harassment if we don't give in to their demands.

Also there are the ways in which we are constantly undermined by the social institutions we are forced to relate to as mothers. From an early age our children have been confronted with and confused by anti-lesbianism at school by both teachers and pupils. Even today there are probably very few lesbian mothers who feel able to be out to the school. Where the health services know we are lesbians, our children's health problems have been blamed on our lesbianism, implying that if there was a man around, our children would not get ill!

Our refusal to present ourselves as 'normal', or to imitate the heterosexual nuclear family pattern with our children, has created further problems with the social institutions. At the beginning of the seventies there were few women with whom to share all this – fortunately, this situation has now much changed. The accounts which follow illustrate the politicization of some of these struggles: there are, however, many issues we still do not feel safe to discuss publicly. Lesbian mothers still face harassment from many different quarters and the possibility of losing custody solely for being a lesbian is still very much with us. Furthermore, judges are still making court orders preventing lesbian mothers and their children from having any contact with lovers or with lesbian friends.

At present there is a strong 'back to the family' movement which aims to put the authoritarian father back into his 'rightful' place, and this includes the rise in propaganda for 'parents' rights' in determining what can be learnt at school – that is, *only* ideas about heterosexual family life, with all alternatives again suppressed. Such a movement seems to have strong adherents in all the major political parties. This is bound to make the struggles and survival of lesbian feminist mothers increasingly difficult.

Sue Allen: 1972-8: how it started

The history of lesbian mothers searching each other out for support has its origins in the hostility of a society which finds us, rather than its own hypocrisy, a problem. Since this society is set up to promote and protect heterosexuality and the heterosexual family (just watch the TV ads for an hour), it has particular difficulty dealing with the notion of lesbians bearing and/or parenting children. Nowhere is this prejudice more clearly shown than within the legal processes around custody cases, processes which have ramifications outside as well as inside the court.

There have probably been custody cases involving lesbians for a very long time, but to my recollection it was a case that began to go through the court process in 1972, and didn't finish until 1975, which started some of us thinking about taking collective action. This was the first time, I think, that lesbianism as an issue in a custody case was taken up in a big way by the media, and it also concerned a woman quite well known in London's Women's Liberation Movement. Until this time, for one reason or another, we'd been silenced and isolated, kept in line by the courts' view of us as 'unfit mothers'. Any lesbian applying for custody would automatically be advised by her solicitor to disguise herself as heterosexually inclined, and to suppress any feminist leanings. So until this case was publicized, we were living our lives under the threat and bias of the law which is dominated by men and institutionalizes anti-lesbian prejudice.

Nowadays there exists a supportive and efficient network of advice and friendship, although that bias has not by any means fundamentally changed. But setting this up hasn't been easy, and we have experienced considerable anguish as well as joy in choosing our directions. As with all oppressions, the burden of responsibility in seeking change has rested on those most affected: lesbian mothers themselves. It has been hard graft both organizing politically, and in our homes raising our children, against unremitting opposition and with little help from those we might have thought ourselves to be in alliance with.

Broadly speaking, the gay pride movement of 1970–3 was the only forum in which lesbians could express their identity. Lesbians already in the Women's Liberation Movement – still then in its early stages in Britain – did not find that their identity as such was endorsed there until considerably later. During that period politically active lesbians found themselves in either one or the other of the two groupings, with little contact between the two. The Gay Liberation Movement enabled many of us to meet, come out, connect up politically and make a public presence. But the overriding sense was that it was good to be gay: it was our gay rather than our lesbian selves that was affirmed. In the male-dominated movement, lesbianism became submerged beneath the gay male identity and incorporated into an overall gay image. Lesbians found we could not raise our own issues or develop our own identity. Meanwhile in the Women's Liberation Movement we were affirmed as women: we put our efforts into issues we saw as affecting the lives of all women, like equal pay and abortion, domestic violence and childcare facilities.

For me what the early years of the seventies meant was that lesbians in both movements were starting to ask where they should put their energy as lesbians, and where their identities lay. I was asking myself how my feminism affected my working with men – gay or straight – and how lesbian strength could become acknowledged as such in the women's movement.

I was already a mother, but through those years the issues of lesbian parenting were totally peripheral. We simply suffered the situation in silence without recognizing the political significance of our position.

Spring 1974 brought the first lesbian conference, held in Canterbury. It signified a coming together of lesbianism and feminism: lesbians were leaving the Gay Liberation Movement en masse, dissatisfied with male control. Later that year saw the women's liberation conference in Edinburgh, where the discussion around the 'sixth demand' emphasizing women's right to determine their own sexuality, became a crucial stepping-stone towards lesbian feminist politics. From then on we were more confident to talk about ourselves, and think about who we are in the world. We began to discover things we had in common: some of us were lesbians, feminists *and* mothers. The significance of this was soon to take on a concrete reality.

During 1975 there were three notorious anti-lesbian custody judgments, all involving women we by then knew or knew about. Subsequently an article was published in the *Guardian* highlighting the anti-lesbian bias of the courts. In late 1975 a group of us met in London and formed Action for Lesbian Parents (ALP). The first meeting was huge: forty women came. But even at that very first discussion I could tell there would be a serious political split. Half the women wanted to campaign around specifically lesbian custody cases whilst the other half wanted to make it a matter for women in general. This was partly because your feminism, whatever your sexuality, was now part of the court's method of branding you unfit for custody. But mainly, I am sure, it was because some lesbians were nervous to name the campaign as a lesbian one knowing there was so little support for us around. At the end of the meeting we had divided into two distinct groups. The 'generalized' campaign, in fact, never got off the ground, and the other became Action for Lesbian Parents.

We were a variety of women, all lesbians, some mothers. Only two of us were experiencing actual custody troubles at the time, but we all felt equally threatened and equally outraged at what was happening in the courts. We were a small but very active group. We formed a telephone link for isolated lesbian mothers, and for those going through the courts. We gave talks, set up a symposium, and responded to pressures from solicitors and barristers to find evidence showing how children fared psychologically being raised by lesbians. We became involved with radical British and American psychologists to produce this 'evidence', and there were even pieces in the Sunday papers about how our children grow up 'normal' (as the media saw it).

Meanwhile, and equally effectively, our presence as lesbian mothers became very visible within the Women's Liberation Movement. From now on, and this was in the heyday of conferences, there were always workshops on the issues of lesbian custody, on the raising of boy children, and on the difficulties mothers have in attending conferences, let alone social events. In those days there was very little input on the need for crèches. The women who came to such workshops were mainly lesbian mothers and our discussions would often bring up the fact that we got so little support from our sisters.

Although the issue of motherhood had wide implications for all feminists, many women felt it was the last role they wanted to play, and saw it as standing in the way of everything liberation would mean: independence and freedom from imposed roles as women. Women would often say, 'I've never chosen to be involved with children,' the implication being that we had, so it was our problem. Another response was that they did not want to put energy into our children when they had no real power in the relationship. It is true that mothers are powerful through their ultimate responsibility for their children's lives, but we felt it was hard to share that responsibility in a climate where it seemed impossible to get discussion going about what raising children involves or means. Nor was the issue of seeing children outside the context of 'possessions' ever really raised, or perhaps most importantly, how to bring children into a future that is not bound up with the nuclear family and all the oppression that places upon women.

Throughout 1975-8 we attempted to raise these matters,

and the central concern of lesbian custody, at conferences throughout the country. During early 1978 the media again brought lesbian motherhood into the forefront of the news. The *London Evening News* printed an 'exposé' concerning lesbians acquiring artificial insemination by donor, a story they built up by using a journalist pretending to be a lesbian wanting to become pregnant, seeking help and support from lesbian groups. Their attitude to lesbian pregnancy, the sensationalist presentation of the story, and their exposure of vulnerable lesbians they had tricked, infuriated much of the London lesbian community. ALP and other women staged a sit-in at the newspaper's offices and demanded (successfully) the right to reply. We subsequently lost a complaint to the Press Council who deemed the paper's journalistic methods acceptable. There were other related responses: the journalist had her home spray-painted, and pro-lesbian slogans appeared in Parliament Square, at the law courts and, where it can still be seen faintly today, outside the British Medical Association, from whence some hostile quotes had emerged. One woman was arrested and later convicted for spray-painting the newspaper's delivery vans: her court case was also the scene of a huge and lively picket. All these events regalvanized activity around our issues and brought them to a much wider public.

However, they caused a turning point for ALP. Firstly, it caused a serious rift in the group. Half the members felt that using ALP's name as a key one for the action of the sit-in was a suitable political stance, both in advertising our existence and supporting those lesbians who were having artificial insemination. The other half wanted ALP to remain in the background focusing on research and maintaining a respectable front for future contacts with the courts and the media. We parted company. The first group kept up the telephone link, the second group pursued research. Secondly, artificial insemination (AID as it was then called) became a serious possibility for lesbians and the whole issue became a topic of discussion and action within the lesbian feminist movement and supportive self-help insemination groups were formed, out of which new networks of lesbian mothers soon began to flourish.

Lyne Harne: 1978–87: the continuing story

Although I have been a lesbian, a mother and a feminist since 1971 I found few possibilities to talk with other lesbians with children about our situation or our identity as lesbian mothers until almost ten years later.

In the early lesbian feminist movement of the seventies it felt as if you were not a real lesbian if you had children. There was still the idea around that a real lesbian was one who had never been in a heterosexual relationship. There was also, and still is, the idea that having children is anti-feminist and against our current interests as lesbians – that having children drains us from organizing our own lives. Although this is a concept I can feel a lot of sympathy with, it does not and did not allow for those of us who had children because we felt at the time that there were no other options open to us: it was just what women did, and because we did not know any better. Also at that time lesbians making the choice to have children as out lesbians through self-insemination or through artificial insemination by donor (AID) did not seem a possibility.

So as a lesbian throughout the seventies having a child was something I often kept quiet about in both the lesbian and feminist movements. (As Sue has mentioned, the lesbian and feminist movements did not seem to come together until the mid-seventies, when, after the Edinburgh conference of 1974, we became a recognized force within the Women's Liberation Movement, many lesbians by this time having disaffected from the gay movement.) When I had problems over childcare, or the school, or with the child's father it was not something I felt I could raise as a political issue, or ask support for. I felt I had no right to ask for support, because I had stupidly brought it all on myself.

I had support and commitment on a long-term basis from an individual lesbian, in terms of sharing childcare, and occasionally from others who were around at the time. But it felt that on the one hand I was a lesbian and on the other I was a mother, and that being a mother was my own problem and politically un-right-on. I also knew very few lesbians with girls of my daughter's age. This was important to me since I needed to know and meet other lesbians with children, and it would also have been important to her in terms of validating our lifestyle.

Looking back, the change appeared to come at the beginning of the eighties and from two different directions. More lesbian mothers were coming out in the lesbian feminist context as mothers, and demanding better childcare facilities at conferences and meetings. This was no doubt helped by the existence of organizations such as Action for Lesbian Parents. Also more lesbian mothers were openly fighting custody battles for children as lesbians. In fact the lesbian movement appeared to have gained such strength that there were lesbians – especially in London – who were surprised that you could still lose your children on grounds of your sexuality.

From the other direction some lesbians had been having children through self-insemination (SI) and AID from the late seventies. They could afford to be more open as lesbian mothers since there was no father around to claim custody of their children. However they too were affected by the hostility they began to meet from the heterosexual world, and there are situations other than custody where the 'authorities' continually try to intervene; for example, if you have a child with disability, or if you choose to live with your child with a lesbian who *is* involved in a custody case. However, the existence of SI/AID lesbian mothers did mean more women being able to campaign more openly.

In 1981, for the first time, I began to meet other lesbians who described themselves as lesbian mothers. Now I could talk about all the previously internalized oppression which I'd had to hide from the heterosexual world and to a certain extent from the lesbian community itself. In 1981 there had been a large workshop of lesbian mothers at the National Lesbian Conference. A week later there was a conference in Edinburgh on feminist childcare practice, which was largely attended by lesbian mothers. One of the most significant things about this conference was that daughters of lesbian mothers had their own workshop.

After this, networks of lesbian mothers began to develop up and down the country, and there was also a lesbian mothers' newsletter. The following summer, in 1982, there was a lesbian mothers' holiday organized at the women's holiday centre at Oaklands (Hereford/Wales border). We began to raise issues like the heterosexism we were having to deal with from schools and other institutions like the health services, as well as supporting the growing number of out lesbians losing custody of their children. What we were doing was creating support for each other and also what in the old days would have been called consciousness-raising. It was also crucially important that our children could meet each other, and could share their experiences.

For me the whole political implication of lesbian mothers losing custody, and understanding how this was an attack on all of us as lesbians, only became clear when friends became involved in custody disputes and then lost custody themselves. It was apparent that the idea of lesbians bringing up children without any direct male control was untenable to male supremacy, both in terms of the example we were setting – showing that men are not necessary – and in terms of their fears that we might subvert our children (if only we could!). The phenomenon known as male-bonding became very obvious as judges, lawyers, welfare officers and fathers united together in custody cases. Furthermore some heterosexual feminists (sometimes lovers of the custody-seeking male, sometimes in other roles) were giving (and still give) evidence against lesbian mothers in their efforts to gain male approval. There were socialist men, and their socialist feminist lovers, fighting lesbian mothers for custody through the courts and using the mother's lesbianism as the reason why she should not have the children.

In order to challenge the state of affairs where probably 90 per cent of lesbian mothers were losing custody, they needed much more support, and much more information about what might come up in a custody case. Also there needed to be much better legal representation. Many lesbian mothers had homophobic lawyers. Even where they'd used feminist lawyers, these had sometimes turned out to be ignorant of the issues. In addition, there needed to be a higher profile of the oppression facing lesbian mothers both within and outside the women's movement. All these matters had been raised in the seventies by lesbian mothers, and there had been little progress. It seemed important to try again: now the lesbian movement had grown substantially within feminism, there were more lesbian mothers able to make their presence felt, and there were a few lesbian feminist lawyers prepared to give their support.

In early 1983 a lesbian custody conference was held in the north of England, planned jointly by a northern group of lesbian mothers with lesbian lawyers, and other lesbian mothers and lesbians without children from London. At the same time, Rights of Women (ROW), a feminist legal workers' organization, had been approached by the London group to set up a lesbian custody group. They wanted this to research, advise and campaign, and also to liaise with lesbian mothers' groups and with any national campaign that might be set up. The idea was to get the project funded by the Greater London Council (GLC), and to employ a full-time worker. It would provide a legal resource for lesbian mothers facing a custody or access dispute, and would set up a referral list of well-informed feminist lawyers around the country.

The northern conference was attended by over a hundred women, many of whom were lesbian mothers, some of whom had already lost custody of their children. Although this conference was fraught with the pain of those who had lost their children, or who were going through the courts, there seemed to be an overall sense of gaining strength as a group, and being able to move forward. From this conference more local groups and support networks were set up.

The following year a film (*Breaking the Silence*) was made about lesbian custody which was shown on Channel 4 television both in 1985 and during the 'gay season' of films in 1987, bringing in many more inquiries. It involved much work from women who courageously came out on film, and their children, and many others who could not participate so openly.

In June 1983 the ROW Lesbian Custody Project got its funding from the GLC Women's Committee. It began some research to detail the experience of lesbians going through custody disputes. The project sent out detailed question-naires to lesbians who had been through, or were going through, the courts. It published its report in a booklet, *Lesbian Mothers on Trial*, based on the experience of thirty-six women, and it makes depressing reading. It made clear that there had been little change in the attitudes of the courts between 1974 and 1984. It also amply illustrated the intense discrimination experienced by lesbian mothers who are out, from institutions such as schools and the health service.

Nowadays the oppression of lesbian mothers, and the discrimination suffered by their children, is firmly on the agenda of the lesbian feminist movement, even if support is patchy. But custody issues themselves still do not attract much attention. A few more lesbians are winning custody, but many are not. The Lesbian Custody Project continues to receive many phone calls a week for legal advice and support. The Project has also published a legal handbook for lesbian mothers which gives legal advice on custody, the importance of making wills, adoption and fostering and many other issues of concern to lesbian mothers.

Future funding is uncertain, but it seems that the Project will keep going as a lesbian feminist advice and referral agency. Meanwhile, support groups and networks are growing and there are lesbian mothers' discos and holidays. It also seems as if daughters of lesbian mothers may be beginning to organize their own support networks. They produced their first newsletter from London in 1987.

At the lesbian mothers' conference held in 1986, the idea of a charter setting out some basic demands was adopted. This could then be discussed widely; for example, it could be presented to social service departments. It calls for an end to discrimination against lesbian mothers, for the same rights for lesbians to foster and adopt as heterosexuals, rights for lesbian co-parents, an end to the myth of the normal family, and for recognition of the particular discriminations towards working-class lesbian mothers, those who are Black, and those who have disabilities.

The future is uncertain. A charter would enable a campaign to present more publicly the issue of lesbian mothers' 'rights'. But at present the government is making an all-out attack on lesbians and gays, and many Labour-led local authorities are backing down on their manifesto commitments for fear of losing votes. This in turn has led to a new alliance of lesbians and gays, and lesbian feminist issues are becoming once more submerged in some current campaigns. However, we have learnt a great deal about our issues: whatever the pressures, from the right, from the left, or within mixed struggles, we will not again allow the issue of lesbian custody to become lost.

17 Parrot cries

Andrew Lumsden

Jacquitta used to work behind the bar of that pub beloved of
Daily Mirror journalists. I've forgotten its real name. It was
always referred to as the Stab, short for the Stab in the Back.
She was of South American origin, I suppose. There were
tales of her having been on the crew of a tramp steamer and
then there she was, for thirty years, the life and soul of the
Stab. The landlord retired and she retired too. She went to
live with the editor of the *Daily Mirror*.

He had a little house in an Earls Court mews where I'd
been visiting for three years when the sixties ended. It
became 1970 and Gay Liberation Front came to Britain and
I was twenty-nine. I'd been out for only two years. I'd been a
Fleet Street journalist since I was twenty-one and by then
was on *The Times*. Also living with the editor of the *Daily
Mirror* in his Earls Court house at the end of the sixties,
when I came to know them all, was his wife Sheila, another
journalist, who wrote in her maiden name of Sheila Black.
She had written to the editor of the *Financial Times* in the
early sixties pointing out that though women spend vast
sums in retailing, and since the Victorian age have been
managing their own property, the paper had no women
writers on the great industries.

An amused editor, Gordon, now Sir Gordon, Newton,
gave her an interview and hired her on trial. By the mid-
sixties she was a star of the paper. Her style was and is
unmistakable, conversational and direct. At first, until
Newton forbade it, the sub-editors 'corrected' her.

We had become very close and it was to see her that I was

in and out of the house. Lee Howard – that was her husband's name, the editor of the *Daily Mirror* – was usually at the *Mirror* offices in Holborn till all hours, but sometimes he was at home. And one day I tackled him about gays. You must picture an enormous man. Six feet four, or something of that sort, in height, twenty stone or thereabouts in weight, a White Russian by ancestry, an on-board bomber photographer during the war, a great Buddha of a man with grey locks, and generally, when at home, in a flowered caftan for comfort, which Sheila had made him. The growling voice of a giant. The growl too of a man who habitually sat whether in Earls Court or at his office with an open box of a hundred cigarettes, a soda siphon and a bottle of whisky, all of which he got through each day. Except that I never heard him foul-mouthed, he was a piece of Hollywood dream-casting as a newspaper editor.

The *Mirror*, then, was the largest-selling daily newspaper in Britain, perhaps in the western world, as it had been for years. The *Sun*, under Rupert Murdoch, wasn't to overtake it till 1976. The *Mirror* always campaigned for Labour at general elections and saw the Labour Party and the trade unions as the natural allies of the 'ordinary folk', its readers. This was despite the fact that a man like Lee Howard and the *Mirror*'s owners, his bosses – Robert Maxwell wouldn't be the owner for another generation – were as courted by Harold Wilson and the other Labour leaders as Tories in the media are courted today by Mrs Thatcher. Just as the Tory media are today as often as not scathing in private about Mrs Thatcher and her Cabinet, even though in public they generally support them politically, so the *Mirror* people would often despair of Wilson, but rally to Labour in a public crisis.

So there I sat on the sofa one evening in the Earls Court living-room while Sheila made a meal for the three of us in the kitchen, she and I with a glass of champagne each, he with his Scotch seated in an immense winged red armchair. To one side of him on her perch sat Jacquita the parrot, scarlet and emerald, dreaming of South American forests, of cargo-boats, of the Stab, where for so long she'd been a vaudeville turn and an inducement to charitable donations. She had – for at last she did turn up her claws, seventy years old if she was a day – two specialities. One was an imitation of the bronchitic old landlord of the Stab. She would do this if she was alone in the room and wanted someone to come and pay attention. You heard a ghastly sobbing, hacking, gurgling cough and breath drawn in like the last breath ever drawn in the world and you rushed, if you hadn't been warned, expecting to have to summon police, ambulances, priests. Her other turn, which she might do when you were sitting there, was a whistle of unimaginable volume, a ship's siren. Your ears so ringing that you could hardly find your balance to walk, you staggered over to the perch and first she ducked her head so that you could scratch the back of her neck between the green feathers, and then she bit your finger, pushing with her stubby tongue, until you yelped.

All this never disturbed Lee Howard. 'There's a new organization for homosexuals, or I should say *by* homosexuals,' I said to him. He knew that I was 'queer', the word people of his age used – in his case, as in Sheila's, though she was younger than Lee, purely descriptively. Their lives, he in newspapers, she on the stage and then in newspapers, had brought them so many homosexual colleagues and social acquaintances, women and men, that even when I cried out that it was offensive, they quite truthfully said they didn't mean it to be. In newspapers alone they had known, after all, Nancy Spain, a celebrated popular columnist and journalist of the fifties whose lesbianism was so unmistakable that even though she didn't *write* about it there wasn't a saloon bar in the country that didn't know (where is any modern version of Nancy Spain today?). They had known the popular columnists Godfrey Winn and Beverley Nichols, whose 'queerness' also, though they too didn't *write* about it, was known in every pub.

'This organization,' I ploughed on, feeling myself sweating a bit as I approached with a gulp the word I was still hardly familiar with – *gay* – 'has been meeting at the London School of Economics for the last few weeks. Two LSE students, Bob Mellors and Aubrey Walters, obviously they're very bright as you can guess, brought the idea from New York – they're English, they went on a visit – it's called Gay Liberation Front, or GLF. Gay means homosexual.'

I halted. Lee's great face watched me, benignly, from above the incongruous flowing caftan.

'The idea is that homosexuals should learn to feel self-respect,' I continued. '"Gay" is our own word; that's to say it's more American than ours, but we're hoping to make it the word everywhere. It doesn't sound psychiatric like "homosexual" or unpleasant like "queer". It's three years now since 1967, and the legislation, when we stopped being completely criminal.' I could hear a pleading note enter my voice. 'It was Labour, it was Leo Abse, Lord Arran, Roy Jenkins, who improved the law.'

He knew where I was driving. Was the *Mirror* not the great Labour paper? He squirted soda into another Scotch. I drank my champagne. I reached the point: 'Couldn't the *Mirror* write about it?'

The editor of the *Daily Mirror* gazed at me attentively, looking I am sure as he did umpteen times a day in Holborn when people brought him features proposals.

'You tell me,' he rumbled, 'that these people, you people, are having meetings in London?'

'Yes, though people have been coming from as far as Scotland -'

He held up a great hand.

'How many of you?'

'It's hard to tell. It's in a lecture hall. Two hundred? Four hundred?'

He contemplated the possibly absurd figure of myself sitting there all eagerness, all innocence, filled with my youthful passion for something of interest to myself.

'No', he said, 'no. The *Mirror* is a national paper. We don't write of events confined to London.'

It was absolute, the verdict of a man who had been bearded, had listened, and had decided against. Sheila brought in our dinners. That was 1970.

On 2 January 1971 the *Spectator*, then edited by George Gale, ran an article of mine headed 'Gay Liberation' which complained of the lack of serious quality press attention to the wildfire impact among homosexuals of the Gay Liberation Front. It began: 'As an adult homosexual of fixed abode, work, and way of life ...' I'd been dismayed when *The Times*, my own employers, refused to publish a first draft of the article. It went all the way up I was told to the then editor William, now Sir William, Rees-Mogg. It was in my irritation that William wouldn't print it that I added for the *Spectator* what had not been there before, the opening come-out.

The allegedly 'permissive' sixties had come and gone, and yet Labour's greatest paper, the proudly anti-establishment *Mirror*, wouldn't prepare a friendly feature telling 'the common people' of an extraordinary change occurring among many of the sons and daughters of 'the common people'. Nor would 'the top people's' greatest paper, the nearly 200-year-old *Times*, pride of the establishment and self-proclaimed newspaper of record, give house-room to a development which has since, in some sort, entered the universal awareness.

That's how low, from my own experience, the standards of British journalism were when 'gay' first appeared: no reportorial inquisitiveness, no sense of an obligation to let the people – 'common' or 'top' – *know*. Two heads of British journalism whom I knew, and who weren't muck-rakers, tucked their tails between their legs when, instead of a familiar queer, a gay first appeared before them telling them an old age was over, like a child before the elders in the Temple. Everyone I had come to like or to love or to admire in Gay Liberation Front, the 'working–class' drag queens, the women steeped in feminism before GLF was ever thought of, the trained Marxists, the mind-blowers dealing (or as often, to those they liked, giving away) acid and cannabis, was way ahead of me. 'Whatever else do you expect?' they said.

Nothing for it but to launch a paper. Within sight of where I'm writing this, if it weren't for the seven-storey St Stephen's housing estate which blocks the view, is All Saints Hall in Powis Gardens, Notting Hill Gate. I could wander over, but it wouldn't be the same. I do in fact sometimes pass by, but all that happened there is long gone, and there seems no connection.

1971. The vicar of All Saints lets GLF take weekly sanctuary in his hall after first the LSE throws us out, fed up with the crowds, and then 'Middle Earth', a catacomb in Covent Garden which had briefly been a Tolkien-titled arts-lab-rock-pop-venue no longer allows us to meet.

GLF has spread everywhere in Britain and in Western Europe. It's on campus, it has gathered radical chic, the 'theft' of the word gay is denounced in Tory papers, the lesbians are fed up with the self-absorption of the gay men, moves are on to disband the centralized London meetings in favour of a plurality of GLFs all over the London boroughs, there are GLF publications and a GLF paper, *Come Together*. The joint is jumping. I'm still on *The Times* (I leave the following year) and am anxious about the repeated complaints of people beyond London and even of people in London that they never know what's going on beyond their own doorstep. And I'm furious about my own profession, as it continues to lock gays out. A newsletter is already being organized by others, just as concerned. I have larger ideas since I came from a large paper. I know nothing about problems of distribution, typesetting, paste-up, photographic facilities, newsprint costs, advertising, financing. After all, I've been pampered for my whole working life, shielded as national journalists are from any such considerations.

Leaning against a pillar in All Saints Hall on, I think it was, a November evening and probably looking, I remember thinking, negligently condescending – or rather in danger of sounding, with my BBC-ish accent, negligently condescending. Self-consciously slurring my voice, I propose that we devise a national paper. To be by and for gay women and men (I don't then say 'lesbians and gays'). To be partisan for gays, but not between gays. To be spun out of GLF, but not to be by GLF. The notion drifts away. It has hopped for a moment without breaking the surface of the meeting, like one of those insects, a waterboatman, on the surface of a pond, and then drifts away on the strong currents of other, urgent, 1971 business.

It would have come to nothing (though the need is there, and felt, and someone else would have fulfilled it), if it hadn't been for the lanky character in stars-and-stripes pants, hippy hair to the shoulders, huge eyes, and a bad back, who comes loping over to the pillar when the evening's meeting is breaking up and says, 'I want to work on creating a newspaper like that.'

I already know Denis Lemon. He's about twenty-four.
He's been making the rounds of the radical non-gay
London listings and other papers cajoling, urging, shaming
them into giving space to gay news. He works in a record-
shop. He has no 'journalistic credentials', he wants to get
into journalism. He's hyper. He cruises with demonic
energy. We never get anything together but a paper, but I
grow very fond of him. Kissing and embracing people, as
was the way, we work our paths out of All Saints Hall that
winter night, talking furiously. He has a friend who might
(and who does) offer a small office near Paddington ...

Eight months later, in the summer days of 1972, the
fortnightly *Gay News* hits the pubs. Many are to come
forward, I remember a Canadian composer, and David
Seligman who went on to help found London Lesbian and
Gay Switchboard, and my own lover Peter who was a shy
School of Oriental and African Studies student who had to
force himself to bear these daringly out activities, and
Glenys Parry, who was chair of CHE in Manchester, and
Jean-Claude Thevenin, whom Denis fell in love with in
Paris and persuaded to move to England, and ... oh, many,
many.

The demonic mover and shaker is Denis, who as the
conservative fight-back against 'permissiveness' gains
strength in the mid-seventies, laying a carpet of flowered
tussore and foulard for Mrs T. to tread gratefully on her way
to Downing St in 1979, is to be hauled before the Old Bailey
as editor of *Gay News*, charged and found guilty of
publishing a blasphemous libel – a gay man's reverie on the
crucified Christ. Without Denis, no *Gay News*. Something
else, no doubt.

A young woman walks firmly along the pavement
towards the newsagents but at the last instant her will fails
her, and instead of turning in through the door, she carries
on, until outside a Woolies she leans against the plate glass,
trembling and sweating.

It's her fourth attempt. She looks at the road with the cars
and buses, and at the shoppers scurrying up and down
either pavement, and she sternly says to herself:

'That woman in her bulky coat and boots, cluttered with
shopping bags and pushing her child in the stroller, may be

homosexual. That young builder's mate in the paint-stained overalls sitting in the cat's cradle with his legs swinging, staring down at us as he breaks for a tin mug of tea, may be homosexual.

'The driver of that Daimler, tapping his fingers on the steering-wheel to a sound system I can't hear, may be homosexual. Or perhaps the elderly bus-driver, clambering from his cab and holding up the traffic so he can walk back and have a row with a taxi. Any one of those four office-workers sitting on the bench sharing a cream-slice and talking loudly of their boy friends may be.

'They can't *all* be heterosexuals. They can't *all* be looking at me and suspecting me. I am *not* alone. I *won't* be defeated.'

Light-headed, afraid she may faint, she leaves the security of Woolies' windows and puts one foot in front of another until there's the newsagents again, and she walks on in, and going to exactly where she has known for weeks that it's to be found she picks out a *Gay News*, and she takes it to the cashier who, paying no attention, takes her money.

It isn't only that the paper seems to her to scream gay, gay, gay. It will be about men, she's sure, mainly about men, and though she's desperate for contact with any of the homosexuality that she's convinced is going on out there somewhere, she's had to claw up her courage twice over: to cross a Rubicon in her own heart and to buy it, yes, but also to intrude on the world of homosexual men, so unknown to her, so alarming to her, not at all what her spirit and body long for.

She finds a large literary section, filled no, not filled, but extensive, spacious – with women writing. Lesbians, gay women, dykes. She has already torn out the endless guide to gay and lesbian events and venues around the British Isles, prepared, though she doesn't know it, by Jo, a lesbian, to pore over, seeking some meeting, some place, she'd like to go.

She has folded back the interminable pages, as they seem to her, of ads for gay male clubs and pubs, with their pictures of semi-naked men, and men in harness, and men in women's clothes, from which her eye shrinks, curious yet appalled, apprehensive ... what money the men do seem to have ... what revels ...

In another town, on the selfsame day, a young man has nerved himself at last, as she did, to become a first-time reader of *Gay News*. His heart has almost stopped with the excitement of blazing repetitions of 'gay men, gay men, gay men'. People from straight papers, the best of them, spread themselves in *Gay News*, talking at last as the gays they are, openly to gays, their wings filling in an air where they no longer have to remember that 'most of the readers aren't gay', 'won't understand', 'shouldn't be told'.

The unique books pages are run by Alison Hennegan, the black hair flowing down her back, from the smallest room in the known universe. In the next cubby-hole, Michael Mason, now of *Capital Gay*, runs the news pages, diving at the phone: 'You say there were three police in plain-clothes. . .' Roger Baker, Peter Burton, Emmanuel Cooper, Gillian Hanscombe, Kris Kirk, Edward Lucie-Smith, Graham McKerrow, Glen Platts, Tony Reeves, Vito Russo, David Shenton, Wendy Simpson, Simon Watney, Bob Workman. . .

Names, just names. Names you may know, names you may not. But that's the point. Openly self-named names, detailing the new age. There are other magazines, for ten years there is *Sappho* for women only, but for most of the time it is the only newspaper, until the end comes.

So it goes for eleven years, 1972–83.

The cries of parrots rend the ears: the *Sun*, the *Star*, the *Daily Mail*, the *News of the World*, the *People*, the *Express* group, cackle the words gay and lesbian from morning till night.

For it is now March 1987. The *Sun* has just published a stolen letter in which Patricia Hewitt, press secretary to Labour leader Neil Kinnock, blames the loss of a previously safe Labour seat in Greenwich in part on 'the lesbian and gay issue costing us dear among the pensioners'. Exulting, the *Sun* banner headlines on its front page that even the Labour party ('the socialists') are now rounding on the GAYS.

I sit at my desk as associate editor of the *New Statesman* – a desk from which I'm soon to be evicted, the editor declaring both me and my special subject-matter of collisions between heterosexual assumptions and lesbians and gays to be 'redundant'. I'm pondering whether there isn't any wholly democratic way – any way that doesn't open the doors to a Parliamentary censorship of the media which might rebound – in which a hood might be dropped over the parrots of the press as they cry GAY GAY GAY.

Politically, Rupert Murdoch, Lord Rothermere and the other owners of the conservative mass media are colluding with the establishment British hunt for scapegoats. They wouldn't do it, though, it there wasn't money in it. They have traduced GAY into a three-letter word for VICE, and tales of vice sell papers. Crowds will pack the streets to see a hanging, and the fell execution of GAYS virtually every morning in the press is now vital to shifting hundreds of thousands of bales of newspapers a day. Surely, I ponder, the solution must be to leave them free to do as they choose, but insist they pay for it. Let those who profit, pay.

I conceive the idea of a Finance Bill. Murdoch, Rothermere and the rest are newly defined (solely as a tax-matter) as partly living off immoral earnings, unless they can prove otherwise to the tax inspectors. I draft a tax-scale: a special £200 levy (say) to be payable by newspapers for every naked female breast per 100,000 of circulation per day of publication.

A further £200 to be payable for every use of the words 'gay' or 'lesbian', or any synonym, *unless the news story or article is by someone clearly identified to the readers as being themselves lesbian or gay.* A further £200 levied on each headline use of the words SEX or VICE.

It doesn't sound much, does it? A feather with which to tickle a mountain. Well, in fact, it would tickle the mountain to death. On a typical six-day output of the *Sun* in early 1987 (28 February to 6 March, to be precise) Murdoch would have been liable to pay up £550,000 of special duty on the *Sun*'s outpourings. Let the *Sun* keep up the same rate of pimping off homosexuals and women throughout 1987, and the special tax payable would be ... some £29 million.

The parrots would grow eerily quiet indeed when their owners contemplated such an invasion of their financial privacy as that. At a Campaign for Press and Broadcasting Freedom conference in London on 4 April 1987, I laughingly outlined the idea, admitting that no House of Commons we know or are likely to know is going to do as I suggest. To my surprise, people linger over the idea, turn it over yearningly in their minds: 'Is it really so utterly impracticable?' they ask.

But it will not be for me to try to persuade the Alliance or the Labour Party of any merits it may have. For on 3 April, the day before the CPBF conference, I have been sacked from the *New Statesman*. The article in which I was to have laid out my train of thought on how perhaps best to oppose the defacement of lesbian and gay lives by Fleet Street has been banned (30 March) by the editor.

Never mind, I've always thought we won for all time when we took to calling ourselves lesbian or gay. I don't care if those words one day fade. Defining ourselves in our own terms, that's all. That's all it needs.

18 Normal channels

Bob Cant

The Lesbian and Gay Pride march in 1985 was the largest London had ever seen. Among the 15,000 people gathered together in Hyde Park, a particular place of honour was given to members of the mining communities of South Wales, and lesbians and gays who had supported them in their year-long struggle against pit closures. I had not been a member of Lesbians and Gays Support the Miners (LGSM) but I joined that part of the crowd because I wanted to identify with this alliance between my own community and one of the most active sections of the organized working class.

As I joined the group they were singing the LGSM version of 'Glad To Be Gay':

> Sisters and brothers we supported the strike
> We stand with the miners, their fight is our fight
> The women fought hardest with so much to gain
> They stood on the picket, they showed us our aim
> Making the links with LGSM
> Trade union women, children and men
> Brought us together, united we'll win
> Thatcher called us – the enemy within.

The expressions of mutual solidarity between organizations of lesbians and gays and organizations from mining communities was unprecedented and seemed to me to represent the hope of the emergence of a new kind of politics. I had felt torn for years between the demands of gay politics and those of socialism. I had never had any doubt that they could be reconciled, strengthened and both transformed but it had often seemed that it would never happen.

I had been a socialist for over twenty years and had become particularly active since I joined the Gay Liberation Front and come out openly as gay. It is difficult to explain why I – a white, middle-class Scotsman who went to a right-wing university – became a socialist; but there is undoubtedly some connection with the fact that as I discovered my own gayness, I realized it would make me an outsider in this society. I began to identify with other groups of outsiders, people who had no control over the wealth and power in society, let alone control over their own lives. I identified with women in their struggles against oppression, with the working class in their struggles against exploitation and with the Third World in their struggles against imperialism and poverty – but I did so in ways that were confused and irrational. I often did not understand why I was acting as I was, but I had no real doubts about the general direction I was going in. It was while I was doing Voluntary Service Overseas in Tanzania that I began to understand very clearly that outsiders did not need to be victims. Socialism seemed to me to offer the only hope of enabling all these outsiders to change the world. As a gay man, I made it part of my socialist project to raise the question of lesbian and gay oppression – in the revolutionary left, in my trade union, in the Anti-Nazi League and in the Labour Party. I was prepared to work in this way because I accepted the claims of the left that it represented a world view rather than just one sectional interest. I worked within the left on the terms laid down by the left – through what they called normal channels.

Being with LGSM on the Pride march brought back memories of my political involvement during the previous miners' dispute in 1973–4. At that time I was a fairly hyperactive member of the International Socialists (IS) a neo-Trotskyist group which later transformed into the Socialist Workers' Party (SWP). I had been attracted to such an organization because in the early seventies revolutionary change seemed to be a real possibility. I belonged to GLF, which was then an international movement; we were greatly influenced by the growth of feminism, I was involved in solidarity work with the anti-imperialist struggles in Southern Africa and Vietnam; the British working class was taking action on its own behalf by, for example, the occupation at Upper Clyde Shipbuilders. Major social change seemed to be on the agenda. If it was to happen, however, it had to be fought for through organized activity; if I was to be part of that struggle, then I had to be part of an organization. The Labour Party of Harold Wilson offered no hope; the Communist Party was too compromised by Stalinism; IS seemed to me to be a group of committed, energetic Marxists who were making advances in the traditional, organized working class. I joined IS early in 1973.

That period in IS's history proved to be one of the worst for sexual politics. IS was, as it put it, turning to the class and was becoming increasingly occupied with economic issues to the exclusion of much else. People who were active around sexual politics and the politics of everyday life were regularly denounced as 'middle class' or '*petit bourgeois* intellectuals'. Racism was taken more seriously than sexual politics but most of the opposition to it was based on the fact that it was divisive of the working class. The politics of any form of oppression were trivialized. Inconveniently, however, for the leadership of IS, this was a period when large numbers of lesbians and gays, politicized and strengthened by GLF, decided to join socialist organizations. Many of us joined IS; many others joined the Communist Party or the International Marxist Group.

The debate on lesbian and gay politics had already been going on for some months when I joined IS. More than anything else, the leadership wished it would go away. It had been discussed in the fifties at the time of the publication of the Wolfenden Report, when a prominent member had written:

> It is only when there is complete equality between the sexes in all respects, beginning with economic equality between the sexes and extending throughout all aspects of life ... that homosexuality would disappear naturally. If nature then produced an abnormality, which it might do in a

number of cases, medical treatment would take good care of it. (C. Dallas, *Socialist Review*, December 1957).

Clearly, some comrades continued to believe that we were indeed such an aberration but we seldom got the chance to discuss even that with them. People who would use the Marxist method to interpret almost anything else were, when it came to sexual politics, bourgeois liberals and even reactionaries.

The IS Gay Group was set up in Lancaster in 1973. We organized extensively and wrote a document for the *Internal Bulletin*, which was supposed to be open to all members, but it was never published. We called, among other things, for an end to discrimination in jobs and housing, for an end to aversion therapy, for equality in the age of consent, for gay parents' right to keep their children and for an honest sex education programme. The National Committeee, however, produced another document which, while it said that IS was 'utterly and vehemently opposed to attacks on homosexuals' instructed us to 'withdraw from work in GLF'. We were not allowed to set up our own group in IS nor were we allowed to belong to the major radical gay organization in the country. We tried to organize a conference on sexism and were instructed not to do so. The letter which instructed us to cancel the conference also said: 'IS does not take a position on what you describe as "sexism", and also contrary to your opinion we have not found the issue to cause any concern among the working-class members of IS.'

How they could have established the views of working-class members when no open discussion of the issue was permitted was hard to understand. I later succeeded, however, in persuading the staff of the *Socialist Worker* to let me write an article. After five months of negotiation an article appeared. Everything that I had written about either ideology or lesbianism was edited out, the word 'gay' was replaced by 'homosexual'; it was, in effect, an article about the civil rights of gay men. I was never sure whether I was right to agree to it appearing in that form. I did agree because the alternative seemed to be no article at all.

We got a lot of support, on the other hand, at local level, in my own branch in Tottenham and, most particularly, in

Lancaster. Resolutions were sent from these branches to the Annual Conferences in 1974 and 1975. Both times they were defeated without any discussion.

Someone once threatened us with expulsion but there was no need for that. The campaign of vilification, mis-representation and silence worked far better. Members of the unofficial Gay Group felt that they were being made to choose between gay politics and socialism; some opted for a life of self-oppression within IS; some opted for gay politics outside IS; many simply dropped out – and that was particularly true of working-class members who did not have the same kind of job mobility as their more educationally-qualified comrades.

I was able to stay in IS for as long as three years, longer than many others in the group, because of the level of support I received from a number of quarters. The most important source of support was, of course, the IS Gay Group itself but most of them were from outside London and so, on a day-to-day level, I was very isolated. I was a hard-working member of my IS branch, partly because of the need I felt to prove myself. I did trade union work, anti-racist work, strike support work and newspaper selling and I was on good terms with other members of my branch. It was often a great strain to have to explain the whole politics of sexuality to people who appeared never to have thought about it before, but my arguments were taken seriously and these discussions seemed worthwhile. Par-ticularly supportive were other members, mostly women, who were in disagreement with the leadership over sexism, over racism, over Ireland. None of us was a separatist, but because we were all involved in politics which were not simply and straightforwardly economic, we made common cause and supported each other. Without all those forms of support, I would have left IS much sooner.

Another source of support came from the fact that I lived in London. I was the only out gay person at my place of work but several of the others were involved in, or at least influenced by, sexual politics. London has, of course, always attracted lots of lesbian and gay migrants and there were a number of gay groups that I participated in. I was most involved in the Gay Teachers' Group and the LSE Gay

Culture Society. But I tended to adopt IS's general outlook towards such groups and I rather looked down on them, for much of the time, as 'lifestyle politics'. Nonetheless, I made contact at these meetings with other lesbian and gay socialists. Most of these friends thought that I was crazy to remain in IS but, as socialists, they were supportive of what I was doing there.

I had affairs and sexual relationships with some of the gay men in IS and also with some of the men from the London groups that I belonged to. Although I thought that I wanted a longer-term relationship with another man, I never succeeded in forming one during this period. My behaviour probably made it impossible. My job and my activity in IS were so time-consuming that I approached my leisure time and my relationships in ways that were often less than creative. IS's social activities were really designed for youngish, childless, able-bodied heterosexuals. I looked for gay company not just in radical gay pubs like the Prince Albert but, more and more, on the gay scene in pubs like the Champion and also in the Catacombs late-night coffee bar. There are lots of different features to the gay male scene but I used it largely as a place to pick up men rather than to make friendships. I also met men on the streets, in parks and in cottages much more than I ever had done when I was in GLF. There was a real edge of desperation to my search which had not been there before. Ironically, many of the men I picked up were working class – from this island, from Ireland, from the Mediterranean, from the Caribbean. We met as one-night stands and so that was what we remained. But there was a warmth to many of these encounters and as we talked about other parts of our lives and about the ways that we coped with an anti-gay society, it struck me as ironic that I was making far more contact with working-class gay men than ever I was permitted to do through IS.

Bitter would be one word to describe my feelings when I left IS. But bitterness is destructive of the person who feels it and I had to get over it. IS's decision to adopt a policy on gay rights six months after I had left, when there were almost no members of the original group left, did not, however, tempt me to rejoin. It was, in any case, a policy that seemed to be interested only in the victimization of gay workers and did not address itself to the issues of coming out as gay in a culture that promoted heterosexuality. Workers who hide their own gayness can still be victimized on account of their sexuality but are hardly likely to initiate a campaign around it when prejudice against gayness is rampant and, for the most part, unchecked by socialists.

I remained a socialist but I now had a lot lower expectations about the comradeship of most heterosexual socialists and, therefore, about socialist organizations. I still, however, shared the view of IS that priority should be given to organizing rank and file workers at the workplace rather than focusing on elections to positions of power in trade unions or Parliament. Without rank and file support, elected leaders of the Labour Movement are able to do very little on their own terms. So I continued to work (although a lot less closely) with IS/SWP members in the Rank and File group in my union, NATFHE, the college lecturers' union. In the early years after I left IS I concentrated on issues like workplace conditions, pay, education cuts and racism in education. I was also secretary of my union branch for a number of years. My political activity was now much more clearly divided between the gay and the traditional.

One of the projects in which I was involved which tried to address itself to both these political concerns was the Gay Left collective. We were a group of nine gay men when, in 1975, we produced the first of ten issues of the *Gay Left* magazine. We declared our twofold aim as being 'to contribute towards a Marxist analysis of homosexual oppression' and 'to encourage in the gay movement an understanding of the links between the struggle against sexual oppression and the struggle for socialism'. Lively, hard-working and often turbulent, the Gay Left group met weekly for most of a five-year period. My involvement with the traditional left made it difficult for me to identify with some of the political developments in the group and, in fact, I left after issue number six over what I saw as a difference over personal politics. The debates which took place in the pages of *Gay Left* were just one reflection of the vitality of gay politics in the late seventies.

One of the most important advances for gay politics in this period came from outside the movement itself with the establishment of the Anti-Nazi League (ANL). Set up, initially, by members of the SWP and some Labour leftists as an organization to oppose the National Front, it captured the mood of the times and grew into a mass movement. A particularly important feature of it was Rock Against Racism (RAR). Their gigs were enormously popular and played a major role in establishing an anti-racist and anti-Facist culture. Their success was such that people felt confident enough individually to identify themselves as supporters of the ANL even when they were away from the demonstrations and the gigs. Anti-Nazi badges could be seen everywhere. Prominent among these were the Gays Against the Nazis badges. Not only was the culture of ANL and RAR anti-racist and anti-Fascist, it was also welcoming of lesbians and gay men. The music of the gay singer and ANL activist, Tom Robinson, played an important part in generating that atmosphere. When he sang anti-Fascist songs everyone joined in; when he sang 'Glad To Be Gay' everyone joined in. Being gay in that atmosphere was much less isolated than being gay anywhere else on the Left had been and many lesbians and gay men came out and became politically active through this whole experience. In that period, it was possible to be openly gay, to be politically active and to have a good time. A period to be cherished.

My single major political priority throughout the rest of the seventies remained my union work. I took steps to set up a nationwide union gay group in 1974. With the support of Rank and File, the gay group campaigned to get NATFHE to adopt a policy supporting their lesbian and gay members. It was a time when similar work was going on in a number of other unions and in 1976 both NATFHE and NALGO took tentative steps towards acknowledging the employment problems facing lesbians and gay men. The NATFHE policy was opposed to discrimination on grounds of sex, race and sexuality at interviews. It seemed like a real victory for a time but the union generated no publicity about it and, despite lengthy consultations with the group, it produced no report on the implications of this policy. Nothing changed – the group became very demoralized.

The union conference in 1980 proved to be a turning point in my perception of gay politics in the union. That year the conference was held in Scarborough, despite the fact that it was the object of a boycott because of its council's refusal to allow the Campaign for Homosexual Equality to meet there. A number of protests had been made to the NATFHE Executive, but all to no avail. I had written a leaflet of protest which my regional council had agreed to endorse but, while I was glad of this support, it seemed much too polite and rather futile to confine ourselves to this form of protest.

A woman member of Rank and File suggested that we should use some GLF tactics to heighten the consciousness of delegates about meeting in such an avowedly anti-gay atmosphere. We had stickers printed saying, 'Glad to be Gay in Scarborough' and about half the delegates wore these; some were shocked to find that bar staff refused to serve them drinks while they were wearing them. We gave out songsheets with the words of 'Glad To Be Gay' and encouraged delegates to sing this when the Mayor gave his welcoming address. A couple of us unfurled a Gay Teachers' Group banner and successfully interrupted his speech. The protest made the front page of the *Scarborough Echo* and NATFHE has never been back there for its conference; nor has it gone to any of the other resorts that have been the object of boycotts because of anti-gay policies.

The action was regarded as a success by everyone who took part. I was particularly pleased that Rank and File members, all apparently heterosexual, had so openly and willingly identified with lesbian and gay rights. Five years previously, they would never have contemplated participating in something so gay-identified. But, for me, it was a much more personal statement about the politics of my sexuality than I had ever made in the union before. As someone, rather pompously, said to me, 'Your name is now synonymous with homosexuality in NATFHE circles'. I was, in fact, a total wreck after that conference. For days I was physically trembling and was hardly in control of my own behaviour. I realized that if I was to do anything similar again, it had to be part of a lesbian and gay initiative. I would welcome – and positively seek – the support of heterosexual socialists. But where our oppression was the issue, lesbians and gay men must take the lead collectively.

Later that summer, one of the members of the group returned to London inspired by the lesbian and gay politics of California and was eager to revive the weary NATFHE Gay Group. His enthusiasm generated a new lease of life in the group and it became much more active again. We organized a picket of the National Council of NATFHE about their failure to produce a policy statement from the conference resolution of four years earlier. We invited heterosexual supporters to take part and many did so but it was on our terms of reference. We got some press coverage and the NATFHE leadership whispered sweet nothings in our ears. The group was, in its small way, on the road again.

Focusing as we did so specifically on union politics was probably the major factor in making us less mindful of our own sexual politics. The revived group was all male whereas the earlier group had been mixed. Lesbians were withdrawing from many mixed groups at that time, and while we regretted that we never really addressed ourselves to the question of whether the practice of our group was, in fact, oppressive of women – we wanted women to join but we made it easy for them not to – it was easier to focus on the power of others rather than examine our own power and the problems it raised.

After the success of the picket the group decided to campaign for the union to adopt a policy on job protection and positive coverage of homosexuality in educational materials. The regional council which I attended as my branch delegate was one of the three which we targetted as being likely to submit such a motion to annual conference. The leadership there was left wing – not Rank and File, but Broad Left. Broad Left in this case was an uneasy assortment of Stalinists, Eurocommunists, Labourites and careerists. I attempted to win support on the common ground of our socialism but although I got considerable formal support I underestimated the strength of cultural resistance. On the one occasion, in 1981, where they did agree to support a lesbian and gay resolution for conference, they did so only on condition that the wording in the section on homosexuality in the curriculum was changed from 'positive' treatment to 'constructive' treatment. I agreed to the compromise with grave misgivings, but it was never debated due to its position on the agenda and lack of time.

The greatest difficulty about seeking support for this kind of resolution was that the regional council was a context where no one ever talked about their own personal sexuality, although the atmosphere was often heavy with heterosexual nuances. Many of the delegates often came from colleges in small towns where they did not, consciously, know any lesbians or gay men. Talking about the social meaning of the sexuality of people like myself, I was assumed to be talking about my own sexual *activity*. Some men found this so strange that they could not even look at me. Others seemed to think that I had agreed to make my own sexuality, and that of men thought to be my lovers, valid subjects of humour in semi-public situations. These 'jokers' defined themselves as supporters of gay rights and were careful never to use any words in public that were positively anti-gay. But there was no doubt about the atmosphere that they were permitted to generate. It was an atmosphere where even a seasoned campaigner like myself felt isolated and threatened; an atmosphere where no one else would have felt encouraged to come out as lesbian or gay. Some women identified with what was happening to me but I never saw anyone challenge these 'jokers'; some even endorsed the 'jokes' by a whole body language of looks and gestures; but most of them were simply tolerant – tolerant of the gay and the anti-gay alike without distinction.

The lesbian and gay group thrived, however, during this period, particularly among lesbians and gay men from London colleges. We became a mixed group again; we tried to provide support for each other; we organized meetings; we continued to leaflet and lobby conference delegates. In 1984, the Inner London region submitted a resolution on lesbian and gay rights to the annual conference. It was by no means easy for the gay delegates who promoted it in that region but they were assisted by the fact that, by then, lesbians and gay men had become an increasingly visible part of everyday life in London. This visibility of the lesbian and gay communities helped the resolution to be seen as a matter of public concern rather than the reflection of a personal problem. A number of openly gay delegates made speeches to that conference and, at last, NATFHE had a policy on lesbian and gay rights. There were still further struggles to get it publicized and to make it part of the union's common sense but that conference decision was a major move in the right direction.

I was unable, however, to attend that conference as a delegate. Despite my long record of activity in the region, the Broad Left group that year decided not to support my election as a delegate. It was not manifestly, at least, because of lesbian and gay rights but because of racism. A Black lecturer, John Fernandes, teaching at the Hendon Police College, had become involved in a dispute with the Metropolitan Police about anti-racist teaching that he had planned to do with the police cadets. The issue was a complex one but his course was eventually stopped by the police and he was banned from the college. NATFHE was enormously embarrassed over all this and wanted John Fernandes to treat his dispute with the police as a matter of individual casework. He refused because he said that the issue at stake was not an individual one but one of institutionalized racism. From 1982 to 1984 the issue tore the union apart. I agreed with John Fernandes' refusal to accept that the issue of racism should be treated as though it were his personal problem. I could also envisage a time when a lesbian or gay lecturer might be put in a similar position where the union saw the individual, and not the general issue of oppression, as the problem.

When I took resolutions of solidarity with John Fernandes from my branch to the regional council I was met with interest from many delegates, concerned about the lack of real debate in the union, but with hostility from the leadership of the Broad Left grouping. Avowedly anti-racist, they saw John Fernandes' approach to racism as being, within a union context, divisive. But it seemed to me that they were denying the right of the oppressed to define the nature of their own oppression. There was very little the Broad Left could do to me, but by failing to support me as a conference delegate they made sure that I felt even more of an outcast.

I continued to be active in my union branch. I was involved in a particularly successful campaign to win job security for eight part-time lecturers. But the degree of depression that I felt about my regional union work, not to mention the post-Falklands war climate of rampant Thatcherism, was mitigated by my growing awareness of the activities of the Labour-led Greater London Council which had been elected in 1981. Its commitment to public accountability, to job creation, to cheap transport, to anti-racism, to anti-sexism and to lesbian and gay rights helped to make me consider joining the Labour Party. Throughout the seventies I had been very critical and dismissive of Labour but by the time I joined in 1982 I felt the situation was so desperate that I would either have to join the Labour Party or disappear into political nothingness. Most of its membership was reformist; some did not even define themselves as socialists; but it did represent collectivism on a scale that none of the smaller parties did. It was hardly in favour of lesbian and gay rights and its treatment of Peter Tatchell up to and during the Bermondsey by-election was blatantly homophobic. There was, however, some degree of self-organization among lesbians and gay men. In fact, I joined the Labour Campaign for Lesbian and Gay Rights (LCLGR) first and it was only after that that I felt confident enough to join the Party in Haringey in north London. The man I share a house with had been a member for some years; I knew other lesbian and gay members in the locality; I felt much less isolated than I had done in any political organization for a very long time.

I was quite seriously ill for much of the time from late 1982 to early 1985. I eventually agreed to have a major operation which transformed my health and gave me the chance of a fresh start. I was determined not to return to the old patterns of hyperactivity. I remained a socialist but the individual stress I had experienced as a result of the consciously and unconsciously homophobic elements on the left was not something to which I was willing to submit myself again. I knew that there was a role for me, along with other oppressed people, in the struggle for a contemporary socialism. Nonetheless, decisions had to be made.

The decisions, in fact, proved to be much less difficult to make than I had anticipated. Much of that was due to the activities of Lesbians and Gays Support the Miners. I soon discovered after my operation that although LGSM was a successful fund-raising body, it was also much more than that. They recognized that they had common enemies with the striking miners; they identified with the struggles of these working-class people to save their livelihoods and their communities. The insecurity experienced by the lesbian and gay communities was one of the factors which made them sensitive to these issues. But the way in which they offered their solidarity was important because it was neither covert nor through normal channels. Lesbians and gay men offered their solidarity to the striking miners on their own terms. Particularly strong links were established between LGSM and some of the Women Against Pit Closure groups. Struggle, even when it is defensive, is never static. The struggles of LGSM helped not only to provide support to particular mining communities but also to bring about a considerable shift of opinion in our favour in the whole Labour movement. That, in turn, was to have a major impact on my political activity.

LGSM had succeeded in making possible lesbian and gay self-organization on the Left. I became involved in setting up a local group of LCLGR in Haringey in 1985. The Labour Council, following the example of the GLC, was consulting the lesbian and gay communities about their needs and LCLGR joined in that process. We persuaded both the constituency parties in Haringey to put forward resolutions on lesbian and gay rights to the 1985 Labour Party Conference. Lesbian and gay rights were widely discussed in the Labour movement in Haringey and while not everyone was happy about this, it had become possible to participate in left politics as openly identified members of the lesbian and gay communities without being subjected to constant marginalization and intimidation. Nor was our experience in Haringey an isolated one. Many such local groups were set up that year all across Britain. The TUC and the Labour Party Conference both passed resolutions calling for an end to discrimination in employment and housing, changes in our legal status and further developments in equal opportunities policies. After fifteen years' struggle the Labour movement had put lesbian and gay rights on their agenda. While this was a major advance, those of us familiar with the history of that agenda tried not to get too excited.

In Haringey the major achievement of this period related to the fact that we succeeded in putting lesbian and gay rights onto the Labour manifesto for the 1986 council elections. We addressed ourselves to the heterosexist assumptions that underpinned the provision of housing, of education, of social services, of leisure and Labour undertook to begin to redress this discrimination. Despite hostile coverage of these policies by much of the local press, Labour won the council elections with an increased majority. But after the election a local campaign, with Tory support, was set up to challenge and oppose the introduction of positive images of lesbians and gays in schools. The ferocity of that campaign has made it clear to everyone how central the ways that young people learn about lesbianism and gayness are to the struggle to end our oppression. If we succeed in introducing positive images, we will be faced with both an alliance of bigotry and fear and the panic of liberals; if we fail to introduce positive images, young lesbians and gays will continue to learn to hate themselves and young heterosexuals to despise them. The atmosphere in Haringey has at times been horrendous but lesbians and gay men, in a number of different contexts, continue to organize and struggle – more than ever before.

Although my political activity is increasingly devoted to lesbian and gay issues that is not the only factor that motivates me to be a socialist. I am still convinced that the only solution to the material and emotional poverty of people's lives is a collective one brought about by the oppressed and the exploited themselves. I am a member of the Labour Party largely because they alone seem capable of organizing any short-term defence against the onslaught of pauperization and competitive individualism that faces us.

But my experience on the left in relation to issues of oppression has made me much more critical not of the aims of socialism but of the nature of much socialist struggle. Many of the debates which periodically grip the left have little relevance to me or many of the other oppressed people who are drawn towards socialism, for they are conducted in the language of seventy years ago. In the wake of the Russian Revolution of 1917, socialists in Europe divided into two camps – the reformist camp and the revolutionary camp. Both camps, whatever their other differences, are fiercely centralized. Whatever historical circumstances justified that then, they no longer do so today. Not only has centralization engendered bureaucratic politics, it has also succeeded in excluding from mainstream socialist activity all those who struggle against oppression – and particularly against racism, against sexism, against ableism and against heterosexism. The left has not always ignored these issues but it has habitually failed to address them in the terms defined by the oppressed themselves.

The left could do worse than look to socialist models in other parts of the world and in other periods of history which have challenged specific forms of oppression in a class context. The Jewish Workers' Bund in Tsarist Russia, the Industrial Workers of the World (Wobblies) in USA, the Women's Co-operative Guild, James Connolly's Celtic Communism, ujamaa socialism in Tanzania all provide models for us, not to copy, but to learn from. Only those of us who experience the particular forms of oppression and exploitation of the advanced industrialized world at the end of the twentieth century can create forms of organization appropriate to this period. All socialists have to become involved in this process if there is to be any hope of socialist change.

This process will be slow – slower than ever I imagined when I first came out in 1971. But our greatest advances have taken place when we have organized on our own terms. Lesbian and gay self-organization will be the key to making our struggle part of the commonsense of socialism.

19 The should we, shouldn't we? debate

Femi Otitoju

Waterloo Station

Nineteen eighty-two and nothing much seemed to be happening. Booed out of the OWAAD* conference, frozen out of the Black Women's Centre and utterly perplexed by the distant rumblings of the sado-masochism debate as it seethed across the Atlantic like some bubbling boiling mist that no mere mortal lesbian could hope to enter and emerge from unscathed. It seemed to a Blacklesbian that there was nothing but gloom in the air. I mourned the passing of the GLF and hated my mother for not having me years earlier in order that I might have been there and seen real struggle and change, but ruefully I acknowledged that as a lesbian my space in that movement would have been limited. I had made one or two forays out into the wilds of CHE and found men horrified at the thought of coming out at work and intimidated by this strident harpie in their midst and concerned lest my political ramblings would go on past closing time.

I had always subscribed to the train of thought that went along the lines of working to change the system from within was nothing but a fantasy for those people who were outside of the system. Once you got in you forgot your good intent and simply knuckled down to surviving and resisting attempts to brainwash you entirely. It was, then, this firm

* OWAAD is the Organisation of Women of African and Asian Descent which held major conferences in the early eighties.

belief which kept me working in small organizations, constantly struggling for resources and wondering if there would be a next pay packet at all let alone what the size of its contents would be. The establishment was something to be avoided. Mainstream party politics were nothing to do with the aims of my struggle as a feminist and a woman-identified woman. Local government was a smaller version of government, and both were to be fought, demonstrated against and challenged at every available opportunity with the everlasting hope that that one day it would be thrashed, overthrown, replaced with . . .? Well, replaced anyway. Most alternatives would surely be better.

It was in this frame of mind that I was ambling through Waterloo Station. On my way to catch a 171 bus and frantically scouring my memory for anything that would help me remember what meeting I was supposed to be at tonight, I saw a familiar face and banished my worries instantly knowing Mark was always good for a little distraction. When we ran out of political arguments, when neither of us could remember the original point we had been trying to prove or disprove, we could always go out on the piss. Things were looking up; I beamed at the tiny man as he half-walked, half-skipped in my direction and began talking before he was really close enough to be heard. 'Coming to County Hall?' he asked. I stared blankly, faintly aware of the strange sight we must have made: me, a six foot tall Black dyke, be-Kickered and dungareed, utterly motionless in the still busy walkthrough of the station, apparently mesmerised by . . . he, as beautiful as a miniature Vogue model, tiny tam on his head, 'tache carefully shaped, jeans once seductively slit under left buttock and over one knee, now looking simply as though the leg was about to fall off entirely in either of these two places. But it wasn't his physical appearance that captivated me so: he had suggested that I might be going to County Hall. Alarm bells rang as I tried to fathom what I though Mark could possibly be about to do in County Hall. The threat of a sweat began across my forehead and upper lip as I strove to recall just what exactly had happened to Guy Fawkes. I opened my mouth to say that I was a member of the peace movement and that blowing up County Hall would be terrorism in my book when he said, 'Yeah c'mon, Andy Harris has said that it is possible that they may fund a centre.'

Everything fell into place. County Hall, home of the GLC, hitherto just another home of the white male-dominated bureaucracy which dominated our lives, had thrown open its doors to the community, our community. I beamed at Mark again. Up until now the community had been relatively suspicious. There had been little take-up of the offers to consult and resource. I had heard of some small lesbian and gay organizations which had received funding, but they had seemed fairly distant and I suspected that there was nothing fair about the way in which their selection for funding had come about. A few boys in the know maybe, fully paid-up members of the Labour Party pulling a few strings and getting a few favours for their loyalty. What Mark was proposing called for a rethink of my position of no collusion with the establishment, so I slipped my arm through his, making a mental note to talk to him about it in the pub after the meeting and worrying only the tiniest bit about my credibility as a Blacklesbian, almost separatist feminist.

The Wellington

The meeting was relatively short. After it ended there was no doubt that 'The Political Commitment' existed to make a lesbian and gay centre more than the dream of the few lesbians and gays who dared make like the ant and the rubber tree plant. In the pub afterwards a varied selection of activists, many of whom had steadfastly shunned main-stream politics in the past, discussed the depth and breath of this 'Political Commitment' and the motivation behind it, and, most importantly, although this wasn't reflected in the time it was apportioned, what exactly we were going to do with it.

I was suspicious. I had heard all sorts of tales about what happened to small voluntary organizations that were funded by bigger statutory organizations, and I didn't like the prospect of our movement being co-opted in this way. My sisters in the women's movement had shunned many of the open meetings set up by the GLC's Women's Committee in order to 'get the views of women in London' and the best attended one had been packed out by members of the Wages Due Lesbians, Wages for Housework campaign, which is as distanced from most women in London as was the GLC itself at that time. Feminists in London were generally wary and to me it made sense for us lesbians and gays to be wary too. Local government grants tied you up in all sorts of ways. You were accountable to the council, and they controlled what you could and couldn't do once you had their money. It undermined the very idea of autonomy and could well turn into a monster that could devour us. I voiced my reservations to our small gathering and was met with earnest faces, some bobbing in agreement and others grimacing and shaking with dissent.

One of the shaking heads tried to explain that this wasn't really a problem since all the lesbian and gay projects had their very own guardian angel in the form of Ken Livingstone, who was of course gay himself or at the very least bi-sexual, and who was personally committed to ensuring that lesbians and gays should finally have a voice in local government. I suspected a crush but couldn't bring myself to lower the tone of the discussion, so held my tongue. He went on to hypothesize that these new initiatives were completely wholesome because they, like the changes in the type of food that was being served in the County Hall canteen, had been brought about out of a genuine wish of various individuals to make the council's services better for everyone. I couldn't buy it, and so shifted my gaze to the prim-looking bespectacled man to his left who was muttering about *naïveté*, in order to encourage him to keep talking.

Specs began by saying that all politicians were manipulative and pathological liars and that we shouldn't trust any of them. I thought this was a bit strong but it would have seemed rude to interrupt him so soon, and besides other people had begun to look interested so I waited. Specs went on to say that the only possible reason could be that of gathering political support from those sections of the community that have in the past felt neglected and often shat upon by the various politicians of the day. I reckoned that this made sense. But, continued Specs, we must not be so puritanical that we don't recognize the potential gains that are to be made for the movement here. It is entirely possible for us to take advantage of what is on offer and still maintain our integrity and independence so long as we remember that if such forces ever get to the position where they feel that they no longer need our votes, they will drop us like the proverbial hot potato. We should use it, he urged, while we can to strengthen our morale and our spending power. With a year of good financial backing we could create a campaigning force to be reckoned with. It was beginning to sound like my kind of fighting talk when he began to choke on a peanut that he had thrown too vigorously into the back of his throat and grasped desperately for his beer.

The momentum was seized by a woman who had been smiling at me across the table during the meeting in the awe-inspiring room on the principal floor of County Hall. I smiled my encouragement, not that she seemed to need it. 'Oh yeah, great,' she pitched in, 'And before you know it the movement will be filled with overpaid unmotivated so-called activists who don't know how to filch a pencil or scavenge a few photocopies. We'll have organizations filled with dead wood drawing hefty pay cheques and when they do "the proverbial hot potato number" they'll have achieved what is probably exactly what they want, the total destruction of a cohesive lesbian and gay movement and a community that is totally dependent on the establishment, that could no more set up and run a centre or support service than it could run a bath.' There was definitely something in what she was saying so I leaned forward on the edge of my seat and struggled with a roley (I never did get the hang of those things). She, however, seemed to think that she had said enough and set off, blushing furiously, towards the bar. While I toyed with the idea of dashing up and offering to buy her a drink someone else clambered onto the soapbox.

What we all seem to be forgetting, he was saying, is that what we are discussing here is no big deal. It feels that way to us because since the beginning of this government structure we have never had the rates that we pay spent on us. 'I think,' he said, 'It's only right and fitting that the days of the overworked, exploited and eventually burned-out activist are finally coming to an end.' There were one or two hear-hears and right-ons. The speaker didn't look like some kind of traitor but what he was saying was surely treason against every dyke and faggot that ever fought for their rights. Local government *should* be taking over, he ventured. They have a duty to cater for the needs of every member of the population, and let's face it, no matter how different many people try to make us feel, we are all members of the wider population. So what if we no longer have to beg, borrow or steal the paper to get out a newsletter telling people about lesbian and gay events? 'I happen to think,' he continued, 'that every one of us has a right to a genuine timewasting hobby, like hang-gliding or flower-pressing, instead of spending every second of our spare time trying to grab our fair share. Counselling other lesbians and gays because society has fucked up their heads and provides no services to help them get over it . . .' he paused for breath. 'I say let's take their money and work towards the day when we won't need the grants because such services are provided directly by the council.' I decided to go and buy the woman with the smile a drink after all, and left the group to the sound of the others falling on his argument and ripping it to shreds.

So how did it happen?

I was very excited about the idea of a Lesbian and Gay Centre situated in the heart of London funded by local government and run by us for us. The should we take the money? shouldn't we take the money? discussions continued over beer, herb teas and Cokes, but for a long time no one could work out what Londons' lesbians and gays had done in order to gain favour with the GLC. Some of the mysteries were explained by those of us who were active in the Labour Party prior to the August of 1981 when Ken Livingstone was appointed leader of the GLC. There had been much activity at a local level with many branches working hard to get resolutions about lesbians and gay issues to Labour

Party Conference. They told of work at local level percolating through the main body of the party.

Inside County Hall itself lesbians and gays worked solidly for recognition. The adoption of the pro-lesbian and gay stance was first openly stated by Ken himself (he was always called Ken after that, our big adopted brother) at a packed meeting of Harrow Gay Unity. This resulted in lesbians and gays already on the staff, working in other capacities, taking a growing interest in the work the council could begin to undertake for lesbians and gays. The announcement also resulted in a massive onslaught by the right-wing press. Banner headlines told of parties on the rates and campaigns against 'normal sex'.

The Gay Working Party was formed. It was made up of representatives of the lesbian and gay communities, some emissaries of organizations, and others simply individuals determined to have a say for once. It was to the chairs of this Working Party – first Andy Harris and later Jenni Fletcher – that the task fell of ensuring that views aired at the Working Party meetings were taken on into the wider forum of the members.

Despite the flak it took, or maybe because of it, the GLC never gave the Gay Working Party full committee status. Despite constant pushing from lesbian and gay staff lured into coming out with the promises of the 'political commitment' to continued support for the struggle for lesbian and gay rights, the GLC never provided resources in the form of a group of officers with the sole responsibility of combatting discrimination against lesbians and gays in the way it had for challenging racism, sexism or able-bodied chauvinism. Only towards the very end of its reign was an officer appointed within the general Equal Opportunities Unit to identify ways of countering the discrimination faced by those lesbians and gays who were employees of the council.

Outside of the council, the various community organizations worked out their positions in the should we, shouldn't we debate. Most of those which could get it together enough to work out the complexities of the methods of application applied for and got funding and this resulted in some of the most important work done on lesbians and gays in this decade. Most notable was the research undertaken by the London Gay Teenage Group, later publicized under the title of *Something To Tell You*, which highlighted the appalling experiences of so many young lesbians and gays at the hands of education services everywhere. A few organizations declined taking on paid workers, preferring instead to rely on capital funding for one-off items that they could never otherwise afford – like computers and photocopiers, thereby gaining but retaining independence.

Summer of 1985 saw the launch of The Charter: a document named in the typical GLC fashion in keeping with its underlying ethos of never doing things by halves, *Changing the World*. The London Lesbian and Gay Centre Project was able at last to hand over to the first management committee and the centre was open.

For the first time for me, being a lesbian in London was fun when I was in the heterosexual community as well as within the lesbian and gay community. Londoners were saying the words lesbian and gay more times in a day than they would previously have said them in a year. New words filtered into the vocabulary of ordinary folk. I can't begin to count the number of times I was asked, 'But what exactly does heterosexism mean?' and 'Could you give us a definition of homophobia?' Voluntary organizations began to request training on lesbian and gay issues, many of them, it has to be said, because it was a condition of their grant aiding that lesbians and gays be catered for as well as any other section of the community. Others, however, were making genuine attempts to redress some of the imbalances that have existed for so long.

To this Blacklesbian it felt as though the breakthrough had finally come and it was simply a matter of waiting till the others had seen the light. Something that had managed to have such an enormous effect on the everyday lives of lesbians and gays in London could surely see off the threat of abolition. Couldn't it? But it couldn't.

Stickers, Badges and Balloons

After the last meeting of the Gay Working Party I again

found myself in the Wellington with many of the same people as the first time. Specs was there again spreading gloom and despondency, his enthusiasm seemed to have waned with the life of the GLC. I needed cheering up so I tried to goad him into optimism; 'Well at least this'll make sure that we don't forget how to cope on our own,' I offered.

'I don't know,' he whined, 'It's too late. We've been distracted. Lesbians and gays have put time and energy into fighting abolition that should have been put into ensuring our own survival. There's been too much money for too long and we'll never manage without now. We need time to get all set up again and this newfangled Richmond scheme won't support us while we do it.' There was much nodding and a collective swigging of beer.

The one who'd had a crush on Ken was obviously still carrying a torch. He banged down his glass and remonstrated: 'Hardly that bad, old thing. It's not as though Ken and co. will take it lying down. After all you must remember the degree of personal as well as political commitment that went into making all this happen ...!' 'Pah!' interjected Specs, 'And where are they now, your Ken and co.? Just weeks before abolition and they're scurrying around looking for safe seats for the next local elections.' He belched unapologetically.

I pondered for a while, blotting out the sounds of the bickering activists dissecting the past and trying to ascertain whether we had been wrong to jump on the equal opportunities bandwagon. My attention was commanded by a raised voice, a middle-aged man who hadn't been with us on that first evening. 'You're leaving something out here,' he insisted. 'There is a new breed of campaigner in your midst now. I'm one. I came out in 1981. I've worked for the GLC for thirteen years, most of that time in the closet, fearful for my job and grateful to have it, concentrating only on keeping my head down and my nose clean. I came out at work shortly after the council adopted the new equal opportunities policy which included lesbians and gays. One or two people in the department couldn't hack it but in the main everyone was really supportive. I felt so good I wanted to help other lesbians and gays outside of work and started working on a voluntary basis with my local lesbian and gay youth group. There are hundreds of people like me for whom this past five years has been a source of great inspiration. Lesbian and gay issues are really on the agenda in local government now. What Margaret Thatcher hasn't allowed for is the fact that we've all been nestling in County Hall, drawing experience, strength and courage ...' 'Spare me,' groaned Specs, 'Or I shall need a paper bag.' 'But think about it,' he said, 'We've all been here working together and soon we're going to be scattered, into other boroughs, and into the voluntary sector, scattering far and wide like the seeds of a single dandelion that eventually cultivates a whole field.' He finished out of breath. 'I'm with you brother,' I said, I grabbed his glass and made off to the bar to get it filled.

20 One step to heaven?

John Shiers

What changed for gay men in the seventies? As time goes by, it becomes increasingly difficult to fully understand or appreciate just how dramatically things did change, and the number of people who, in one way or another, were affected by the changes. The casual use of the term 'gay men' is itself a product of the climate of the seventies. Before then we were, even to ourselves, at best 'homosexuals', more often 'queers', 'poofs' or 'nancy-boys'. The idea that we constitute a minority group in society with a right to live visibly gay lives as equal members of society no longer seems radical. But less than twenty years ago you could almost count on two hands the number of people who were prepared to affirm this principle, and, probably on one finger those who were prepared to state this openly as gay people.

For those of us who have grown up since the late sixties and came out in the seventies and eighties it is very hard to have a real idea of what life was like for men with homosexual desires before. For us there may have been a long period of personal crisis, of denial and of attempted repression. But there is a gay consciousness and culture pre-existing our individual decision to come out to ourselves. This consciousness and culture gives us an anchor-point and a sense that being gay is a shared experience. In other words, it gives meaning to our desires. We might go on to reject that meaning and the forms of consciousness and culture which are dominant at any one time, but at least it is there to start with. The problem lies in gaining access to it, given the prejudice, lack of information, and lack of recognition about being gay which is still widespread in British society.

Before the seventies gay consciousness and culture in the form we know it today were just not there, except in 'pockets of resistance' which developed amongst small numbers of men living, usually, in the large cities. These 'pockets of resistance' were able to grow up wherever men with homosexual desires were prepared or able to meet outside specifically sexual situations. Where, in other words, they could socialize as well as have sex with one another. Jeffrey Weeks, in his book *Coming Out* (Quartet, London, 1977), has written what still remains the only well-researched account of the development since the late nineteenth century of a sense of homosexuality as an identity, and the attempts of a small number of homosexuals to create a place for themselves in society. But we know that homosexual friendship circles have existed throughout the century behind the closed doors of many large homes of the privileged. We also know that certain occupations such as the theatre, hairdressing and catering have had at least their fair share of men who socially relate to each other as homosexuals, even in the bleakest moments of repression. There have also been, throughout the century, a small number of pubs and clubs which have catered for this homosexually-defined group, even though they may have gone to great lengths to conceal the fact.

There are three important things about homosexual identity before the seventies. First, even the small number of homosexually-defined people were forced to keep very quiet about it. With the law, until 1967, making male homosexual relations completely illegal, men risked literally everything if they were discovered. Second, only very few men appear to have seriously considered that they did have a right to anything better: by and large they accepted the inferior status given to their sexuality in society. Third, and most significant, the vast majority of men who had homosexual desires never defined themselves as homosexual. Indeed, they were highly likely to violently resist such a definition. All the evidence from the accounts of older gay men about the earlier decades of this century point to there having been a massive amount of homosexual activity. Toilets, parks, swimming pools, open spaces have always been important meeting places for men who desire other men. But most of this activity was furtive, casual and undefined, with the majority of the men engaging in it being married.

Working-class culture, the majority experience in society, had no space and no role for the homosexual, except as an object of hatred and ridicule. Hence the even greater invisibility of working-class homosexuals (but not working-class homosexual activity) than amongst the minority whose wealth could buy themselves privacy, or men who were able to 'de-class' themselves by working in 'effete' occupations.

The seventies blew open this restrictive, repressive and stultifying environment. A combination of two social forces intermeshing was responsible for what was a transformation in what it meant to be a homosexual man.

Much has been written about the centrality of the Gay Liberation Movement in organizing homosexuals around our own oppression; in challenging a society which denies us visibility and legitimacy; and in affirming our sexuality as every bit as good and valid as heterosexuality. The Gay Movement clearly emerged at a key moment throughout the USA and Western Europe. It followed on directly from all the other radical protest movements of the late sixties: in particular the Black movement and the women's movement. It mercilessly attacked every institution and symbol of homosexual oppression, whether it was in the form of psychiatrists meeting to discuss the 'problem' of homosexuality without us being there, or local councils denying us the right to meet in their buildings. Its tactics were direct action and confrontation with heterosexist authority. This is why, although smaller in numbers, 'liberation'-style groups were always more effective in challenging prejudice than the larger, but more polite and respectable Campaign for Homosexual Equality was able to be.

Gay Liberation presented a new way of being homosexual. We could determine our lives for ourselves. We were from now on 'gay'; a term which we had chosen. We no longer had to live in the closet, furtively meeting in the shadows. Our sexuality could be expressed openly. If heterosexuals were not able to cope with it, that was their problem, not ours. At least until the mid-seventies when radical, possibly revolutionary, change looked like it was distinctly on the horizon, the transformation of society, with women and gay men in alliance against the white heterosexual male establishment, was seen by most gay liberationists as inseparable from the transformation of ourselves into strong, positive lesbians and gay men.

The gay movement has impinged on the lives of most gay men indirectly, however, rather than directly. At a political level it may have succeeded in opening previously closed doors and in broadening out the social climate, and progressive opinion generally. Of greater significance to the majority of gay men has been the very factor which early seventies' gay liberation thought impossible. Business interests began tapping into a seemingly ever-growing 'gay market' and provided far better social facilities for gay men to meet in. The signs were all there from the mid-sixties onwards, if only we had cared to see them. Sex was becoming a marketable commodity. The (always mis-named) new era of 'permissiveness', and relaxation of the old sexual mores, gave enterprising enterpreneurs new oppor-tunities to make money. The gay market was particularly lucrative because gay men had nowhere else to go, and were therefore prepared to pay more for often a lot less in the way of provision than a heterosexual market would accept.

The years from the late sixties to the mid-seventies were also significant because, in some respects, they were a testing ground for these ambitious businessmen to see how far they could push the boundaries in the provision of services and facilities, catering both for sexually adven-turous heterosexuals and also for the previously untapped gay market. The boundaries for some things became clear very early on. Highly explicit pornography with 'action' shots was not going to be tolerated if it was home-produced, although imported pornography of this kind was available in sex shops up until the early eighties. Bathhouses or saunas similar to those that developed in the USA and most Western European countries were, similarly, beyond the pale for Britain. Gay saunas allowing sex on the premises had all been raided and closed in London by the mid-seventies. A few managed to survive outside London, but only with the greatest difficulty and a lot of discretion. No 'fantasy palaces' such as 'Man's County' in New York or even the bar/gym/sauna/restroom complexes which have been an important element in gay subculture in other European cities have ever been allowed in this country. Attempts to set up 'backroom-style' clubs, where a part of the area is given over to sexual activity for anyone who wants to go in, have also been curbed from the start, except for very brief moments until the police find out about them!

In comparison with what was able to develop in most countries in mainland Europe and in the USA, the commercial gay scene in Britain has always been very tame. It has consisted, by and large, of pubs and clubs catering for a gay clientele. Local Authority Licencing Committees, always heavily influenced both by the police and the attitudes of councillors in the area, have had varying responses to applications for licences for pubs or clubs aimed at gay people. Pubs with established licences have been easier to 'turn' gay than clubs. If, that is, the brewery is willing to suspend its 'principles' for hard cash (which most are!). Clubs are more precarious because they need to apply for fresh licences every time they open or reopen. Another factor sometimes mentioned, but difficult to confirm, is the persistent rumour that many club owners have close links with organized crime. In general, however, the role that Licencing Committees have played, up and down the country, in facilitating or inhibiting the growth of a gay subculture in their areas is another unwritten chapter of gay history which requires further investigation.

Huge tracts of the country never had, and still remain without, any gay pubs or clubs. Sometimes a really old style pre-seventies-type pub with the 'discreet' atmosphere, which presumably was the norm of that time, survives. Gay-identified men living in these areas increasingly tend either to flee the area altogether or to get together to make frequent trips to a more congenial 'big city' scene. By and large in these areas, which still cover the majority of the land space in the country, visible gay identities are much harder to develop and sustain. Connections made through contact adverts and dating agencies have played a particularly important role for gay identified people living in these places.

In the early years of the seventies, attempts to create a new style of gay male environment by gay businessmen were few and far between. This was the period when gay groups were able to organize what were usually very tacky and amateur discos in public halls and attract surprisingly large crowds.

The commercial scene was still very undeveloped. I remember in Lancaster in 1972 my absolute wonder at being taken, just after I had come out, to a monthly party held in a café called the Oddspot, owned by a gay man in CHE. This was my first venture in to the commercial gay scene (or the gay ghetto as I then considered it!). That monthly social event was at the time the only gay facility in the whole area of north-west England from Carlisle down to Preston.

The organizer of the Oddspot parties, a man called Malcolm, is one of the unsung heroes of gay liberation. For although his political perspective was rooted in an earlier era (and, at the time, was gross heresy to me!), he had been struggling against constant and violent police harassment since the mid-fifties to create some space for gay men to meet in. He had attempted to run various hotels with a private gay bar in Morecambe, only to be raided and closed down by the police. His attempts to run a gay pub there in the sixties also resulted in relentless police pressure on him. Even his café in Lancaster was a constant source of police attention. Malcolm was one of the people who organized CHE's first National Conference in 1973 on Morecambe Pier, which was the only place he could persuade a hostile and fear-ridden Morecambe to hold it. He died in 1977, having barely reached middle age, worn out, I'm sure, by the years of struggle.

Until the advent of *Gay News* in 1972 there was no easily accessible national guide to gay facilities, and certainly no gay switchboards, which did not begin to develop until after 1974. *Gay News* was, for the first few years, quite hard to get outside London. I remember trailing round Leeds one day in 1973, having read a piece of grafitti on a toilet wall saying 'Charlies is a homo dump'. I realized that Charlies must be a gay facility, but mistakenly thought it would be a pub. I arrived at 7 p.m. down an extremely grotty backstreet, having had to pluck up my courage and ask a passing policeman where it was, only to find a locked building with an absolutely tiny sign on the door saying 'Private Club'. It didn't open for another three hours!

The ambience in most pubs and clubs I visited in the early seventies was a sobering experience to say the least, after the heady world of Gay Liberation consciousness-raising groups, and socials full of radical drag queens and ideologically pure young women and men. The first time I went into the Union pub in Manchester, the doorman asked me jokingly if I 'give it or take it'! He was immediately subjected to a ten minute lecture from me about the oppressive and male-defined nature of penetrative sex and how he needed to escape from restrictive role-playing! I could not cope with so many men in pubs who not only referred to themselves as queers, but used female names to talk to each other. (That was all right in the right-on world of radical drag in GLF, but right-off when it came out of the mouth of a distinctly non-radical homosexual who probably hated drag queens anyway!)

What began to change the gay scene from the mid-seventies in London, and the late seventies in other large British cities, was the influence of increasing numbers of gay men who went to other European cities, and in particular the USA, for 'gay holidays'. In New York and San Francisco in particular there were very large out gay populations, and few state constraints on gay commercial enterprise. Consequently, a new style of gay man was in the process of emerging: one who was distinctively different from both the effete stereotypes of the pre-seventies' homosexual, and from the hippy-inspired gay male styles of the Gay Liberation Movement. In many respects these new gay images were calculatedly the opposite of the old stereotypes. Homosexuals in the past had been considered very middle class; the clothing styles of the 'new' gay man borrowed much more from classic American working-class clothing: the workboots, the Levi 501 jeans, the check shirts, the short hair, often accompanied by a (carefully constructed) moustache ... the perfect clone! Homosexuals had previously also been characterized as effeminate. Now the use of leather, military or police uniforms, and increasingly open interest shown in various forms of sado-masochistic sexual practices and in body-building symbolized a big break with past images and self-concepts. Even if the hard-faced leatherman was really a screaming queen with his mates, 'on stage' he aspired both to being himself, and to meeting, the ... ultimate man! What in essence began to happen was the appropriation of heterosexual male symbolism and imagery, and its sexualization into gay male style. The process led to frequent clashes with many lesbian feminists over whether this amounted to the reinforcement of an oppressive form of masculinity, with overtones of Fascism. This is an issue which is still far from being resolved politically.

Accompanying this new personal style was a different type of gay meeting place. Bars and clubs became increasingly sexualized places, both in their general ambience and their internal décor. A dinstinctively gay male form of music style also emerged, later to become the highly successful hi-energy genre which has so effectively dulled our hearing throughout the early eighties. The use of recreational drugs (hash, speed, amphetamines and, of course, poppers!) became more open and more widespread in gay venues. A visit might be made to an all-night sauna/bathhouse, after a night dancing at the disco, where sexual fantasies heightened by a combination of loud music, drink, drugs, flashing lights and dancing, could be worked through in a clean, pleasant and safe environment. Indeed fantasy is probably the key concept in all of this. What the commercialized gay culture in America really successfully achieved was to enable men who desired other men to escape from the real world of continuing (if slightly less severe) oppression and discrimination, into a fantasy world where they could be whoever and whatever they wanted to be, without fear of anybody outside finding out.

In the late seventies in the USA, novels such as *Faggots* by Larry Kramer and *Dancer from the Dance* by Andrew Holleran, and analytical books with titles like *Which Way out of the Men's Room?* began to question whether all this was *really* what the new generation of gay men wanted for themselves. Back here in Britain, however, we were, by the late seventies, only just beginning to get a slice of the action

... and then only in an extremely weakened form. The new gay male styles were very much borrowed from the States, as was the music we listened to, and even the way we talked about our lifestyles. Our pubs never really managed to take a form remotely similar to American cruise bars. An era of bigger, more overtly sexual clubs did, however, begin in London with Bangs in the late seventies and continued through into the whole Americanized atmosphere created by the highly successful London club Heaven. By 1980 a particular formula for successful gay clubs had emerged: they were dark; they played very loud fast disco music; they had good light shows on the floor; and above all they felt like sexually-charged environments. Out of London, clubs such as Heros in Manchester, Part Two in Nottingham, and Rockshots in Newcastle upon Tyne copied this style and created a winning formula from it.

For those of us who could not or did not take advantage of the cheap fares to the USA in the mid-seventies, there was also the experience of European cities like Amsterdam and Berlin. I remember how my first visit to Amsterdam in December 1978 transformed my whole sense of what it meant to be gay. I just could not believe what I was seeing ... and finding myself doing! A whole world of possibilities for exploring my sexuality was available: things which were not even options in the restricted commercial facilities provided in Britain. Gradually, as more gay men also came to experience the pleasures and possibilities of what became defined as a recreational sex lifestyle, so our sexual lifestyles in this country began to broaden out too.

A major element in this broadening out lies not, I think, in the fact that gay men began to have more casual sex. It lies more in the changed attitude towards casual sex itself. Casual sex has been a constant in the life experience of, I would guess, the majority of men who have desired other men and done anything about it down the ages. It takes place whether the participants define themselves as homosexual or not. It is a direct consequence of living in societies which deny men the right to openly love other men. If we did live in a world where homosexual relationships were treated in every way as equal and valid as heterosexual relationships, I strongly suspect that the pull to casual sex would correspondingly decline because men would grow up without any taboos or inhibitions about being close, sensual and warm with one another. A lot of male sexual activity, gay or heterosexual, is, I would risk suggesting, the result of displaced desires for intimate contact which, as men, we find hard to get in other ways. We remain, at present, a long way from a non-gender-determined sensual world, and simply becoming open and positively gay is not, in itself, sufficient to change the organization of sexual desires which have been constructed throughout our pre-gay identified days.

What has changed about casual sex in Britain is partly that it has, since the seventies, been easier for a particular generation of gay men to get it in safer places, meeting people in pubs and clubs as opposed to toilets and parks. But equally important has been the development of an ideology, linked both to more liberal attitudes toward sex generally, and also to the successful commercial exploitation of it in gay facilities. This is that recreational sex is a perfectly valid option for the organization of a gay man's sexual and emotional life. Men who desire other men have always had to split off the sex from the emotion, with the probable consequence that neither has been really satisfying because each has been cut off from the other. The new gay consciousness, backed up by the culture of commercial facilities, has allowed us to be openly gay; develop strong and emotionally-supportive friendship networks; drop in and out of relationships as we choose or are emotionally able to sustain, and to have a positive attitude towards the purely sexual encounters we may pursue, at varying times, with greater or lesser enthusiasm, in a whole variety of different places.

But of course many gay men do not have and do not want a large variety of sexual partners; they desire and sustain one-to-one relationships with varying degrees of success. Age, income, and degree of self-confidence, as well as class and race experiences, play a large part in how successfully recreational sex as a lifestyle can be pursued. Guilt remains in the background, particularly for gay men who have had strong religious backgrounds, even as they are plunging headlong into their journey of sexual exploitation. Many men desiring other men in this country also still remain closeted about it, and continue to resist a gay self-definition. Despite all these qualifications, however, there has been a deep and profound shift in sexual attitudes, with a whole variety of new role options, apart from the aping of heterosexual 'family life' as the ideal, emerging from the post-seventies' gay consciousness and culture. The commercialization of sexuality has had, I consider, more to do with the extension of these role options than the gay movement has had. The extension of 'the scene' was very much geared to gay men. While it did not, for the most part, exclude lesbians, it marginalized them. Separate rather than shared social spaces because the norm – although, paradoxically, many gay men enjoyed taking their heterosexual women friends for a night out on the scene.

So what kind of stocktaking can done from the perspective of the late eighties? There can be no escape from the fact that AIDS has cut a deep wound through all of the post-sixties' changes in gay consciousness and culture. In America, the home of the specialized sexual fantasy and of recreational sex as a lifestyle, the seventies' generation of new male homosexuals has been precisely those people most affected by the health crisis posed by AIDS. The funeral pyre has replaced the hi-energy music for literally thousands of gay men who have met painful, premature and such senseless deaths. Not surprisingly, the new right has had a field day, using AIDS as a central plank in its attack on the liberalism of the sixties' generation in general and on homosexuality in particular. By and large, by the mid-eighties in the USA they had done a fairly effective job in turning the worried masses of middle America more strongly against the new gay consciousness, and reintroducing the concept of homosexuals as sad, sick people in a new guise.

But what has also developed is a new sense of gay solidarity and togetherness, which would have been impossible in the bad old days when fear, guilt and secrecy reigned unchallenged. Gay men have been at the forefront of the battle against AIDS and in supporting and caring for one another. AIDS organizations have sprung up throughout the USA, but particularly in the most affected areas of

San Francisco, Los Angeles and New York. Gay men are changing their sexual lives to prevent the further spread of the virus. But they are doing it the typically ingenious way that has characterized the new gay generation. While some people have opted for monogamy or chastity, the signs are that new forms of recreational sex which are safe but still raunchy are emerging. Sex over the phone has become a major gay American pastime. Jack-off parties, where groups of men meet to explore (safe) fantasies with each other are replacing the dark backrooms and potentially risky bathhouse sex scenes. Talk-based sexual explorations, combined with less genitally-based physicality, have developed into popular forms of sexual expression. Although in San Francisco the old-style gay facilities around Castro Street are all closing, new social environments which are less overtly sexual, and which have more emphasis on friendliness and a relaxed atmosphere are emerging. More gay men are getting into healthier lifestyles through a better diet, and various holistic techniques for stress-reduction and more integrated living. None of this of course minimizes the sheer devastation and human misery that AIDS is responsible for causing, but it does show that the new gay consciousness will not be easily destroyed by right-wing moralists. The hard truth about the AIDS virus, which is that it does not choose whom it attacks according to their sexual preference, is already resulting in an increasingly large amount of heterosexual infection. The days when it can be dismissed as the consequence of a sick way of life are clearly numbered. The danger, in the longer term, is that the right will shift from an attack principally on gay sexuality to *all* sexuality which is non-monogamous and non-procreative. This is already happening in the writing and speaking of the 'moral majority' ideologists in America. If unchecked, it could roll back many of the progressive gains made in the recent past over attitudes toward sex and relationships.

In Britain, our AIDS crisis is several years behind the USA. Things began to go the same way, however, when AIDS first became big news at the beginning of 1985. Here was a gay plague that was a result of a lifestyle which all of us good citizens had really known all along to be wrong. It

was God's (or Nature's) punishment for departing from the
straight and narrow. Not only did this type of publicity
succeed in linking AIDS, in popular consciousness, with
gay men, it also conveyed the dangerous message to all good
heterosexuals that it was not an issue of concern for them,
unless, that is, they were drug addicts or haemophiliacs. But
by the end of 1985 it was all too clear that internationally, it
was heterosexuals, not just gay men, who were being
infected with the AIDS virus. Although in the West, it had
initially spread among gay men whose lifestyles contained a
wider range of sexual partners than did the average
heterosexual, this did not mean any long-term heterosexual
protection.

So it was that the sorry saga of the Thatcher Government's
AIDS campaign began. In March 1986, Mrs Thatcher could
resist any Cabinet discussion, saying she found the matter
'distasteful'. By March 1987 her Minister of Health was
appearing on TV extravaganzas, accompanied by blown-up
condoms and *Spitting Image* puppets to reinforce the
message that AIDS is a risk to us all.

While it is harder now for gay men alone to be scapegoated
for the spread of AIDS, our immediate position still remains
precarious. At least into the early years of the next decade,
the statistics will show that it is primarily gay men who are
developing AIDS. We have also been deeply linked in the
public mind as the initial carriers of the disease. The Tory
Government of Mrs Thatcher has also been profoundly
anti-gay, and has seen its future in reversing what it
propounds as the decline in traditional family values and
morality. The right has been able to seize the initiative on
matters relating to sexuality, like so many other social
issues, because the Labour Party has been so unwilling, at a
national level, to face up to them. Labour in Parliament was
not vocal when the media launched their vicious 'gay
plague' attacks in 1985. Labour has not been out at the
forefront either in explaining that AIDS is a health issue,
not a moral issue, nor has it been urging safe sex rather than
straight sex as the most important means of reducing its
spread. Labour at present shows every sign of copping-out
on carrying out its official policy to legislate for our
equality in society. The Liberals have, for a decade, been

running away from their paper commitment to gay rights and, in any case, it is far too risky to push, when in alliance with the responsible 'moderate' face of the SDP!

British licencing laws can also be very easily used to close down gay establishments. It is likely that those parts of the country that have the fewest facilities and weakest gay self-organization will be the easiest targets. There are many signs that the police are straining at the leash to attack more openly the presence of gay pubs and clubs in their areas. This has even been the case in London when, at the end of 1986, they exercised astonishing nerve in entering a long-established bar, the Royal Vauxhall Tavern, and arresting over a dozen men for being drunk *inside the premises*!

The consequences of having perhaps as many as 50,000 gay men who are HIV-positive, having to exercise great care over their mental and physical health, and the relentless increase in the conversion rate from HIV-positive to AIDS, have yet to be seen in terms of major changes in British gay male culture and consciousness. With negative messages being communicated from the state about the consequences of casual attitudes towards sex, coupled with a continued refusal to take the political steps necessary to create greater integration and acceptance of gay people into society, gay male self-confidence could be severely dented by the early nineties. The task in the immediate future must, therefore, be to build stronger and more effective mechanisms of support and defence than we have had previously. Gay politics has to be broadened out to include whole layers of people who in the past have shunned it. It also needs to become far more caring and supportive on a personal level than conventionally political organizations are usually able to be. Those of us whose experience comes out of Gay Liberation are going to have to accept that this new gay movement will be a broader church than anything we have been prepared to work in to date. It will also need to be organizationally tighter and better able to identify and gain support from non-gay allies than has been the case in the past.

For what is fundamentally at stake is the continued growth in the social space which has allowed a gay identity to develop. In order to meet the challenge that we, collectively, face, we have yet to take ourselves more seriously. Through the experience of the seventies, the gay movement's role and the commercial development of the gay scene, we began the shift away from an identity which was a purely sexual one. This shift led to a sense of ourselves as a social group with at least some common interests. Our sexual desires were, however, the motor-force behind the form that our social identity took and the expression of it in consciousness and culture. Without in any way denying that it is sexual desires towards our own sex which are at the root of being gay, our sense of identity has to shift further towards feeling part of a social group, with rights and expectations about our position in society. The adoption of safe sex practices will not, in itself, be enough to achieve this shift. Living in a social space with considerable numbers of us who are HIV-positive or who have AIDS is, in itself, a major challenge to our ability to relate to each other in an emotionally supportive as well as a sexual way.

AIDS need not inevitably usher in an era of new puritanism. Whether or not it does is dependent on political choices. The interventions which we as gay men make will affect the outcome. In America, after increasing numbers of men were beginning to get worn out by the big 'sex explosion' but before AIDS became a major issue, there was an important shift towards viewing sexual and emotional experience and desire as a series of options and choices: you explore different options, as you feel the desire, at different points. There is no 'fixed state' or one 'right way' to live. We all need to find the way of life which suits us best and harms others least, at any stage in our lives. The sexual 'big bang' which accompanied homosexuality emerging out of the shadows is just one stage along the way. It should not be seen as any more permanent, or be considered more authentically part of our 'real selves' than the era when desire was stamped on if it was not monogamous and heterosexual. Both have their contradictions, and out of the opposites clashing – new possibilities emerge.

AIDS inevitably means major changes in the organization of our sexual lives, and, in some respects in sexual desire itself. It does not, however, have to imply monogamy, celibacy, or a return to 'traditional' moral values, either for

HIV-negative or HIV-positive people. Dealt with in a humane, rational, and non-panic-inducing way, it can as much mean opening-up a whole new set of options and possibilities for sexual and emotional relationships, as it means the closing-off of other, now unsafe, ones. Equally important, the crisis forces us all to face up to the quality of our emotional lives and how emotional as well as sexual needs can be satisfactorily met. We now have to ensure that it is ourselves as gay men, and not the right-wing moralists who emerge the victors from the political battles to come, as we enter the nineties.

21 Somewhere over the rainbow ...

Ann Tobin

Over the past five years or so lesbian and gay male activists have made a considerable impact upon the policies and programmes of the Labour Party and trade union movement. The Labour GLC produced the Lesbian and Gay Rights Charter and funded the London Lesbian and Gay Centre. Labour administrations in local authorities throughout the country have taken up the issue of lesbian rights at a number of levels. The Labour Party itself, following years of work by lesbian and gay members, passed a major resolution on gay rights at its 1985 Annual Conference.

The presence of a contingent from the South Wales NUM on the Gay Pride March in 1985 was just one of the most outward and visible symbols of the support given by lesbians and gay men to an issue which moved far beyond the confines of gay rights. During 1986 at Wapping the presence of lesbians and gay men on the picket lines indicated that the same connections were still being made by us, although the notoriously macho print trade is apparently finding it more difficult than the miners to respond to our support.

Why then, as a lesbian and a committed socialist, and as a longtime member of the Labour Party do I feel so ill at ease with my Labour Party membership? Why do I wonder so frequently what I am doing as a lesbian in the Labour Party? Why does being a lesbian in the Labour Party often seem to be a denial of my lesbianism and commitment to lesbian and feminist politics, rather than a reaffirmation of the links and connections between my sexual politics and my socialism?

In part, of course, the unease can be traced to my own personal history as a member of the Labour Party and my history before coming out as a lesbian.

I first joined the Party when I was sixteen largely out of a sense of family tradition – not in itself a bad thing, since tradition is a mainstay of our sense of our history and our history should be a vital part of our present. In my case, family tradition was handed down from my grandmother, Chair of East Ham's Housing Committee and one of London's first women mayors, and from my aunt who was a longtime member of the Communist Party and who remained a passionate and committed socialist after she left the Party in 1956, and it was almost inevitable that I would join too as soon as I was old enough to do so.

My involvement in the Labour Party coincided with my first sexual relationship and the connection between sex and politics has remained intact ever since.

Looking back it now seems to me that as important as the fact that John and I were sleeping together was our political relationship. Had John not been secretary of the local Young Socialists and me the chair I doubt that we would have done it. My experience of sex signified far more than the act of sexual intercourse. Apart from the fact of actually doing it (no small thing in 1961, of course) the most exciting thing about sleeping with John was that it led to my admittance to the inner sanctums of the Socialist Labour League (SLL), the sixties' equivalent of today's Militant. This horizontal conversion, a standard tactic of male lefties, took place during a period when the Labour Party was engaged in trying to expel the left, mainly in the form of at its height during the National Conference of the Young Young Socialists, from its ranks. Our sexual affair was still Socialists at which Reg Underhill, the Party's National Youth Officer, assured the YS that the NEC would never close it down – a statement which bore little relationship to the document that I had personally typed for an NEC meeting. This document examined the NEC's plans to 'phase out' the Young Socialists. I 'leaked' the document to the Socialist Labour League and its 'youth' paper *Keep Left*, an act which was followed not surprisingly by my expulsion from the Labour Party.

That Conference was therefore one of high excitement and tension, both politically and sexually. But both experiences proved remarkably similar. On the one hand sex, whilst exciting in the anticipation was in reality rather boring. On the other hand, while there was an undoubted pleasure and excitement at being in the centre of the political and revolutionary turmoil of the Conference, I retained a lurking though unarticulated suspicion that the revolution was not in fact just around the corner and that the working class showed little sign of engaging in an armed uprising that would overthrow the state.

However, I threw myself wholeheartedly into the pursuit of both sex and politics with an apparent enthusiasm, gaining apparent emotional fulfilment from both. In practice both were rather hollow and tawdry. And so both continued to be for a number of years.

A series of men passed through my life, most of whom seemed to believe that they were the one who could solve my problem. Unfortunately they all appeared to think that athleticism or staying power was the answer. What had initially been a rather unfulfilling but vaguely pleasant sensation was long overridden by boredom at best, combined with a strong wish that my sexual partners would stop trying to prove their sexual prowess and go to sleep. Moreover, I became convinced that it was all my fault. We may not have been too familiar with the word 'orgasm' in the years before the swinging sixties, but the word 'frigidity' was never too far from men's lips. Women who didn't enjoy it, even when their partners kept at it for hours on end, were obviously frigid.

In the meantime politics were just as unsatisfying. Following my expulsion from the Labour Party I was recruited by the Socialist Labour League, who turned out to be a rather dour group of activists convinced that the crisis of capitalism was just around the corner. Comrades were exhorted to dedicate every waking hour to building a mass movement of the working class ready to seize the opportunity presented by the crisis of capitalism. That meant turning up at dock gates first thing in the morning, standing outside factory gates at lunchtimes and leafletting or party meetings in the evening. Crucial in these exercises was the fact that we never really took part in the grassroots activity on the factory floor, or participated in the struggle itself. We merely turned up at the time of industrial disputes in the hope of manipulating the people involved towards our own ends.

Apart from these endless meetings and leaflets my most vivid memory of the Socialist Labour League is of attending a Camp somewhere in Surrey. One night we watched a film in the main tent, showing great moments from our past – mainly of the YS on various marches and demonstrations. At the head of one demo was Roger Protz, one of the first and most prominent Labour Party Young Socialists, who was at one stage editor of *Keep Left*. He had, however, left the SLL and denounced its politics. The film show swiftly became an Orwellian hate session with the ranks of Young Socialists screaming abuse at the figure of Protz up on the screen. But whilst this surface impression of the League's politics was disturbing, equally unsatisfying were the theories lying behind its political approach. The literal and devoted interpretation of the words of Lenin, Marx, Engels and Trotsky as holy writ appeared to be more and more irrelevant to the realities of Britain in the sixties. In particular, the League had little or nothing to say about the increasingly public face of racism (particularly in the form of Powellism) that was emerging at that period. They merely insisted that this was just another sign of the impending crisis of capitalism, and that Black and white workers should unite. This response took little notice of the fact that the white working class was light years away from uniting with the Black working class in common socialist cause. The hatred that emerged during the vilification of Roger Protz appeared to indicate the dominant nature of this particular version of Trotskyist politics. We knew what we hated, knew what we opposed, but I found it difficult to work out what we wanted to replace it with.

I left the SLL shortly after that summer school. By now, the new dawn of sexual permissiveness had risen, but beyond the fact that it had now become more or less acceptable to try it out with more and more men, my sexual life remained largely unaffected.

Throughout this period homosexuality was still the great unspoken factor. I was happiest in the company of women and with women friends. I had found no great satisfaction in the sex I had with men. But I didn't make any connection between these two facts. It's difficult now to convey just how unimaginable being a lesbian seemed. It was not that the thought was abhorrent, more that the thought never entered my head. I just never knew about lesbians.

My first contact with homosexuality was in Australia, when I became friends with two gay lovers. The friendship arose largely because of the fact that Australia was still the land of macho men and their mateship. What this meant in practice was that men would take women to parties and then dump them for the evening as they proved their virility to each other by drinking crates of beer. The aim was to drink sufficient beer to make you throw up and then start drinking again. It was the drinking again after vomiting that proved virility. By then sex was no longer particularly entrancing as far as I was concerned. But it lost any magic it still retained in Australia the night I was invited to share a cockroach-ridden bedroom by a man who had a few minutes before demonstrated his virility to his own and his mates' beery satisfaction.

(In case anyone is wondering whether this is untypical, I can only say that most of the Australian men I knew were involved in the theatre and/or the Australian Communist party – all dedicated to improving the lot of their fellow man. They were, in other words, not at all typical. They were the best.)

By the time I left Australia most of my friends were either gay men or women and I had effectively stopped going out with heterosexual men. The initial connection had been made and homosexuality was no longer unthinkable.

However, it was still to be some years before I came out as a lesbian. I returned to England and rejoined the Labour Party. But although I had rejected the revolutionary politics of the left, the Labour Party still seemed less than adequate. The most frustrating thing, however, was that I couldn't really work out why. I could not resolve the contradictions between rejecting the revolutionary approach to socialism, and the weaknesses of a Labour Party which totally accepted the structure and limitations of a parliamentary democracy and which failed to grapple with the problems of how to set about genuinely transforming society. So I put most of my activity into trade unionism, which appeared much more direct and clear cut, and involved immediate responses to set circumstances.

I also embarked on a new bout of sexual activity with various men, but by this time I had a faint, though unstated, consciousness that I was a lesbian. By then gays had come out, the Women's Movement had taken off and the images of homosexuality had changed. But although I knew about myself by then, I still resisted the possibility of acting upon that knowledge. Apart from anything else I didn't really know what to do about it. Then in 1976 I went to Sussex University and possibilities changed almost overnight. Sussex had an active Gaysoc, full of individuals and groups flaunting their gayness and proud of it. Not that it became easier overnight. In my first year there, during Gay Pride Week, there was a Gay Bonfire Night. I spent the evening circling around the bonfire from a distance, trying to summon up nerve to join in, but failing. For if I joined in the circle everyone would know I was one too! Next morning, of course I found that it would have made no difference at all, for all my straight friends were there anyway. At Sussex, supporting Gay Liberation was the trendy and right-on thing to do.

Eventually a woman asked me to spend the night with her. And I woke up the next morning asking myself why I had wasted the last fifteen years. I was a lesbian and it felt good.

It wasn't just my personal and sexual life that was transformed. My politics were transformed too and I soaked myself in feminist theory and practice, and like many other lesbians I became involved in the separatist politics of the radical feminist wing of the movement.

However, although that experience was crucial to me personally, I could never set aside for very long my underlying commitment to socialism – to working-class politics.

Most important though was the confidence I gained

through coming out as a lesbian, the new strength I had in my own self-definition, which arose directly from my involvement in lesbian and feminist politics. I felt able to go back into Labour Party politics on my own terms.

The precise turning point, however, was in 1982 when the Thatcher Government announced its plans for the National Health Service. It was quite clear that whatever lipservice the Tories paid to the NHS, they intended to effectively dismantle it. They were out to destroy the concept of good health for all, a concept central to what still remains one of the supreme achievements of the post-war Labour Government. It seemed very clear to me then that if my own and other people's parents and grandparents had fought for things like the NHS the least people like me could do was to join in the fight to retain them. So I became active in the Party again, becoming secretary of the local Ward Party, sitting on the Constituency Party's Executive and serving as vice-chair in 1985.

There can be no doubt that what made it easier to become active was the strength of women in the Labour Party, and the involvement of the Women's Sections in Party business and activity. The strength and commitment of the women in the Party I belonged to also made it possible for me to be open and out as a lesbian from the start.

Women in the Labour Party have been at the forefront of pushing forward the Labour Party's policies into the eighties, and have been a crucial part in helping create the new coalitions that have informed and affected Labour politics. But most important has been the support given by and to the various groups. Women involved in the campaign to get the autonomous election of women on the NEC have been supported both behind the scenes and on the conference floor by Black activitists raising the issue of Black sections in the Party. Black members have supported the struggles of lesbian and gay men to get their needs placed onto the conference agendas, and lesbians and gay men have supported the calls for Black sections.

But whilst the impact of that coalition has been profound and cannot be overlooked, it is as yet an impact which has gained an all too often superficial, but rarely practical, support. There are plenty of sounds made by the leadership in support of anti-racist, anti-sexist and anti-heterosexist campaigns, but little or no practical changes taking place.

Even in the GLC, the most public supporter of lesbian and gay rights that there has been in the Labour movement so far, the reality tended to lag behind the rhetoric. Thus the Gay and Lesbian Charter was launched in October 1985 and was followed in November 1985 by the Housing Committee's rejection of policy work looking into the housing needs of lesbians and gay men. The Labour Group on the Inner London Education Authority (ILEA) hastily ditched its work on lesbian and gays in schools in the run-up to the 1986 election fearing that it might be too controversial.

The campaign for women's rights in the Labour Party has been met year after year by outright hostility from the trade unions and much of the Parliamentary Labour Party. Black section campaigners are stamped upon with even more ferocity by the Labour leadership. In my own borough the adoption of a Gay and Lesbian Charter was denounced by the leading shop steward as a charter for deviants and perverts and he went public in the local papers promising that he would never allow the employment of perverts in the Council.

There are obviously a number of contributing factors that make the Labour Party and trade union movement unable to take on all these issues – not least of which is the massive move to the right that has taken place in Britain as a result of Thatcherism and the recession, a rightwards lurch that has affected all our political activity.

But the basic structure and politics of the Labour Movement itself militate against the possibility of the Labour and trade union movement taking on board these issues and organizing actively and practically around them.

For the Labour Party and the trade union movement is in essence a movement devoted to protecting and upholding the purely sectional and rather limited interests of the white working-class male who is unionised and who works in the manufacturing industries. Those of us who do not fit into that rather narrow spectrum – women, the Black and ethnic minority community, the unemployed, part-time workers, homeworkers, unionised workers in the service industries –

none of these groups are of any real interest to the majority of trade unionists who still rule the Labour Party by virtue of the block vote and the political levy. Nor, of course, are the needs of the gay and lesbian community of particular concern.

Labour Party meetings are conducted according to the methods and practices established by the Labour movement in the nineteenth century, which were themselves based upon the methods and practices of a reactionary Parliament. They are ancient rules polished into intolerant rigidity by generations of the working class anxious to prove their respectability and respectfulness to the institutions of power handed down from Victorian England. Their importance in maintaining the power of the hidebound hierarchs of 'local democracy' means that they are clung to with as much tenacity as the apron-wearers of Freemasonry cling to their only slightly more inane rituals. All debate is conducted according to these rules. It is a method which imposes confrontation and opposition rather than allowing understanding and consensus. In fact the rules often positively prevent discussion, even confrontational discussion, taking place. During the rate-capping farce of 1985 where the situation was to say the least rather fluid, I sat in endless meetings where we were unable to discuss what to do because the 'rules' did not allow us to do so.

Trade unions make little effort to go out and recruit the people who still remain un-unionised. There are millions of part-time and homeworkers whom the unions could recruit – but their needs and claims, apart from being simply unfamiliar to the men who run our trade unions, could challenge the traditional concerns of the male unionists, so recruitment is half-hearted or non-existent. Perhaps most shameful of all – in the days of four million unemployed – is the failure of the trade union movement to take any notice of the unemployed. The problem is, of course, that the trade union movement doesn't actually know how to respond to workers who are not working. The rules do not permit the unemployed to join a trade union.

But, if you manage to join a trade union, or join the Labour Party, you don't exactly get the greatest of welcomes. Labour Party and branch meetings are held at night, and tend to go on endlessly and tediously about nothing much in particular. If you are a woman with no private transport, if you have caring responsibilities, then meetings are not merely boring, they are inaccessible.

The cultural and social life of the Labour Party is built around the pub or club, the cultural realm of the white working-class male. If you don't fit into that culture – because you choose not to, or because your own culture and background is in opposition to this lifestyle – then the Labour Party and trade union movement is doubly inaccessible.

When resolutions are passed that uphold lesbian and gay rights, and Black rights and women's rights in a generalized and non-specific way, then the Labour movement is happy to fall in with them. When, however, demands are made which if accepted would challenge or alter the existing power structures of the Labour Party, they are ferociously and utterly rejected. The Labour leadership makes noises on behalf on women, but will not support rule changes that would permit women to elect their own representatives to the NEC – because that would mean the trade union hold on the NEC was lessened and its majority influence would no longer exist. The Party is quite happy to make noises on behalf of its Black members, but not to allow its Black members to establish their own sections and participate directly in the existing structures – because that too would challenge existing forms of power.

The Labour leadership might sit back and acquiesce in resolutions on lesbian and gay rights, but the GLC's practical actions in this direction were at best ignored and at worst subjected to hostile attack from the trade unionist and Labour leadership – for fear that the white working class may have been alienated by the GLC's policies.

Like my parents and grandparents before me I joined the Labour Party initially because of a moral imperative, a belief in the paramount necessity to transform our society into one in which freedom, justice and equality was the right of all. It is a transformation which cannot and will not happen without the concomitant and fundamental transformation of the economic and material bases of our society. But a socialism which bases itself upon just the economic

well-being of the white working-class male is in the end not
worthy of being identified as socialism. And a Labour Party
which is either indifferent to or scared of identifying itself
with the needs of lesbians and gay men, and of Black and
ethnic minorities, and of women is not worthy of calling
itself a socialist party.

Reading this through I realize that I have not given any
good reason for remaining in the Labour Party. What it
amounts to in the end is that as a lesbian, and as a feminist,
and as a socialist I can find no other forum in which I can
work politically and which encompasses all my political
beliefs. When I concentrate all my political activity into just
gay politics, or feminist politics, I lose contact with my past
and with my commitment to socialism. If I concentrate all
my activity in just the Labour Party or other areas of the
Labour movement I lose touch with my lesbianism and my
feminist politics. So I constantly move uneasily to and fro
between all three, and live in hopes of a new political
initiative in which all these and the other spectrums of the
rainbow are joined together.

22 No going back

Jan Parker

Time has run and is running away with this chapter. I wrote the first draft in February 1986 arguing that it was the time for lesbians and gay men to go more on the offensive. Be Offensive – the new slogan. I'm on my third version. It's now two weeks until 11 June 1987, polling day. Shiver. Shudder. Our lives – and our deaths – have never before been such a political issue. Like it or not politicians are talking about us, defending us or ridiculing us, when in the past we've been ignored. Tebbit's remarks a year ago tipped us off and, sure enough, the Tories are stirring up anti-gay feelings to attack Labour with as well as attacking us. Lesbians and gay men are on the *mainstream* political agenda. If we're organized we can ensure that lesbian and gay rights get on the mainstream political agenda. We put our demands there and developments over the last few years have been rapid. The hairy pace has been stepped up by unpredictable events and organized opposition. Whichever way the election goes, AIDS backlash to boot, there's no going back. So how well are we doing at going forward?

Many (white, male) gay writers, like Jeffrey Weeks in *Coming Out* (Quartet, London, 1977), have often asserted that our social situation makes it impossible to build a large-scale movement, that 'homosexuality and lesbianism are not stable enough factors on which to build a movement', that 'we are torn apart by conflicting class, gender and racial allegiances'. The extent of gay men's misogyny and white lesbian and gay men's racism in the lesbian and gay 'movement' leaves only a narrow path to tread, but it is a path nevertheless, and a path that more and more of us are *trying* to tread. When setting out on what is hopefully a new journey it's useful to learn our own 'movement's' history, proper to pay tribute to those who've travelled before us and important to learn from their mistakes.

Coming Out tells the story of (mostly) male homosexual organization in Britain since the late nineteenth century, through the 1940s and then the limited change in the law in 1967. Jeffrey Weeks traces the birth of the Gay Liberation Movement which, by challenging traditional gender roles, had a profound influence on the left and on feminists. The story of the Gay Liberation Front is also a story of perpetual identity crises. GLF was terrified of organization, was tyrannised by its own lack of structure and, despite a euphoric birth in the autumn of 1970, was all over two years later. Then CHE came to the fore, one of the oldest and at times biggest organizations.

CHE was established in mid-1969 as the Committee for Homosexual Equality and significantly changed its name to 'Campaign' in 1971. By the end of 1972 it had 2,800 members in sixty local groups. It has been notoriously concerned with its own structures and has reorganized itself several times. It has been even more notorious for its failure to win over and then to keep women members and in the seventies it vacillated over the most basic level of solidarity with women, for example on whether to affiliate to the National Abortion Campaign. Activists have criticised CHE's emphasis on non-political stances and its fear of an over-militant stand that would alienate 'respectable' support. It offered no analysis of our position in society: its message was integration. Writers in the *Gay Left* journal described CHE in the summer of 1977 as 'a massive apparatus of papers and committees erected [sic] on an apolitical base'.

Coming Out concluded that 'the days of a euphoric rally to arms is over and it is more likely that the most creative work of Gay Liberation in the immediate future will come from a multiplicity of relatively small groups burrowing through their specialized concerns than from a massive new national initiative. A strong national organization is indeed necessary ... but becomes less, not more, likely as the 1970s stagger along their downhill path'. The last ten years has indeed seen the emergence of a growing number of 'specialist' groups and services encouraged, amongst other things, by local government funding.

CHE has changed but, on its own, is still unable to adequately respond to the situation. Attempts to improve the state of lesbian and gay organizations have been made before. One example in 1978 was the Gay Activists Alliance which was formed out of the National *Gay News* Defence Committee to provide a campaigning and co-ordinated national structure. It didn't last long and never really took off in the first place. The story of lesbian-only organization is no better. Time and time again women have individually joined organizations dominated by gay men and then left when they realized it was, at best, all give and no get. In 1977 women left CHE in a block move and set up NOOLS, the National Organization of Lesbians, which held one conference and collapsed. Lesbian feminists who preferred to join forces with heterosexual women in the Women's Liberation Movement for the most part haven't felt bowled over by the solidary on offer from those women.

Although lesbians have met with increasing regularity in conferences in recent years, the agendas have focused on questions such as ethics and sexual practice. One exception has been the conferences on lesbian mothers and child custody but it has proved difficult to sustain a campaign on this issue, especially in isolation from the broader agenda. Lesbians, as the saying goes, are indeed everywhere, there is a resurgence of lesbian activism but, organizationally speaking, we're no more together than we've ever been.

It's difficult to freeze moments in time but 1985 was a very signficant year for lesbian and gay rights, if not a turning point. That was the year we went more public with our vision. The first Lesbian and Gay Centre in London opened. The Pride march was the biggest ever with 15,000 on it, including contingents from mining communities returning the solidarity and support of lesbians and gay men during the 1984-5 miners' strike. That was the year we, at last, *began* to get on the mainstream political agenda. The 1985 TUC and Labour Party Conferences not only debated, but passed resolutions on lesbian and gay rights for the first time. The GLC, in co-operation with the GLC Gay Working Party, produced *Changing the World: A London Charter for Lesbian and Gay Rights* containing 142 social policy recommendations. Despite the abolition of the GLC and the Metropolitan Authorities, despite Nottingham Equal Opportunities Unit facing closure after the Tories gained control in the May 1987 local elections, lesbian and gay work in local government is continuing and consolidating.

All these events are indications of a growing confidence amongst lesbians and gay men, of a sense that new strategies are in order, and of the imagination, commitment and skills we have collectively built in order to keep progressing our demands at the same time as defending ourselves from increasing attacks.

We've also made progress in our political analysis. We've moved beyond being accommodating and pleading for understanding and forgiveness. Works such as Adrienne Rich's *Compulsory Heterosexuality and Lesbian Existence* (Onlywomen Press, London, 1982) have developed and strengthened the links of multi-oppression. The word 'heterosexism' is entering our vocabulary and its emergence as a part of a theory has offered us an analysis of our position in society and a better understanding of our oppression. At last we've named our oppression and the notion that it is institutionalized in all forms of daily life has been given wider credibility. It has helped us develop programmatically in identifying how these processes work and what demands to make to change them.

What lies ahead depends a lot on what happens on 11 June. First, let's be optimistic and, sadly, unrealistic, and assume a Labour victory. At the 1986 Labour Party Conference a resolution on lesbian and gay rights was passed again, this time with a massive 79 per cent. Their policy includes a commitment to legislation and action in local authorities, housing and the police. There's been virtually no *national* Labour Party action on this policy until the LP shot itself in the foot over Patricia Hewitt's infamous 'loony left' letter after the Greenwich by-election in early 1987, where she said that the 'gay and lesbian issue' was turning people, especially 'pensioners', off Labour.

Nevertheless Labour has put a commitment in its 1987 Manifesto, albeit a vague one: 'We will take steps to ensure that homosexuals are not discriminated against.' After talking to Kinnock, Chris Smith MP assured *Capital Gay* readers of the Labour leader's commitment to introduce anti-discrimination legislation but probably not until year two or three of a Labour Government. Chance would be a fine thing.

As for the Liberal/SDP Alliance, there's been very little positive action at all. On paper their 1987 manifesto pledges to establish a 'Human Rights Commission that would take over the work of the Equal Opportunities and Racial Equality Commissions and counter all discrimination on grounds of race, sex, creed, class, disability or sexual orientation and be able to initiate action in the courts.' As a suggestion and approach it's similar to proposals from independent civil rights organizations for a new and general anti-discrimination Bill.

And then there's the Tories. In May, Tebbit said (in a letter to the Lesbian and Gay Rights Legislation Campaign) that he did 'not envisage the Conservative Party would propose any changes in the law concerning homosexual conduct in its Manifesto.' It must be a sign of the times that some people have taken that as reassurance that Geoffrey Dickens MP and colleagues in the Conservative Family Campaign will not get their way and totally recriminalize homosexuality. Overtly anti-gay speeches and propaganda is being used by the Tories in this election and they mean to go on that way. In May a Bill, brought first by Lord Halsbury in the Lords and then by Dame Jill Knight in the Commons, banning local authorities from 'promoting homosexuality', finally fell after seven months and last-ditch administrative attempts to get it through. Its defeat prompted both Rhodes Boyson and Thatcher to declare their backing for future measures to be introduced.

Whatever happens in the election, the pressure on lesbians and gay men is not going to let up. How then to learn from our history and previous mistakes given the situation now facing us? Where we have not yet succeeded as a 'movement' is in the 'structural arena'. We have only just begun and have a long way to go. We have not yet brought lesbian and gay consciousness, rage and projects into sufficient engagement with existing political structures to create *lasting* changes which would 'institutionalize' some of the new possibilities for the life that we seek. That is exactly where the right wing is trying to stop us. The right are counting on the fact that our ideas are not yet 'institutionalized', or widely enough accepted, and are hoping to prevent our advance now, while they think they still can.

The initiative from the Labour Campaign for Lesbian and Gay Rights, the Campaign for Homosexual Equality and the National Council for Civil Liberties last October, to organize a national two-day conference on legislation for lesbian and gay rights in May 1987, was a timely response by lesbians and gay men. It's an acknowledgment that for example, local authority work is vulnerable because there are neither any statutory duties nor any general anti-discrimination legislation in relation to lesbians and gay men. The conference has helped us educate ourselves and our allies about the nature of our oppression: it brought 500 lesbians and gay men together and was the first gathering of its kind. It's provided a focus for campaigning and helped us stick to the issues amidst all the buffeting.

If the Tories get back in there will be an onslaught on Labour, the left, all radical moves to counter racism and sexism. Local government is near the top of a long hit-list. Lesbians and gay men are likely to retain our high profile in all this because we're seen as one of the weakest links in the opposition's chain. We'll be facing restrictive legislation rather than campaigning for positive legal changes and we need to be more together, to be better organized. This is not impossible.

Lesbians and gay men are by no means a homogenous group, neither are women, Black people, people with disabilities or the working class. However, to concentrate on the differences and divisions between us in a way that breaks, rather than strengthens the link is no strategy for progress. In the last five years or more debates have raged about our differences and divisions in an unprecedented way. Unfortunately a lot of unnecessary guilt-tripping has accompanied this. However personally painful this has been for some people, probably more for women than for men, it has overall been a positive process. It has helped challenge privileged assumptions and positions. Amongst women, for example, it's raised consciousness about oppressions other than gender and how they inter-connect with each other. Political practice as well as political understanding has improved. It's also helped women who are made to feel 'other' or excluded, find each other and led to the formation of groups and networks.

All this makes stronger possibilities for organizing together now. It does not mean the movement is split and dead. As the Legislation Conference demonstrated, it is very much alive. I very much hope that some kind of new national lesbian and gay organization/campaign comes out of all this work. I hope it keeps the issue of legislation on the agenda not least because it provides a focus and an opportunity to shift attitudes in the heterosexual population by raising the level of debate about what is 'legitimate' sexual activity. But going public with our vision *and* countering the right-wing agenda for the future requires us to engage in multiple strategies. A movement cannot be single-strategy, never mind single-issue, without running the danger of losing its overall vision and diminishing its support, since different 'classes' of people feel most intensely the pressure of different issues. Our campaigns must recognize that some of the issues we raise are 'threatening', and we must aim at winning the hearts and minds of large numbers of people as well as convincing the politicians and bureaucrats. We must devise strategies to activate people who care but aren't 'politically active' and provide channels of action for people who have an hour a week, ten minutes a day. And coalitions, with each other as lesbians and gay men and with other progressive groups, will be vital. We must be clear about what makes them viable.

Coalitions don't succeed simply for ideological or charitable reasons. They succeed out of a sense that in specific political struggles we need each other – men and women, Black and white, young and old, able-bodied and people with disabilities. Coalitions are only effective when there is mutual respect, a clearly articulated bottom line –

and when you have your own group mobilized for action.

We are in a position now to influence what life is going to be like at the beginning of the next century. This is what the principle of coalition is all about. On the whole people don't do coalition work because they like it, but because it's effective. We've come to learn that you do not judge a coalition by whether or not it makes you feel comfortable. It won't feel the same as that sense of 'coming home' many of us have experienced once or more within our autonomous liberation groupings, finding our identities alongside others sharing similar histories of oppressions. (In any case, more recent experience has sometimes shown us that we cannot altogether rely on feeling completely nurtured even in those autonomous groupings.)

This doesn't mean abandoning the principle of the fundamental relationship between the personal and political. But if building coalitions feels a strain, it could well mean that difficult, but good, work is being done. This is the way forward for lesbian and gay liberation.